Politics and Economics of the Soviet Union: An Annotated Bibliography

Politics and Economics of the Soviet Union: An Annotated Bibliography

Edited by G.P. Manat

Nova Science Publishers, Inc.

Nova Science Publishers, Inc.
6080 Jericho Turnpike, Suite 207
Commack, New York 11725

Book Production Manager: Denise Engelhardt
Cover Design: Christopher Concannon

Library of Congress Cataloging-in-Publication Data
available upon request

ISBN 1-56072-048-4

Printed in the United States of America

CONTENTS

PREFACE

This compilation represents and attempt to gather descriptive citations concerning the politics and economics of the Soviet Union. The materials presented here form the beginning of a project to regularly publish descriptive citations and lists of articles dealing with this important theme. We have attempted to group the entries in what is hoped will be a logical format and augmented them with subject and author indexes for multiple access points.

G.D. Manat June 1992

A. BUSINESS; FINANCE; ECONOMICS; FOREIGN TRADE

A001. Aganbegyan, A. **MANAGEMENT AND THE FUTURE OF JOINT VENTURES IN THE SOVIET UNION.** *Business in the Contemporary World,* Vol. 2, Spring 1990, pp. 12–24.

A prominent architect of perestroika reveals the importance of economic reform for the Soviet Union in a discussion with Western analysts.

A002. **ALTERNATIVE TRADE UNIONS: POSSIBILITIES AND REALITY.** *Soviet Review,* Vol. 32, Mar.–Apr. 1991, pp. 21–51.

Presents discussion from a roundtable concerning the growth of informal associations that are assuming some of the functions of official trade unions in the Soviet Union. Panel includes members of the Socialist Trade Union (Sotsprof), one of the new informal associations.

A003. Andrews, W.G., 1930– . **THE LAND AND PEOPLE OF THE SOVIET UNION.** New York, NY: Harper Collins, c1991, xv, 304 pp., ill., 24 cm.

Includes bibliographical references (pp. 287–291). Discography, 292 pp. Filmography, pp. 292–293.

Introduces the history, geography, people, culture, government, and economy of the Soviet Union.

A004. Ash, E. and Strittmatter, R. **ACCOUNTING IN THE SOVIET UNION.** New York, NY: Praeger, 1991.

Includes bibliographical references and index.

A005. Åslund, A. **THE MAKING OF ECONOMIC POLICY IN 1989 AND 1990.** *Soviet Economy,* Vol. 6, Jan.–Mar. 1990, pp. 65–94.

Traces principal changes in the anatomy of economic policy from the summer of 1989 through the middle of September 1990....Focuses on the role of institutions and the succession of commissions involving such leading policy makers as Abel Aganbegyan, Leonid Abalkin, Oleg Bogomolov, Stanislav Shatalin, Nikolay Petrakov, and others. Political and bureaucratic infighting at the top is discussed to facilitate insight into the currently worsening crisis.

A006. Aslund, A., 1952– . **GORBACHEV'S STRUGGLE FOR ECONOMIC REFORM.** Ithaca, NY: Cornell University Press, 1991. Studies in Soviet History and Society.

Includes bibliographical references and index.

A007. Aslund, A. **GORBACHEV, PERESTROIKA, AND ECONOMIC CRISIS.** *Problem of Communism*, Vol. 40, Jan.–Apr. 1991, pp. 18–41.

The Gorbachev regime has taken the economic stagnation it inherited from the Brezhnev era and converted it into a severe crisis, as it wavers between conservative and radical proposals for reform.

A008. **ASSOCIATION OF THE BAR OF THE CITY OF NEW YORK.** Committee on Soviet Affairs. Normalization of the U.S.-Soviet trade relationship. *Record of the Association of the Bar of the City of New York*, Vol. 46, Mar. 1991, pp. 104–128.

In 1990, the United States took significant steps to normalize trade relations with the Soviet Union, first by concluding a new trade agreement on June 1, and also by continuing to negotiate treaties on investment protection and taxation and by re-examining legal restrictions on trade and investment. This Report examines these and other issues affecting the U.S.-Soviet trade relationship and concludes that further efforts should be made to remove structural obstacles and repeal obsolete legal restrictions.

A009. Baker, J.A. **IMPERATIVES OF ECONOMIC REFORM: CHANGE IN SOVIET AND EAST EUROPEAN ECONOMIES.** Washington, U.S. Dept. of State, Bureau of Public Affairs, 1990, 10 pp.

A prepared statement by the Secretary of State before the House Ways and Means Committee (April 18, 1990) on the progress of economic reforms in the Soviet Union and Eastern Europe.

A010. Barber, J. 1944– and Harrison, M. **THE SOVIET HOME FRONT, 1941–1945: A SOCIAL AND ECONOMIC HISTORY OF THE U.S.S.R. IN WORLD WAR II.** London (England), New York, NY: Longman, 1991.

Includes bibliographical references and index.

A011. Belykh, V. **MOSCOW TRAFFICKING NETWORKS, SUPPLY ROUTES OUTLINED.** JPRS Report (Narcotics), Mar. 12, 1991, pp. 45 47.

Translation of an article originally appearing in the Soviet newspaper Trud, Feb. 28, 1991, 8 pp.

A012. Bergson, A. **REAL NATIONAL INCOME MEASUREMENT: IN SOVIET PERSPECTIVE.** *Cambridge, Mass., Harvard Institute of Economic Research, Harvard University*, 1991, Vol. 27, 5 pp. (Discussion Paper No. 1541).

Examines the usefulness of Soviet data on national income as measures of real growth and compares these data with those compiled by the Central Intelligence Agency.

A013. Bergson, A. **THE U.S.S.R. BEFORE THE FALL: HOW POOR AND WHY.** *Cambridge, Mass., Harvard Institute of Economic Research, Harvard, University*, 1991, Vol. 25, 7 pp. (Discussion Paper No. 1540).

Comparing Soviet per capita consumption data with OECD countries, finds that the U.S.S.R. ranked just above Turkey at the bottom of the scale in 1985. Claims that consumption levels were "depressed by notably large allocations of the GDP to investment and defense" and by extremely low labor productivity.

A014. Billington, J.H. **RUSSIA'S QUEST FOR IDENTITY.** *Washington Post,* Jan. 21, 1990, B7; Jan. 22, A11.

When Gorbachev turned from economic to political reform, he opened up a crisis of legitimacy that he has not been able to resolve....Gorbachev and any successor in ruling this deeply disillusioned people can probably find only four possible answers to the question of Russian identity.

A015. Birenbaum, D.E. and Racklin, D.P. **BUSINESS VENTURES IN EASTERN EUROPE AND THE SOVIET UNION: THE EMERGING LEGAL FRAMEWORK FOR FOREIGN INVESTMENT.** Englewood Cliffs, NJ: Prentice Hall Law and Business, 1991.

Includes index.

A016. Blackburn, R. **RUSSIAN REVOLUTION: THE SEQUEL.** *Progressive,* Vol. 54, Jan. 1990, pp. 22–24.

The Soviet economy may be headed for a crash as bad as that which struck the United States in the 1930s. The appallingly difficult economic situation and the intractable nationality conflicts that besiege the Soviet government cast a pall over the extraordinary political transformations taking place in the communist world.

A017. Boettke, P.J. **THE POLITICAL ECONOMY OF SOVIET SOCIALISM: THE FORMATIVE YEARS, 1918–1928.** Foreword by Y.N. Maltsev. Boston, MA: Kluwer Academic, c1990, xxi, 246 pp., 24 cm.

Includes bibliographical references (pp. 203–217) and index.

A018. Bogomolov, O. **THE SOVIET ECONOMY ON THE EVE OF THE 1990'S: PROSPECTS FOR INTERNATIONAL COOPERATION.** NATO Review, June 1990, pp. 21–24.

Argues that little significant change can take place without material incentives and entrepreneurial motives and competition. Creation of sound and fully convertible money is the most important step on the road to the creation of true markets and to the introduction of economic incentives for higher output and greater production and efficiency.

A019. Bond, A.R., Belkindas, M.V. and Treyvish, A.I. **ECONOMIC DEVELOPMENT TRENDS IN THE U.S.S.R. 1970–1988: PART II (CONSUMPTION, INVESTMENT AND INCOME REDISTRIBUTION).** *Soviet Geography,* Vol. 32, Jan. 1991, pp. 1–57.

Examines patterns in consumption and investment (national income used) at the union republic level, personal services expenditures (oblast and economic regional level), and level of living (small sample of indicators, republic level). Economic and political issues surrounding the current debate over interrepublican income transfers and commodity flows are discussed and limited parallels drawn between Soviet and global versions of restructuring. For Part One of this article, see LRS90-12040.

A020. Bornstein, M. **SOVIET ASSESSMENTS OF ECONOMIC REFORMS IN OTHER SOCIALIST COUNTRIES.** *Soviet Economy,* Vol. 7, Jan.–Mar. 1991, pp. 14–45.

This study surveys, analyzes, and appraises Soviet specialists' assessments of economic reforms in other socialist countries, mainly in Eastern Europe and China. The aim is to identify what Soviet specialists consider some of the chief features, achievements, and problems of such reform measures - and thus possible lessons for economic reform efforts in the U.S.S.R.

A021. Brady, R. **AND NOW, A CRACKDOWN ON CASH.** *Business Week,* No. 3198, Feb. 4, 1991, pp. 64–66.

Ruble confiscation is the most draconian fiscal measure taken in decades and another demonstration of Soviet President Mikhail Gorbachev's turn to the right. It may also signal the end of attempts to liberalize the economy. Instead of continuing to promote individual initiative with material rewards, Gorbachev is reasserting a traditional taboo: Having a lot of cash is a crime. Companion article discusses the recent surge of Soviet borrowing on the international market.

A022. Brady, R. and Galuszka, P. **500 DAYS.** *Business Week,* No. 3180, Oct. 1, 1990, pp. 138–141,144–145,148.

Reviews the "500-Day Plan" which sets forth a program that marks the nearly complete changeover of Soviet central planning to a free market by April 1992.

A023. Braun, A. and Day, R.B. **GORBACHEVIAN CONTRADICTIONS.** *Problems of Communism,* Vol. 39, May–June 1990, pp. 36–50.

Aside from the fact that the size of the Soviet economy will perforce make Western help marginal at best, there is the larger issue of the proper diagnosis of the Soviet crisis. All indications are that the economic problems are a by-product of a legitimacy crisis of the Soviet system. Unless Gorbachev is able to jettison the Leninist system and rid himself of his own vanguardist mentality, the political crisis is unlikely to be resolved and the Soviet Union's people will not be drawn into participating in the economic reconstruction of the Soviet Union.

A024. Brown, L. **THE SIBERIAN CITY OF TOMSK IS OPENING FOR BUSINESS....AT LAST.** *Business America,* Vol. 112, June 3, 1991, pp. 2–5.

A Commerce Department official recently returned from a two-month assignment in the Commercial Section of the U.S. Embassy in Moscow. She writes about her visit to the Siberian city of Tomsk, as a member of the first official delegation since 1941.

A025. Brun, E. and Hersh, J. **SOVIET-THIRD WORLD RELATIONS IN A CAPITALIST WORLD: THE POLITICAL ECONOMY OF BROKEN PROMISES.** New York, NY: St. Martin's Press, 1990, x, 335 pp., 23 cm.

Includes bibliographical references (pp. 301–322) and index.

A026. Bukovsky, V. **MALTA IN RETROSPECT.** *Global Affairs,* Vol. 5, Spring 1990, pp. 71–82.

Only the emergence of a strong, democratic opposition can stabilize the Soviet Union by replacing the Communist Party in power, dissolving the empire, and urgently introducing a market economy.

A027. Bush, K. **PAVLOV'S ANTICRISIS PROGRAM.** *Report on the U.S.S.R.*, Vol. 3, May 17, 1991, pp. 1–6.

Pavlov's draft anticrisis program was made public by TASS on April 9, only to be withdrawn immediately. It is the fifth attempt at a comprehensive economic reform to be undertaken since Gorbachev's accession. It consists of a package of stabilization measures designed to halt the present recession and disintegration of the economy and a package to enable transition to the market by creating the environment and the infrastructure for limited privatization and for the development of market institutions.

A028. Campbell, R.W. **THE SOCIALIST ECONOMIES IN TRANSITION: A PRIMER ON SEMI-REFORMED SYSTEMS.** Bloomington, IN: Indiana University Press, c1991.

Includes bibliographical references and index.

A029. Carey, S.C. **FOREIGN INVESTMENT** IN THE U.S.S.R.. *Harriman Institute Forum*, Vol. 3, Feb. 1990, pp. 1–8.

Claims that in the next few years a steady expansion of investment opportunities can be anticipated, with foreigners participating in long-term leases of land and other property, as stockholders of Soviet businesses, in special Western-organized investment funds designed to finance new businesses in the Soviet Union, and the Soviet bond offerings, currency auctions, and other financial markets. The rules governing such participation can only be conjectured at this point.

A030. Cohen, R. 1946– and Wilson, P.A. **SUPERPOWERS IN ECONOMIC DECLINE: U.S. STRATEGY FOR THE TRANSCENTURY ERA.** New York, NY: Crane Russak, 1990, xi, 276 pp., ill, 24 cm.

Includes bibliographical references (pp. 258–266) and index.

A031. Cohen, A. **THE DEVELOPING SOVIET MARKET: COMMODITY EXCHANGES.** *Report on the U.S.S.R.*, Vol. 3, May 17, 1991, pp. 11–16.

By the beginning of 1991, about 100 commodity exchanges had either opened their doors in the U.S.S.R. or announced their intention to start trading in the near future. The emergence of a commodity exchange network, so necessary for the creation of price-setting mechanisms and the elimination of the supply bottlenecks left by Gosplan, is a promising economic phenomenon, but the exchanges must overcome formidable obstacles.

A032. Collins, S.M. and Rodrik, D. **EASTERN EUROPE AND THE SOVIET UNION IN THE WORLD ECONOMY.** Washington, DC: Institute for International Economics, 1991.

Includes bibliographical references.

A033. Cook, L.J. **LESSONS OF SOVIET COAL MINER'S STRIKE OF SUMMER 1989.** *Harriman Institute Forum*, Vol. 4, Mar. 1991, pp. 1–10.

Says that the most significant aspect of the summer 1989 strike movement was the miners' pro-reform agenda, their support for enterprise autonomy and self-financing. Questions the long-held assumptions about the inherent conservatism and dependent psychology of Soviet blue collar workers.

A034. Cooper, R. **WHAT ONE SOVIET BANKER SAID TO ANOTHER.** *Euromoney*, Jan. 1990, pp. 25,27–28.

Reform of the Soviet financial system is causing tension between the newly-linked banks and Gosbank, the state monolith-turned-supervisor. It seems that the co-operative banks are leading the drive towards such free market practices as client confidentiality.

A035. Costa, A. **WILL SOVIET PRIVATE ENTERPRISE SURVIVE?** *World and I*, Vol. 5, June 1990, pp. 136–142.

The Soviet Union's privately owned cooperatives are in danger of being strangled by corruption and red tape. U.S. aid should be channeled to them rather than government-run enterprises.

A036. Crow, S. **CASHING THE PEACE DIVIDEND.** *Report on the U.S.S.R.*, Vol. 3, Jan. 4, 1991, pp. 5–7.

A central tenet of foreign policy under Mikhail Gorbachev has been that the Soviet Union can become more secure and prosperous by turning adversaries into allies. To gain the trust of former enemies, Moscow gave up its East European buffer states, began to reconsider nettlesome commitments in Asia, Africa, and Latin America, and started to establish links with countries it had previously shunned....Nineteen-ninety can therefore be characterized as the year in which Moscow cashed in its peace dividend.

A037. Crowfoot. J. and Harrison, M. **THE U.S.S.R. COUNCIL OF MINISTERS UNDER LATE STALINISM, 1945–1954: ITS PRODUCTION BRANCH COMPOSITION AND THE REQUIREMENTS OF NATIONAL ECONOMY AND POLICY.** *Soviet Studies*, Vol. 42, Jan. 1990, pp. 39–58.

A038. Dyker, D.A. **GORBACHEV'S ECONOMIC REFORMS: PERESTROIKA IN CRISIS.** Koln: Bundesinstitut fur Ostwissenschaftliche und Internationale Studien, c1990, 32 pp., 30 cm. Berichte des Bundesinstituts fur Ostwissenschaftliche und Internationale Studien, 8-1990.

Cover title. Includes summary in German. Includes bibliographical references (pp. 28–30).

A039. **EAST–WEST TRADE AND THE ATLANTIC ALLIANCE.** Edited by D.A. Baldwin and H.V. Milner, New York, NY: St. Martin's Press, 1990, xi, 227 pp., ill., 23 cm.

Includes bibliographical references and index.

A040. **ECONOMIC REFORMS AND WELFARE SYSTEMS IN THE USSR, POLAND, AND HUNGARY: SOCIAL CONTRACT IN TRANSFORMATION.** Edited by J. Adam. New York, NY: St. Martin's Press, 1991.

Includes index.

A041. **ECONOMICS-DEPUTIES ON RADICAL ECONOMIC REFORM.** *Soviet Review*, Vol. 31, July–Aug. 1990, pp. 3–20.

A press conference attended by U.S.S.R. People's Deputies - Academician L. Abalkin; Academician O. Bogomolov; V. Tikhonov, Academician of the All-Union V.I. Lenin Academy of Agricultural Sciences; Professor G. Popov, Doctor of Economic Sciences; Professor G. Lisichkin, Doctor of Economic

Sciences - was held on 16 June 1989 at the Institute of Economics of the U.S.S.R. Academy of Sciences.

A042. **THE EMERGING RUSSIAN BEAR: INTEGRATING THE SOVIET UNION INTO THE WORLD ECONOMY.** Edited by J.C. Brada and M.P. Claudon. New York, NY: New York University Press, c1991.

Includes index.

A043. Fairlamb, D. **THE SOVIET BANKING BROUHAHA.** *Institutional Investor*, Vol. 24, July 1990, pp. 185–189.

Describes the ideological battles between the advocates of banking reform and the vested interests within the Soviet banking system.

A044. Fakiolas, T. **SOVIET ECONOMIC COMPETITION WITH THE DEVELOPED COUNTRIES: PAST AND FUTURE.** *Futures*, Vol. 22, Sept. 1990, pp. 740–751.

A critical investigation is made of the data on which the projections by Stalin and Khruschev were based, namely that within 10 to 20 years the U.S.S.R. would outstrip the U.S.A. and the other developed countries both in the total volume of and in per capita production. The reasons why these projections were not attained are also examined. Investigation is also made of the causes that have rendered the Soviets both more reserved and pessimistic today as regards the prospects for the development of the Soviet economy.

A045. Faltsman, Vladimir. **WHAT DO WE EXPECT OF CONVERSION?** Business Contact, no. 2, Mar.–Apr. 1990, pp. 6–7,9–13.

Interviews Soviet economist, Vladimir Faltsman, Concerning the hopes for a beneficial conversion of Soviet defense production to civilian production. Includes companion article, the Pavel Sukhoi Experimental Design Office: From interceptors to Aerobatic Planes.

A046. Feige, E.L. **PERESTROIKA AND SOCIALIST PRIVATIZATION: WHAT IS TO BE DONE? AND HOW?** *Comparative Economic Studies*, Vol. 32, Fall 1990, pp. 1–81.

Proposes one possible path for restructuring the Soviet economy, claiming that such obstacles as inflation, unemployment, and bureaucratic obstruction must be circumvented by a sequence of reforms that assure sustained progress toward the final goal. The path the author proposes is a program of "socialists privatization" - an egalitarian redistribution of the state's custodial assets to its citizens as a prelude to a "contained big bang" introduction of market mechanisms. Includes comments by Michael Marrese and James. R. Millar.

A047. Feige, E.L. **A MESSAGE TO GORBACHEV: REDISTRIBUTE THE WEALTH.** *Challenge*, Vol. 33, May–June 1990, pp. 46–53.

Adopting a program of "socialist privatization" would give each Soviet citizen an equal number of chips and a level playing field before the free market casino opens for business. Article originally presented at the International Conference on Entrepreneurship in the World Economy, Nov. 1989.

A048. Feinberg, R.E. **ECONOMIC REFORM IN THREE GIANTS: U.S. FOREIGN POLICY AND THE U.S.S.R., CHINA, AND INDIA,** New Brunswick, N.J.,

Transaction Books, 1990, 247 pp. (U.S.-Third World Policy Perspectives No. 14).

Three of the largest and strategically most important underdeveloped nations in the world - the Soviet Union, China, and India - are simultaneously in the throes of historic changes. Economic reform in the Giants clearly has profound consequences for their own political systems - and for the lives of the 2.2 billion people (nearly half the world's population) living in their societies. The reform in the Giants are also prompting dramatic changes in the international political and economic order. Concludes implications for the U.S.

A049. Feiveson, H.A. and VonHippel, F.N. **BEYOND START: HOW TO MAKE MUCH DEEPER CUTS.** *International Security*, Vol. 15, Summer 1990, pp. 154–180.

If the U.S. and Soviet governments decided, in a post-START strategic-arms reduction agreement, to accept the infeasibility of counterforce missions requiring thousands of warheads, it would be possible for them to agree on very much smaller strategic forces. To keep the strategic forces as large as is envisioned in the START agreement would be both provocative and clearly unnecessary in view of the changed situation in Eastern Europe and the Soviet Union.

A050. **FOREIGN TRADE IN EASTERN EUROPE AND THE SOVIET UNION.** Edited by M. Friedlander, Boulder, CO: Westview Press, 1990, x, 241 pp., 23 cm. The Vienna Institute for Comparative Economic Studies Yearbook, 2.

Includes bibliographical references.

A051. **FROM TSARISM TO THE NEW ECONOMIC POLICY: CONTINUITY AND CHANGE IN THE ECONOMY OF THE USSR.** Edited by R.W. Davies. Ithaca, NY: Cornell University Press, 1991.

Includes bibliographical references and index.

A052. **FUNDAMENTALS OF MILITARY ECONOMIC KNOWLEDGE.** (Washington) Foreign Broadcast Information Service, 1991, 105 pp. JPRS Report (Soviet Union: Military Affairs); JPRS-UMA-91-003 L, 10 April 1991)

Partial contents - Military economic knowledge and its place in the system of knowledge on war. The interrelationship of war and economics, peculiarities of the economic support for modern war. The role of labor resources in the economic support of a war. Economic preparation of the country for defense. Management of the military economy.

A053. Geron, L. **SOVIET FOREIGN ECONOMIC POLICY UNDER PERESTROIKA.** New York, NY: council on Foreign Relations Press, c1990, x, 126 p., 22 cm. Chatham House papers.

Published in North America for the Royal Institute of International Affairs. Includes bibliographical references (pp. 81–95).

A054. Goldman, M.I. **THE HUNT FOR RED ENTERPRISE.** *World Monitor*, Vol. 3, Dec. 1990, pp. 50–52.

Why is the usually decisive Gorbachev flip-flopping on free enterprise? Because he has to sidestep both communism and Russian tradition if he is to lead his people to the promised land of private property.

A055. Granberg, A.G. **THE ECONOMIC MECHANISM OF INTER-REPUBLIC AND INTER-REGIONAL RELATIONS.** *Soviet Review*, Vol. 31, Sept.–Oct. 1990, pp. 38–54.

Claims that the center of gravity of economic reform in the current year has shifted from enterprises to regions. Warns that unilateral actions by the individual republics such as the introduction of their own currencies and tariff barriers can have a disruptive effect on the all-union market.

A056. Graziani, G. **GORBACHEV'S ECONOMIC STRATEGY IN THE THIRD WORLD.** Foreword by E.H. Preeg, New York, NY: Praeger, 1990, xx, 116 pp., 25 cm.

Published with the Center for Strategic and International Studies, Washington, DC. Includes bibliographical references (pp. 101–109) and index.

A057. Gregory, P.R. and Stuart, R.C. **SOVIET ECONOMIC STRUCTURE AND PERFORMANCE.** New York, NY: Harper and Row, c1990, x, 501 pp., ill., 25 cm.

Includes bibliographical references and index.

A058. Gregory, P., Dietz, B. **SOVIET PERCEPTIONS OF ECONOMIC CONDITIONS DURING THE PERIOD OF STAGNATION: EVIDENCE FROM TWO DIVERSE EMIGRANT SURVEYS.** *Soviet Studies*, Vol. 43, No. 3, 1991, pp. 535–551.

Examines living conditions in the Soviet Union based on two sets of interviews with former Soviet citizens: the Soviet Interview Project (SIP) and the German Soviet Interview Project (GSIP).

A059. Gregory, P.R. **RESTRUCTURING THE SOVIET ECONOMIC BUREAUCRACY.** Cambridge, New York, NY: Cambridge University Press, 1990, xii, 181 pp., 24 cm.

Includes bibliographical references and index.

A060. Hanson, P. **SOVIET ECONOMIC REFORM: PERESTROIKA OR "CATASTROIKA"?** *World Policy Journal*, Vol. 8, Spring 1991, pp. 289–318.

If there is reason for optimism, it lies in the growth of "perestroika from below": the emergence of an embryonic private sector....a process of peaceful decentralization that will allow reform to grow from the bottom up.

A061. Hayes, J.B. **WANNA MAKE A DEAL IN MOSCOW?** *Fortune*, Vol. 122, Oct. 22, 1990, pp. 113–115,117–118.

Offers a first-hand impression by one of the 14 chief executive officers invited to the Soviet Union in Sept. 1990 to investigate potential American investments. Includes accompanying article by Ann Reilly Dowd (Oil from Russia).

A062. Hertzfeld, J.M. **JOINT VENTURES: SAVING THE SOVIETS FROM PERESTROIKA.** *Harvard Business Review*, Vol. 69, Jan.–Feb. 1991, pp. 80–91.

Highlights McDonald's successful investment strategies in the Soviet Union. Maintains that to succeed companies must develop operations that allow for expansion of the Soviet economy and integrate themselves by a top-to-bottom chain of linked or integrated enterprises in command of supplies and with independent access to customers.

A063. Hughes, J.R. **STALIN, SIBERIA, AND THE CRISIS OF THE NEW ECONOMIC POLICY.** Cambridge (England), New York, NY: Cambridge University Press, 1991.

Includes bibliographical references and index.

A064. **THE IMPACT OF GOVERNMENTS ON EAST–WEST ECONOMIC RELATIONS.** Edited by G. Bertsch and S. Elliott-Gower. Washington Square, NY: New York University Press, 1991, xii, 407 pp., ill., 24 cm, East–West European economic interaction, Vol. 12.

Papers from the 12th Workshop on East–West European Economic Interaction held Apr. 1–5, 1989 at the University of Georgia in Athens; organized by the Vienna Institute for Comparative Economic Studies. Includes bibliographical references and index.

A065. Kanovsky, E. **WHY THE OIL CRISIS WON'T LAST.** *Orbis*, Vol. 35, Winter 1991, pp. 79–91.

The Iraqi invasion of Kuwait on August 2, 1990 triggered an oil crisis. By October 1990, crude oil prices had risen from about $18 to between $35 and $40 a barrel. If active fighting takes place in the Persian Gulf, oil prices might go through the roof. But within a few years, prices will decline to levels lower than those prevailing before the invasion of Kuwait, when measured in constant dollars.

A066. Kemme, D.M. **ECONOMIC TRANSITION IN EASTERN EUROPE AND THE SOVIET UNION: ISSUES AND STRATEGIES.** New York, NY: Institute for East–West Security Studies; Boulder, CO: Distributed by Westview Press, 1991. Occasional Paper Series, 20.

Includes bibliographical references.

A067. Khorev, B.S. **ECONOMIC DECENTRALIZATION AND REGIONALISM.** *Soviet Geography*, Vol. 31, Sept. 1990, pp. 509–526.

Another recent geographical essay on regional economic management advocates reestablishment of regional economic councils for the achievement of an optimal spatial division of labor under perestroika and rationalizing competing economic, nationalistic, and economic objectives (see Soviet Geography, May 1990, pp. 366–374). The author criticizes proposals for the further ethnic-based division of the country and questions the economic viability of the Baltic states' drive toward independence and of a "political" (republic-based) system of khozraschet. He also questions the wisdom of "resource payments" as a means of supplementing the income of localities.

A068. Kincade, W.H. and Thomson, T.K. **ECONOMIC CONVERSION IN THE U.S.S.R.: ITS ROLE IN PERESTROIKA.** *Problems of Communism*, Vol. 39, Jan.–Feb. 1990, pp. 83–92.

Examines how the conversion of military industries to civilian production "is vitally linked, in the Soviet conception, to arms reduction and to perestroika.

A069. Kir'yanchuk, V.Ye. and Podkolzin, V.V. **PERESTROIKA AND THE ECONOMIC REGION IN STATE MANAGEMENT AND PLANNING.** *Soviet Geography*, Vol. 31, May 1990, pp. 366–374.

The concept of region-based planning and management bodies, which flourished for a time during Khrushchev's sovnarkhozy reforms, is resurrected, this time under the guise of promoting decentralization and enhancing territorial versus sectoral planning under perestroika. More precisely, the authors argue for devolution of meaningful planning and management functions to a network of smaller and more numerous economic regions, with "regional economic councils" serving as bodies for planning and coordinating the activities of smaller spatial units within these regions.

A070. Klebnikow, P. **IN GOLD THEY TRUST?** *Forbes*, Vol. 145, Jan. 8, 1990, pp. 38–40.

Examines the scenario of putting the Soviet ruble on the gold standard as a quick way of making it convertible.

A071. Korbonski, A. **CMEA, ECONOMIC INTEGRATION, AND PERESTROIKA, 1949–1989.** *Studies in Comparative Communism*, Vol. 23, Spring 1990, pp. 47–72.

Examines the process of economic integration in Eastern Europe, since the creation in 1949 of the Council for Mutual Economic Assistance.

A072. Kvint, V. **RUSSIA AS CINDERELLA.** *Forbes*, Vol. 145, Feb. 19, 1990, pp. 130–108.

Argues that many of the Soviet republics that are agitating for independence are overlooking the substantial benefits they receive from their membership in the U.S.S.R. In the form of low raw material prices and product subsidies. Concludes that, according to my evaluation, out of all Union republics only the Russian Federation, Ukraine and Belorussia can independently solve their problems. They alone could make a viable economic entity. In Russia the ruble can be backed by gold, diamonds, mineral resources. If Baltic republic create their own money, how can they be backed, especially with the existing level of industrial and economic development?....Hence my proposal for a Russian secession....in order to unite, the republics of the Soviet Union should separate.

A073. Kvint, V. **DEAD SOULS.** *Forbes*, Vol. 147, May 27, 1991, pp. 96,100,102.

Workers in the Soviet Union seem lazy and thieving, but the Soviet people are fundamentally honest and capable of hard work. It is the system that has made them bad - and the system is dying.

A074. Kvint, V. **EASTERN SIBERIA COULD BECOME ANOTHER SAUDI ARABIA.** *Forbes*, Vol. 146, Sept. 17, 1990, pp. 130–132.

Explains why the Soviet Union may be exporting more oil than Saudi Arabia in the next century.

A075. LaFollette, K. **GOVERNMENT LOANS FOR THE SOVIET UNION: A DISSERVICE TO U.S. TAXPAYERS AND SOVIETS ALIKE.** Washington, Cato Institute, 1991, 12 pp. (Foreign Policy Briefing No. 8)

Claims that Western aid to the Soviet Union is directly underwriting the Soviet central government's political and economic repression. In turn, if and when the political upheaval in the Soviet Union settles, the United States and other G-7 nations will most likely resume their efforts to place the Soviet economy under the tutelage and patronage of the IMF and World Bank. That will only prolong government retrenchment in the Soviet Union and "hook" the central government, or the governments of the republics, on the same kinds of subsidized loans that have financed big government throughout the developing world.

A076. Lavigne, M., 1935– . **FINANCING THE TRANSITION IN THE USSR: THE SHATALIN PLAN AND THE SOVIET ECONOMY.** New York, NY: Institute for East–West Security Studies, 1990. Public policy papers.

Includes bibliographical references.

A077. Lewin, M., 1921– . **STALINISM AND THE SEEDS OF SOVIET REFORM: THE DEBATES OF THE 1960s.** London (England), Concord, MA: Pluto Press, 1991.

Reprint. Originally published: Political Undercurrents in Soviet Economic Debates. Princeton, NJ: Princeton University Press, 1974.

Includes bibliographical references and index.

A078. Lih, L.T. **BREAD AND AUTHORITY IN RUSSIA, 1914–1921.** Berkeley, CA: University of California Press, c1990, xvii, 303 pp. (5) pp. of plates, ill., 24 cm.

Includes bibliographical references (pp. 275–289) and index.

A079. Litwack, J.M. **DISCRETIONARY BEHAVIOUR AND SOVIET ECONOMIC REFORM.** *Soviet Studies*, Vol. 43, No. 2, 1991, pp. 255–279.

This paper first clarifies the nature of the problem of discretion in planning and taxation, and then discusses the consequences of discretion in Soviet planning. Next it summarizes some pre-Gorbachev reform measures and experiments that aimed at limiting discretion, and discusses problems in implementation, after which it turns to the particular dilemma of discretion in the Gorbachev period, emphasizing an important contradiction between the goals and methods of perestroika.

A080. Lopatin, V. **THE ARMY AND THE ECONOMY: ECONOMIC ASPECTS OF SOVIET MILITARY REFORM.** *Global Affairs*, Vol. 6, Winter 1991, pp. 1–22.

Our goal is modest: to formulate the problem, to examine it more broadly and more rigorously, and to define possible approaches to the solution.

A081. Maggs, P. **BEATING SWORDS INTO WASHING MACHINES**. New York, Council on Economic Priorities, 1990, 5 pp.

A082. Malle, S. **EMPLOYMENT PLANNING IN THE SOVIET UNION: CONTINUITY AND CHANGE.** New York, NY: St. Martin's Press, 1991, xii, 334 pp., ill., 23 cm.

Includes bibliographical references (pp. 305–313) and index.

A083. Malseva, Y.N. **SOVIET ECONOMIC REFORMS: AN INSIDE PERSPECTIVE.** *Freeman Ideas on Liberty*, Vol. 40, Mar. 1990, pp. 88–92.

Claims the Soviet economic reforms will not be effective unless the very foundations of the system are changed, and that requires the establishment of a multi-party system, privatization of the economy, and denationalization of land.

A084. **MARKET SOCIALISM OR RESTORATION OF CAPITALISM?** Edited by A. Aslund. Cambridge (England), New York, NY: Cambridge University press, 1991.
Includes index.

A085. Mihalisko, K. **THE WORKERS' REBELLION IN BELORUSSIA.** *Report on the U.S.S.R.*, Vol. 3, Apr. 26, 1991, pp. 21–25.
Thousands of Belorussian workers have downed tools this month in a series of strikes. The protest action was sparked by economic problems, but it quickly took on a political purpose: its organizers want nothing less than the introduction of political democracy in Belorussia. This is the most serious challenge ever to the republic's Communist regime and adds a Belorussian dimension to mounting labor unrest in the U.S.S.R.

A086. **MILESTONES IN GLASNOST AND PERESTROIKA.** E.A. Hewett and V.H. Winston, eds. Washington, DC: Brookings Institution, c1991.
Readings based on contributions to Soviet economy 1985–1991.
Includes bibliographical references and indexes.

A087. Moskoff, W. **THE BREAD OF AFFLICTION: THE FOOD SUPPLY IN THE U.S.S.R. DURING WORLD WAR II.** Cambridge (England), New York, NY: Cambridge University Press, 1990, xvi, 256 pp., ill., 24 cm.
Includes bibliographical references (pp. 240–247) and index.

A088. **NATIONAL AFFAIRS: DRAFT ACTION PROGRAM ON ECONOMY.** FBIS Daily Report (Soviet Union), Apr. 11, 1991, suppl., whole issue (15 pp.).
Presents an English language translation of the next of the Draft U.S.S.R. Cabinet of Ministers' Action Program for Leading the Economy Out of Crisis.

A089. Nellis, J.R. **IMPROVING THE PERFORMANCE OF SOVIET ENTERPRISES.** Washington, DC: World Bank, 1991.

A090. Noren, J.H. **THE SOVIET ECONOMIC CRISIS: ANOTHER PERSPECTIVE.** *Soviet Economy*, Vol. 6, Jan.–Mar. 1990, pp. 3–55.
A senior CIA economist reviews the performance of the Soviet Union's economy during perestroika in an effort to provide a balanced perspective on the severe and pervasive economic crisis. Incorporated in the paper is a discussion of the reliability of Soviet and non-Soviet measures of performance, an overview of the three phases of perestroika and an analysis of factors contributing to that crisis.

A091. Nove, A. **STUDIES IN ECONOMICS AND RUSSIA.** New York, NY: St. Martin's Press, 1990, vii, 375 pp., 23 cm.
Includes bibliographical references and index.

A092. O'Prey, K. **THE SOVIET PEACE DIVIDEND? TRENDS AND PROSPECTS FOR ECONOMIC CONVERSION.** *Soviet Defense Notes*, Vol. 2, June 1990, pp. 1–7.

Looks at the economic conversion program underway in the Soviet Union. While most Soviet commentators agree that some reallocation of defense resources to civil production is a necessary part of efforts to revitalize the Soviet economy, they also agree that the program has had little success to date. This has provoked an interesting and heated debate over how conversion should be structured and implemented.

A093. Okolicsanyi, K. **DRASTIC DECLINE IN TRADE WITH THE U.S.S.R.** *Report on Eastern Europe*, Vol. 2, Apr. 5, 1991, pp. 1–4.

Soviet-Hungarian trade showed a further decline in 1990 and now constitutes only 18–19% of total Hungarian trade....As Hungary's reliance on the Soviet Union decreases, its independence from trade conducted in the nonconvertible transferable ruble - and true economic freedom - increases. Perhaps the most important benefit of this re-orientation of foreign trade is that state-owned enterprises are now being forced to abandon the inefficient practices associated with production for the Soviet market.

A094. Osakwe, C., 1942–. **SOVIET BUSINESS LAW: INSTITUTIONS, PRINCIPLES, AND PROCESSES.** Salem, NH: Butterworth Legal Publishers, c1991, 2 vols. (loose leaf), 25 cm.

Includes bibliographical references and index.

A095. Owen, T.C. **THE CORPORATION UNDER RUSSIAN LAW, 1800–1917: A STUDY IN TSARIST ECONOMIC POLICY.** Cambridge (England), New York, NY: Cambridge University Press, 1991, xviii, 234 pp., 24 cm.

Includes bibliographical references (pp. 220–227) and index.

A096. Palei, L.V. Radzivanovich, K.L. **HOW TO CARRY OUT ECONOMIC REFORM: POINTS OF VIEW AND REALITY.** *Soviet Studies*, Vol. 42, Jan. 1990, pp. 25–37.

Addresses the difficulties of restructuring the Soviet economy while maintaining the traditional bureaucratic apparatus of existing ministries and departments.

A097. Palmer, M.S.R. **PRIVATIZATION IN UKRAINE: ECONOMICS, LAW, AND POLITICS.** *Yale Journal of International Law*, Vol. 16, Summer 1991, pp. 453–517.

This article examines one important aspect of economic transformation in Ukraine - the process of privatization. It is the goal of this article to provide information and advice about the process by which Ukrainians could, themselves, formulate and implement a program of privatization.

A098. Parker, R. **INSIDE THE "COLLAPSING" SOVIET ECONOMY.** *Atlantic Monthly*, Vol. 265, June 1990, pp. 68–71,74–76,79–80.

Contends that Americans should not predict the demise of the Soviet economy despite continuing outbreaks of ethnic conflict, turmoil in political events, and intractable economic problems. Reviews the progress of economic reforms to date and prospects for the success of perestroika.

A099. Peel. Q. **STICKY TIME FOR A VALUABLE RESOURCE.** Financial Times, Oct. 26, 1990, 18(4 pp.).

The truth is that the Soviet oil industry is itself in a state of turmoil, reflecting the chaos in the rest of the Soviet economy. At the same time it is burdened with an inheritance of technical incompetence, illogical planning, ecological negligence and, above all, a drive for production at all costs, which have left it frighteningly ill-equipped to cope with the technological demands of the coming decades.

A100. Pethybridge, R.W. 1934–. **ONE STEP BACKWARDS, TWO STEPS FORWARD: SOVIET SOCIETY AND POLITICS IN THE NEW ECONOMIC POLICY.** Oxford: Clarendon Press, New York, NY: Oxford University Press, 1990, p. cm.

Includes bibliographical references.

A101. Petr, J.L. **ECONOMIC REFORMS IN SOCIALIST ECONOMIES: AN EVOLUTIONARY PERSPECTIVE.** *Journal of Economic Issues*, Vol. 24, Mar. 1990, pp. 1–15.

Uses the Soviet example of perestroika to illustrate and analyze underlying principles of economic evolution in any society. What motivates change? What leads to successful change? And what separates ideology-based change from evolutionary warranted change (besides success)?

A102. Pitzer, J.S., Baukol, A.P. **RECENT GNP PRODUCTIVITY TRENDS.** *Soviet Economy*, Vol. 7, Jan.–Mar. 1991, pp. 46–82.

Two CIA economists present and analyze data on trends in Soviet GNP and productivity from 1960 through 1990. The developments in the 1980s are suitably emphasized and compared with those in the United States. The author's study and calculations embrace labor and capital inputs as well as total factor productivity.

A103. **POLITICAL IMPLICATIONS OF ECONOMIC REFORM IN COMMUNIST SYSTEMS: COMMUNIST DIALECTIC.** Edited by D.L. Bahry and J.C. Moses. New York, NY: New York University Press, c1990, xiii, 358 pp., ill, 24 cm.

Includes bibliographical references and index.

A104. **THE POST-CONTAINMENT HANDBOOK: KEY ISSUES IN U.S.–SOVIET ECONOMIC RELATIONS.** Edited by R. Cullen, Boulder, CO: Westview Press, 1990, xii, 227 pp., 28 cm.

An East–West forum publication.

A105. **PRIVATIZING AND MARKETIZING SOCIALISM.** *Annals of the American Academy of Political and Social Science*, Vol. 507, Jan. 1990, pp. 5–141.

Partial contents - The Stalinist command economy, by P.R. Gregory. The Soviet economy and the need for reform, by M.I. Goldman. Subrosa privatization and marketization in the U.S.S.R., by G. Grossman. The linkage between economic and political reform in the Socialist countries: a supply-side explanation, by Y.-S. Wu. Reforming the planned economy: the Hungarian experience, by T. Bauer. Economic reform of socialism: the Dengist course in China, by J.S. Prybyla. A property-rights analysis of the Yugoslav miracle, by S. Pejovich. East German traditional centralism: an alternative route to economic reconstruction, by P.J. Bryson.

A106. Pucher, J. **CAPITALISM, SOCIALISM, AND URBAN TRANSPORTATION: POLICIES AND TRAVEL BEHAVIOR IN THE EAST AND WEST.** *Journal of the American Planning Association*, Vol. 56, Summer 1990, pp. 278–296.

Urban transportation systems in the Soviet Union, Europe, and North America are very different. The dominance of public transport in the Soviet Union contrasts strikingly with the almost exclusive reliance on the automobile in the United States. European countries lie between these two extremes....Socialist governments strongly supported public transport. By contrast, the more market-oriented a country's economy, the more it has neglected public transport, and instead subsidized highway construction, auto use, and suburbanization.

A107. Roberts, P.C. and LaFollette, K. 1939–. **MELTDOWN: INSIDE THE SOVIET ECONOMY.** Washington, DC: Cato Institute, c1990, xi, 152 pp., 24 cm.

Includes bibliographical references and index.

A108. Roberts, P.C. 1939–. **ALIENATION AND THE SOVIET ECONOMY: TOWARD A GENERAL THEORY OF MARXIAN ALIENATION, ORGANIZATIONAL PRINCIPLES, AND THE SOVIET ECONOMY.** Foreword by A. Wildavsky. New York, NY: Holmes and Meier, 1990, p. cm.

Includes bibliographical references and index.

A109. **THE ROLE OF FREE ECONOMIC ZONES IN THE U.S.S.R. AND EASTERN EUROPE.** New York, NY: United Nations, c1990, vi, 84 pp., 28 cm.

At head of title: United Nations Centre on Transnational Corporations, March 1990.

A110. Ross, S. **THE U.S.S.R. UNDER STALIN.** New York, NY: Bookwright Press, 1991.

Witness history.

Includes bibliographical references and index.

Examines the social and economic changes in the Soviet Union during Stalin's regime and discusses the nation's devastation by World War II.

A111. Rowen, H.S., Wolf, C., Jr. and Tayler, J. **THE SOVIET UNION AS MILITARY GIANT AND ECONOMIC WEAKLING.** Stanford, CA: Hoover Institution, Stanford University, 1990, 19 pp., 23 cm

Includes bibliographical references (pp. 18–19). Essays in public policy, No. 18.

A112. Rumer, B. **INVESTMENT PERFORMANCE IN THE 12TH FIVE-YEAR PLAN.** *Soviet Studies*, Vol. 43, No. 3, 1991, pp. 451–472.

The investment sphere of the Soviet economy is in chaos. The government has lost control over investment. The gap between investment funds and real resources in construction is rapidly increasing. In the second half of the 1980s, government investment policy went from one extreme to another, and by the end of the decade lost direction completely. Under pressure from society, central authorities are retreating from the goals they themselves set. Today, there is no strategy for investment, improvement of the structure of the economy, or renewal of fixed capital.

A113. Rumer, B. **THE "ABALKANIZATION" OF SOVIET ECONOMIC REFORM.** *Problems of Communism*, Vol. 39, Jan.–Feb. 1990, pp. 74–82.

Discusses the generally pessimistic views of Soviet economist, Leonid Abalkin, director of the Institute of Economics, on the condition of and prospects for the Soviet economy. Outlines the measures Abalkin believes are essential for restoring the health of the Soviet economy.

A114. Rusakova, N. **12.5 MILLION HOMELESS CLAIMED IN U.S.S.R.** JPRS Report (Soviet Union: Political Affairs), July 26, 1990, pp. 49–52.

Translation of an article originally appearing in the magazine Sovetskaya Kultura, May 26, 1990, p. 5. Many of the examples are drawn from the city of Arkhangelsk.

A115. Schroeder, G.E. **PERESTROIKA IN THE AFTERMATH OF 1990.** *Soviet Economy*, Vol. 7, Jan.–Mar. 1991, pp. 3–13.

Assesses Soviet economic performance in 1990 (the worst in the postwar period) and the radicalization of economic reform (featuring significant legislation on destatization of property ownership and decontrol of prices) occurring in 1990. Focuses on increasing efforts by republic and lower-level administrative territorial units to exert greater control over economic activity within their borders, over trade relations with other regions, and over budget allocations to the center. Although economic indicators of reasonably coherent reform legislation that is worthy of implementation.

A116. Schroeder, G.E. **"CRISIS" IN THE CONSUMER SECTOR: A COMMENT.** *Soviet Economy*, Vol. 6, Jan.–Mar. 1990, pp. 56–64.

Analyzes the seeming contradiction between observations of empty shelves in stores prompting perceptions of deteriorating living standards since the beginning perestroika and the fact that CIA and Soviet statistical measures show increases in real consumption. The paper notes that goods have been diverted on a large scale into household hoards, sales through workplaces, and black market channels.

A117. **SELECTED COUNTRIES' TRADE WITH IN U.S.S.R. AND EASTERN EUROPE.** Springfield, VA., U.S. Central Intelligence Agency, Directorate of Intelligence, available from NTIS, 1990, 136 pp. IR 90-10008, RTT 90-10009, July 1990.

This publication provides the most recent, detailed statistics on commodity trade with the Soviet Union and East Europe countries. In this Reference Aid, we show a reporting aggregate, Selected Countries, and seven major countries therein that have reported the most recent data. The aggregate, historically, accounts for about two-thirds of world trade.

A118. Selwyn, M. **THE SOVIET BLOC: OPEN FOR BUSINESS.** *Asian Business*, Vol. 26, Feb. 1990, pp. 20–21,22,24,26,28,30–31.

Discusses the problems Asian businesses confront in doing business with Soviet Bloc countries, including political uncertainty, currency problems, COCOM restrictions, and poor communications. Accompanying articles describe special economic zones in the U.S.S.R's Far East and the concept of countertrade.

A119. Selyunin, V. **THE COLLAPSE OF THE CONSUMER MARKET IN THE U.S.S.R.** *Global Affairs*, Vol. 6, Spring 1991, pp. 22–43.

Details the continuing deterioration of the Soviet economy and the loss of control by Gorbachev who is progressively becoming the president of a non-existent state. Says that the political position of Yeltsin is growing because market reforms can be carried out only by the Union republics.

A120. Seppain, H. **THE DIVIDED WEST: CONTRASTING GERMAN AND U.S. ATTITUDES TO SOVIET TRADE.** *Political Quarterly*, Vol. 61, Jan.–Mar. 1990, pp. 51–65.

Notes that historically West Germany has been a leading force in advocating trade liberalization with the U.S.S.R., while the U.S. has had a cautious, even negative, approach to trade with the Soviet bloc. Concludes that the shift in power away from the United States suggests that the German approach may prevail - at least in Europe.

A121. Shalagin, L. **DOING BUSINESS WITH THE U.S.S.R.: IN CONVERSATION WITH LEONID SHALAGIN.** Freedom at Issue, No. 115, July–Aug. 1990, pp. 20–24.

Presents an interview with Leonid Shalagin, director of Sovamtrade, a Leningrad association that promotes Soviet business ventures with the U.S.

A122. Sheedy, J.F., Dean, R.N. **GAINING A FOOTHOLD IN THE SOVIET MARKET: HOW TO ESTABLISH A REPRESENTATIVE OFFICE.** *International Lawyer*, Vol. 25, Spring 1991, pp. 103–125.

Article describes the new liberalized rules on accreditation for foreign companies wishing to establish a representative office in the U.S.S.R.

A123. Smith, S. **TRADE WITH THE SOVIETS: PROMISE AND PITFALLS.** *State Legislatures*, Vol. 16, Jan. 1990, pp. 22–23,25–26.

Discusses developing trade with the Soviet Union from the State level. Concludes that the Soviet Union offers a vast consumer market to outside entrepreneurs who are able to deal with the vagaries of an underdeveloped nation in political and economic turmoil.

A124. **SOCIALISM, PERESTROIKA, AND THE DILEMMAS OF SOVIET ECONOMIC REFORM.** Edited by J.E. Tedstrom, Boulder, CO: Westview Press, 1990, xix, 239 pp., 23 cm

Published in cooperation with Radio Free Europe/Radio Liberty - T.p. Includes bibliographical references and index.

A125. **THE SOVIET ECONOMY.** *International Economy*, Vol. 4, Oct.–Nov. 1990, pp. 26,28–33,35–36.

Contents - The Soviet's economic apocalypse, by A. Aslund. The case for Soviet membership in the IMF and World Bank, by S.I. Shatalov. Structural failure: anatomy of the Soviet demise, by H.B. Malmagren. Soviet economic rescue plan. Can Soviet oil save Gorbachev? by R. Ebel. Risky business, by M. Lindsay. The Sakhalin Island experiment, by W.F. Kiesner.

A126. **SOVIET FOREIGN ECONOMIC POLICY AND INTERNATIONAL SECURITY.** Edited by E. Stubbs. Armonk, NY: M.E. Sharpe, c1991.

Includes revisions of papers presented at a conference sponsored by the Center for Foreign Policy Development at Brown University held in Dec. 1988.

Includes bibliographical references and index.

A127. **THE SOVIET PREDICAMENT: IS THE ECONOMY AS BAD AS THE SOVIETS SAY?** *Orbis*, Vol. 34, fall 1990, pp. 509–525.

Offers edited excerpts from a conference sponsored by the American Enterprise Institute in April 1990. Among the contributors are V. Belkin, G. Khanin, G. Schroeder, E. Denison, G. Grossman, and V. Tikhonov.

A128. **SOVIET PRICES: WHEN THE PRICE IS WRONG.** *Economist*, Vol. 318, Feb. 2, 1991, 45 pp.

The Soviet government may at last be preparing what it calls price reform. Would this signal the start of real economic change?

A129. Spulber, N. **RESTRUCTURING THE SOVIET ECONOMY: IN SEARCH OF THE MARKET.** Ann Arbor, MI: University of Michigan Press, c1991.

Includes bibliographical references and index.

A130. Stokes, B. **HELP ON HOLD.** *National Journal*, Vol. 23, Feb. 2, 1991, pp. 262–266.

Efforts to help the Soviet Union move to a market-based economy have been put in abeyance as the Gorbachev regime appears to be trying to reverse the movement toward political liberalization.

A131. Sutela, P. **ECONOMIC THOUGHT AND ECONOMIC REFORM IN THE SOVIET UNION.** Cambridge (England), New York, NY: Cambridge University Press, 1991.

Includes bibliographical references and index.

A132. Teague, E. **SOVIET WORKERS FIND A VOICE.** *Report on the U.S.S.R.*, Vol 2, July 13, 1990, pp. 13–17.

Examines worker unrest in the Soviet Union. Includes discussion of recent strike activity, the rise of unofficial worker organizations and worker attitudes toward the economic reforms.

A133. **TECHNOLOGY MARKETS AND EXPORT CONTROLS IN THE 1990's.** Edited by D.M. Kemme. New York, NY: New York University Press, c1991.

Includes bibliographical references and index.

A134. Tedstrom, J. **INDUSTRIAL CONVERSION AND CONSUMER GOODS PRODUCTION.** *Report on the U.S.S.R.*, Vol. 3, May 10, 1991, pp. 3–7.

The Soviet Union has taken an improvised and piecemeal approach to the conversion of military industries to civilian production in the last three years. Local officials and defense-plant managers, who have been left financially in the lurch by major cuts in the procurement program, have had to patch together conversion plans with little or no support from the central government. While Soviet defense plants have not achieved much real conversion, their output of consumer goods and other products for the civilian market in some categories has been noticeable.

A135. Tedstrom, J. **THE OUTLOOK FOR ECONOMIC POLICY IN 1991.** *Report on the U.S.S.R.*, Vol. 3, Jan. 25, 1991, pp. 16–19.

Progress on economic reform since October has been uneven. Kremlin officials have focused their attention more on political relations between the center and the republics, while economic policy-making has tended to be incoherent and generally reactive in nature. It is difficult to predict exactly what measures President Gorbachev will take in the coming months.

A136 Tedstrom, J. **THE 1991 BUDGET.** *Report on the U.S.S.R.*, Vol. 3, Feb. 22, 1991, pp. 5–9.

Examines the 1991 Soviet budget which addresses a serious budget deficit. Assesses the impact of raising revenue from various sources and of different patterns of spending.

A137. **TRANSITION TO A MARKET ECONOMY.** JPRS Report (Soviet Union: Economic Affairs), Sept. 26, 1990, whole issue (190 pp.). JPRS-UEA-90-034.

Presents a translation of the text of the proposal by a working group on the transition to a market economy formed by joint decision of M. Gorbachev and B. Yeltsin.

A138. Tweeten, L., Zulauf, C. and Rask, N. **U.S. AGRICULTURE IN THE NEW INTERNATIONAL ORDER.** Choices, third quarter, 1990, pp. 26–29.

Recent events in Central and Eastern Europe are part of a continuing, world-wide political and economic realignment that is important to U.S. food and agricultural industries. The realignment has greater long-run significance for U.S. agriculture than either the new farm bill of the GATT negotiations.

A139. Unger, A.L. **TOWARDS INTRA-PARTY DEMOCRACY IN THE SOVIET UNION?** The election to the 19th conference of the CPSU. Cologne, Ger., Bundesinstituts fur Ostwissenschaftliche und Internationale Studien, 1990, 60 pp. (Berichte No. 12).

Democratization of the CPSU has been a corner stone of the Gorbachev reforms....As political reform moved to the forefront of perestroika, the introduction....of intra-party democracy became its primary objective.

A140. **U.S. CONGRESS. HOUSE. COMMITTEE ON AGRICULTURE. SUBCOMMITTEE ON WHEAT, SOYBEANS, AND FEED GRAINS. SOVIET AGRICULTURE AND THE OUTLOOK FOR SOVIET PURCHASES OF GRAIN AND OILSEEDS.**

Hearing, 101st Congress, 2nd Session. Sept. 24–Dec. 5, 1990. Washington, G.P.O., 1991, 301 pp. Serial No. 101-72.

A141. **UNITED STATES. CONGRESS. HOUSE. COMMITTEE ON AGRICULTURE. SUBCOMMITTEE ON WHEAT, SOYBEANS, AND FEED GRAINS. SOVIET AGRICULTURE AND THE OUTLOOK FOR SOVIET PURCHASES OF GRAIN AND OILSEEDS.**

Hearings before the Subcommittee on Wheat, Soybeans, and Feed Grains of the Committee on Agriculture, House of Representatives, 101st Congress, 2nd Session, Sept. 24 and Dec. 5, 1990. Washington, DC: U.S. G.P.O. For sale by the Supt. of Docs., Congressional Sales Office, U.S. G.P.O., 1991, iv, 301 pp., ill., maps, 24 cm.

Distributed to some depository libraries in microfiche. Shipping list No. 91-295-P. Serial No. 101-72. Item 1010-A, 1010-B (MF).

A142. **U.S. CONGRESS. COMMISSION ON SECURITY AND COOPERATION IN EUROPE. REFERENDUM IN THE SOVIET UNION: A COMPENDIUM OF REPORTS ON THE MARCH 17, 1991 REFERENDUM ON THE FUTURE OF THE U.S.S.R.**

Washington, The Commission, for sale by the Supt. of Docs., G.P.O., 1991, 46 pp. Mikhail Gorbachev's March 17, 1991 referendum on maintaining the U.S.S.R. as a "renewed federation" was the first in Soviet, or Russian, history.

A143. **U.S. CONGRESS. JOINT ECONOMIC COMMITTEE. SUBCOMMITTEE ON NATIONAL SECURITY ECONOMICS.**

Allocation of resources in the Soviet Union and China. Hearing, 101st Congress, 1st session, Washington, G.P.O., 1990, 220 pp. (Hearing, Senate, 101st Congress, 1st session, S. Hrg. 101-476, Pt. 14). Hearing held Apr. 14 and July 7, 1989.

A144. **U.S. CONGRESS. SENATE. COMMITTEE ON FINANCE.**

U.S.–U.S.S.R. economic relations. Hearing, 101st Senate, 1st session, Oct. 4, 1989, Washington, G.P.O., 1990, 45 pp. (Hearing, Senate, 101st Congress, 1st session, S. Hrg. 101-641).

A145. **U.S. CONGRESS. SENATE. COMMITTEE ON FINANCE.**

Trip report on congressional delegate Bentsen (visit to the Union of Soviet Socialist Republics, Tuesday, January 16, 1990 through Thursday, January 18, 1990). Prepared by the staff for the use of the Committee on Finance, United States Senate, Loyd Bentsen, Chairman. Washington, G.P.O., 1990, 12 pp. (Print, Senate, 101st Congress, 2nd session, committee print S. Prt. 101-87).

A146. **U.S. CONGRESS. SENATE. COMMITTEE ON FINANCE.**

U.S.–U.S.S.R. economic relations: hearing before the Committee on Finance, United States Senate, 101st Congress, 1st session, October 4, 1989, Washington, DC: U.S. G.P.O.

A147. **U.S. GENERAL ACCOUNTING OFFICE.**

Soviet refugees: processing and admittance to the United States: report to congressional requesters. May 9, 1990, Washington, G.A.O., 1990, 26 pp. GAO/NSIAD-90-158, B-238005.

The Foreign Operations Appropriations Act for fiscal year, Public law 101-167....Section 599D, referred to as the Lautenberg Amendment, requires the Executive branch to establish refugee processing categories for Jews, Evangelical Christian, Ukrainian Catholics and Ukrainian Orthodox Church members.

A148. **U.S. GENERAL ACCOUNTING OFFICE.**

Soviet energy: U.S. attempts to aid oil production are hindred by many obstacles. Report to the Chairman, Committee on Foreign Relations, U.S. Senate. May 24, 1991. Washington, G.A.O., 1991, 28 pp.

GAO/NSIAD-91-214, B-243667. Provides information on (1) the decline in Soviet oil production and the reasons for this decline and (2) the principal obstacles to U.S. trade and investment in Soviet oil exploration and production.

A149. **U.S. GENERAL ACCOUNTING OFFICE.**
Export controls: U.S. policies and procedures regarding the Soviet Union; fact sheet for the Chairman, Committee on Finance, U.S. Senate. May 24, 1990, Washington, G.A.O., 1990, 19 pp. GAO/NSIAD-90-185FS, B-239423.
Provides information on U.S. export controls regarding the Soviet Union. Specifically, it contains information on export control policies and procedures, the current level of control on exports to the Soviet Union, and U.S. plans to liberalize these controls.

A150. **U.S. GENERAL ACCOUNTING OFFICE.**
Soviet refugees: issue affecting domestic resettlement; report to the Honorable Charles E. Grassley, U.S. Senate, June 26, 1990, Washington, G.A.O., 1990, 24 pp. GAO/HRD-90-106BR, B-239117.
The domestic costs of resettling refugees admitted to this country particularly Soviet refugees.

A151. **U.S. GENERAL ACCOUNTING OFFICE.**
International trade: Soviet export data; briefing report to the chairman, Committee on Finance, U.S. Senate, July 18, 1990, Washington, G.A.O., 1990, 23 pp. GAO/NSIAD-90-209BR, B-239716.
This report (1) provides data on Soviet exports to the United States and the rest of the world, (2) compares the similarity between leading Soviet exports to the United States and other selected countries, (3) provides data on tariff rates for U.S. imports from the Soviet Union, and (4) compares them to rates for countries granted MFN trade status.

A152. **THE U.S.–SOVIET TRADE DIRECTORY.** W.S. Loiry, ed. Chicago, IL: Probus Pub. Co., c1991, 283 pp., 24 cm.

A153. van Ham, P. **SOVIET ECONOMIC REFORM AND EAST-WEST ECONOMIC RELATIONS.** *Problems of Communism*, Vol. 40, Jan.–Apr. 1991, pp. 144–149.
Reviews recent books which provide an understanding of past and present efforts at Soviet economic reform.

A154. Van Winkle, J., Zycher, B. **FUTURE SOVIET INVESTMENT IN TRANSPORTATION, ENERGY, AND ENVIRONMENTAL PROTECTION.** Santa Monica, Calif., Rand Corporation, 1991, 49 pp. (Rand Note N-3173-USDP)
Partial Contents - Introduction. Transportation in the 12th five-year plan. Condition of the Soviet railroads. The biggest constraints on economic growth. Railroad capacity and maintenance. Motor vehicle transportation. Energy. Investment in the fuels and electricity sectors. Nuclear safety retrofit. Environmental issues and resource demands in the Soviet economy. Water supply. Air pollution. Overview of Soviet environmental policy. Prospects for future investment in environmental protection.

A155. Van Atta, D. **BACK TO THE FUTURE IN THE SOVIET COUNTRYSIDE?** *Problems of Communism*, Vol. 40, Jan.–Apr. 1991, pp. 155–164.
Reviews recent works which examine the role of the collective farm in Soviet politics, government, economics, and culture. Considers directions for this institution under Gorbachev.

A156. Vlachoutsicos, C. and Lawrence, P. **WHAT WE DON'T KNOW ABOUT SOVIET MANAGEMENT.** *Harvard Business Review,* Vol. 68, Nov. –Dec. 1990, pp. 50–52,56,58–59,62–63.

Presents results of a study comparing managerial behavior in the Soviet Union and the U.S. Claims that despite the problems of chronic shortages and centralized planning, a remarkable number of Soviet enterprises produce usable, sophisticated products and care for their workers as well.

A157. Volkov, Y.E. **PERESTROIKA, EDUCATION, AND THE SOVIET ECONOMY.** *Forum for Applied Research and Public Policy,* Vol. 6., Spring 1991, pp. 89–97.

Argues that in order to tailor the Soviet education system to the needs of the scientific and technological revolution, it is necessary to make radical economic changes, reorganize the education system, and improve education and training methods. Within the next few years, the Soviet Union must increase education's share of the national budget from its present two percent to 10 to 12 percent - the level in most industrialized countries. Without this investment, Soviet education will continue to decline, and the economy and living standards of the Soviet people will continue to fall as well.

A158. Ward, C. **RUSSIA'S COTTON WORKERS AND THE NEW ECONOMIC POLICY: SHOP-FLOOR CULTURE AND STATE POLICY, 1921–1929.** Cambridge (England), New York, NY: Cambridge University Press, 1990, xvi, 304, (2) pp. of plates, ill, 24 cm.

Includes bibliographical references (pp. 275–290) and index.

A159. Warner, G. **THE INVISIBLE THREADS: INDEPENDENT SOVIETS WORKING FOR GLOBAL AWARENESS AND SOCIAL TRANSFORMATION.** Washington, DC: Seven Locks Press, c1991, xi, 249 pp., 23 cm.

Includes index.

A160. Westbrook, C. and Sherr, A.B. **U.S.–SOVIET JOINT VENTURES AND EXPORT CONTROL POLICY.** Providence, RI: Center for Foreign Policy Development, Brown University, c1990, 30 pp., 28 cm. Briefing paper, No. 3.

Includes bibliographical references.

A161. Winiecki, J. **RESISTANCE TO CHANGE IN THE SOVIET ECONOMIC SYSTEM: A PROPERTY RIGHTS APPROACH.** New York, NY: Routledge, 1990, p. cm.

Includes bibliographical references and index.

A162. **WORKSHOP ON U.S.–U.S.S.R. COMMERCIAL RELATIONS (1989 Apr. 17).**

Workshop on U.S.–U.S.S.R. Commercial Relations: April 17, 1989: a report to the committee on Foreign Relations, United States Senate, by the Congressional Research Service, Library of Congress, Washington, DC: U.S. G.P.O. At head of title: committee print. June 1990.

A163. World Bank Conference on Development Economics (1991, Washington, D.C.). **PROSPECTS FOR ECONOMIC REFORM IN THE U.S.S.R.** Washington, The Bank, 1991, 47 pp.

Contents - Monetary and fiscal problems. The destruction of economic policy-making. Attempts at stabilization and system change. Prospects.

A164. Zaslow, D. **TRUCKING IN THE SOVIET ECONOMY.** *Soviet Geography,* Vol. 31, Mar. 1990, pp. 173–194.

Investigates constraints in the U.S.S.R. to the greater use of trucking during the 1980s, low road density and quality, insufficient trucks, a narrow variety of vehicles, inadequate repair facilities, and fuel shortages. These problems reflect in part the lack of incentives both for the trucking industry to satisfy demand for transport and for machine-builders to improve truck quality, limited investment in road construction, and the neglect of requirements for spare parts.

B. FOREIGN POLICY; FOREIGN AFFAIRS; MILITARY

B001. **A U.S. STRATEGY FOR THE UNPREDICTABLE 90'S; SPECIAL REPORT.** *World and I,* Vol. 5, Jan. 1990, pp. 108–139.

Contents - Helping Gorbachev: the right thing to do? by M.I. Goldman. Working with the new Europe, by R.L. Pfaltzgraff, Jr. a niche for NATO in the 90's? by M.T. Clark. Setting priorities in a changing Asia by N.D. Palmer. The Third World: proceed with caution, by M. Radu.

B002. **A NEW GERMANY - A NEW EUROPE?** *World and I,* Vol. 5, Feb. 1990, pp. 18–51.

Contents - The Cold War has ended, by R.E. Hunter. A changing Germany: what it means, by W. Kaltefleiter. Europe casts an anxious eye, by G. Frost. Gorbachev seeks a trade-off, by C. Jones. The challenge of history, by M.A. Kaplan.

B003. Adelman, K. **HOW GORBACHEV HAS CHANGED US.** *American Enterprise,* Vol. 1, Jan.–Feb. 1990, pp. 22–28.

By discrediting Marxism as a living ideology, Gorbachev has discredited America's ideological thrust abroad. Gone with Messianic Communism is Messianic Democracy.

B004. Adomeit, H. **GORBACHEV AND GERMAN UNIFICATION: REVISION OF THINKING, REALIGNMENT OF POWER.** *Problems of Communism,* Vol. 39, July–Aug. 1990, pp. 1–23.

By Consenting to the unification of Germany, Mikhail Gorbachev has laid the groundwork for Soviet withdrawal from a region....The Gorbachev leadership no longer views a united Germany as a security threat to the U.S.S.R.; Soviet conservatives are harshly critical of Gorbachev's abandonment of the policy toward Europe in general and toward Germany in particular. However, the opposition has no alternative to Gorbachev's policies, which promise not only to remove most of the barriers dividing Eastern and Western Europe but also to pave the way for expanded Soviet cooperation with existing all-European institutions.

B005. **AFGHANISTAN, THE GREAT GAME REVISITED.** Edited by R. Klass, New York, NY: Freedom House, Lanham, MD: Distributed by National Book Network, c1990, 565 pp., maps, 24 cm.

Includes bibliographical references (pp. 521–545) and index.

B006. **AFGHANISTAN AND SRI LANKA: A COMPARISON OF OPERATIONAL STYLES.** *Indian Defence Review,* Jan. 1990, pp. 78–87.

B007. **AFGHANISTAN: UNTOLD STORIES.** *Progressive*, Vol. 54, May 1990, pp. 17–29.

Contents - Journalistic Jihad: a reporter details faked and distorted coverage of Afghanistan. Strained mercy: a "relief agency" for Afghanistan dispenses propaganda galore, but not much medical care. Afghan stalemate: when the Soviet Union pulled its troops out last year, victory for the Mujahideen seemed imminent, but it hasn't happened. Why Kabul didn't fall.

B008. **AGENDA FOR ACTION: AFRICAN–SOVIET–U.S. COOPERATION.** Edited by A.A. Gromyko, C.S. Whitaker, Boulder, CO: L. Rienner Publishers, 1990, xii, 290 pp., 23 cm.

Includes bibliographical references.

B009. Albright, D.E. **VANGUARD PARTIES AND REVOLUTIONARY CHANGE IN THE THIRD WORLD: SOVIET PERSPECTIVES AND THEIR IMPLICATIONS.** Berkeley, CA: Institute of International Studies, University of California, c1990, vii, 126 pp., 24 cm.

Includes bibliographical references (pp. 97–126).

B010. Alekseeva, L. 1927– and Goldberg, P. **THE THAW GENERATION: COMING OF AGE IN THE POST-STALIN ERA.** Boston, MA: Little, Brown, c1990, 339 pp., 16 pp. of plates, ill., 25 cm.

Includes bibliographical references and index.

B011. Alexander, Arthur J. **PERESTROIKA AND CHANGE IN SOVIET WEAPONS ACQUISITION.** Santa Monica, Calif., Rand, 1990, 96 pp.

Contents - Introduction - The plight of Soviet civilian industry. The favored situation of Soviet defense industry. Overview of policy on defense industry conversion. Approaches to conversion. Implementing conversion. Consequences of conversion for civilian production. Soviet defense budgets. The implications of technology and complexity. Soviet weapons acquisition under political reform and technological revolution.

B012. Almquist, P. **RED FORGE: SOVIET MILITARY INDUSTRY SINCE 1965.** New York, NY: Columbia University Press, c1990, xi, 227 pp., 24 cm.

Revised version of the author's doctoral dissertation....Massachusetts Institute of Technology....Introd. Includes bibliographical references (pp. 201–219) and index.

B013. **ALONE AT THE TOP.** *Newsweek*, Vol. 115, June 11, 1990, pp. 14–19.

Gorbachev and Bush established a new rapport at a summit that succeeded without producing breakthroughs on Germany or Lithuania. But a challenge from Boris Yeltsin cast a shadow on the Soviet leader's moment in the sun.

B014. **AMERICA AND THE WORLD 1990/91.** *Foreign Affairs*, Vol. 70, No. 1, 1991, whole issue (pp. 1–249).

Partial contents - The Bush foreign policy, by M. Mandelbaum. The unipolar moment, by C. Krauthammer. Redefining world power, by W. Pfaff. The Soviet Union adrift, by R. Pipes. Latin America: the frustrations of success, by M.A. Uhlig. The Asian-Pacific rim: success at a price, by B.K. Gordon. The year the world economy turned, by C.M. Aho and B. Stokes.

B015. **AMERICAN AND SOVIET INTERVENTION: EFFECTS ON WORLD STABILITY.** Edited by K.A. Feste, New York, NY: Crane Russak, 1990, v, 162 pp., 24 cm.

Includes bibliographical references (p. 147–152) and index.

B016. Amiryar, Q.A. **AFGHANISTAN'S FOREIGN POLICY DILEMMA WITH CHINA AND THE SOVIET UNION: THE TWO ARCH RIVALS.** *Journal of Asian and African Affairs*, Vol. 2, July 1990, pp. 69–85.

Considers the status of events for Afghanistan with regard to that country's relations with both the Soviet Union and China. This study explores the following: Firstly China's perceptions of her relations with Afghanistan, secondly it examines the nature of the Sino-Soviet rivalry in Afghanistan, and thirdly it addresses issues related to polarization of indigenous ideological forces, following the fall of monarchy which in turn inevitably encouraged outside powers to come to the rescue of their patrons.

B017. Amundsen, K. **SOVIET STRATEGIC INTERESTS IN THE NORTH.** New York, NY: St. Martin's Press, 1990, xii, 153 pp., ill., 23 cm.

Includes bibliographical references (pp. 140–147) and index.

B018. Andrew, C.M. and O. Gordievsky. **KGB: THE INSIDE STORY OF ITS FOREIGN OPERATIONS FROM LENIN TO GORBACHEV.** New York, NY: Harper Collins Publishers, c1990, xvii, 776 pp. (24) pp. of plates, ill, 25 cm.

Includes bibliographical references (pp. 729–744) and index.

B019. Arbatov, A.G. **IMPLEMENTING START: POLITICAL, ECONOMIC AND STRATEGIC DIMENSIONS.** *Mediterranean Quarterly*, Vol. 2, Spring 1991, pp. 55–71.

Negotiations between the United States and Soviet Union during 1990 advanced the Strategic Arms Reduction Treaty (START) to what could conveniently be called a 90 percent completion. The time has come, therefore, to make some preliminary evaluations about the significance and consequences of this treaty.

B020. Arnett, R.L. and Fitzgerald, M.C. **RESTRUCTURING THE ARMED FORCES: THE CURRENT SOVIET DEBATE.** *Journal of Soviet Military Studies*, Vol. 3, June 1990, pp. 193–220.

A debate is under way in the Soviet Union regarding whether the Soviet military should switch from the current large, mainly conscript army to a different type of organization....Reform proponents have articulated a variety of proposals, including conversion to an all-volunteer professional army, to a militia system, to national territorial armies, or to some combination of these types....This article examines the nature of the debate, the participants, the reasoning provided, and the likely outcome of the controversy.

B021. Arnett, E.H. **NAVAL NUCLEAR ARMS CONTROL.** *F.A.S. (Journal of the Federation of American Scientists) Public Interest Report*, Vol. 44, May–June 1991, pp. 1–6.

For some time, Administration officials have been effectively refusing to engage in substantive negotiations with the Soviet Union over naval nuclear arms limitations in an area in which the U.S. is superior.

B022. Arnett, R. and Fitzgerald, M. **A VOLUNTEER RED ARMY?** *Orbis*, Vol. 34, Summer 1990, pp. 398–402.

In the summer of 1988, a public debate surfaced in the Soviet Union about whether the armed forces should switch from a largely conscript army to an all-volunteer professional army.

B023. Aron, L. **PREPARING AMERICA FOR THE WAVE OF RUSSIAN IMMIGRANTS.** Washington, Heritage Foundation, 1991, 16 pp. (Backgrounder No. 815).

"The United States must devise a bold immigration policy to help resettle the millions of ethnic Russians who - fleeing economic chaos in the Soviet Union - will look for work in the West this year", says the author.

B024. Aron, L. **GORBACHEV'S CENTRAL ASIAN TIME BOMB IS TICKING.** Washington, Heritage Foundation, 1990, 20 pp.

With 55 million Muslims living on Soviet territory....The Muslim republics of Kazakhstan, Kirgizia, Tadzhikistan, Turkmenia, and Uzbekistan are ready for what could be a violent showdown with the Soviet central government on the road to independence. There are five reasons for this.

B025. Aron, L. and Kosminsky, J.P. **THE BUSH–GORBACHEV WASHINGTON SUMMIT, MAY 30–JUNE 2, 1990: MAINTAINING THE MOMENTUM OF CHANGE.** Washington, Heritage Foundation, 1990, 36 pp.

The Washington summit meeting on May 30–June 2 between George Bush and Mikhail Gorbachev occurs at a crucial juncture in the history of the twentieth century....Denied new ground for expansion, communism in the Soviet Union is collapsing beneath the weight of its own bureaucratic inertia and internal contradictions. What should and could be accomplished at the upcoming Bush–Gorbachev summit? In the enclosed analysis, Heritage Foundation specialists spell out the game plan for George Bush.

B026. Aronson, G. **SOVIET JEWISH EMIGRATION, THE UNITED STATES, AND THE OCCUPIED TERRITORIES.** *Journal of Palestine Studies*, Vol. 19, Summer 1990, pp. 30–45.

B027. **ASIA AND THE DECLINE OF COMMUNISM.** Edited by Y.C. Kim and G.J. Sigur. New Brunswick, NJ: Transaction Publishers, c1991.

Includes index.

B028. Asmus, R.D., Brown, J.F. and Crane, K. **SOVIET FOREIGN POLICY AND THE REVOLUTIONS OF 1989 IN EASTERN EUROPE.** Santa Monica, Calif., Rand Corporation, 1991, 177 pp. (Report No. R-3903-USDP).

The impetus for change in Soviet policy toward Eastern Europe must be sought in the same factors that promoted radical changes in Soviet domestic and foreign policy - the growing recognition of the profound domestic and foreign policy crisis that confronted Soviet policy-makers since the early 1980s. At the same time, Mikhail Gorbachev's attempts to deal with Eastern

Europe were plagued from the outset by the same contradictions and inconsistencies that characterized the first five years of his rule.

B029. Asopa, S.K. **SOVIET UNION AND THE THIRD WORLD: FROM DOGMATIC MARXISM TO GLASNOST.** Jaipur, India: Printwell Publishers, 1990, viii, 186 pp., 22 cm.

Covers the period, 1917–1989. Includes bibliographical references (pp. 177–183).

B030. **ASSESSING THE THREAT.** Edited by S.T. Ross and D.A. Rosenberg, New York, NY: Garland Pub., 1990, 1 v. (various pagings), ill., 29 cm.

America's plans for war against the Soviet Union, 1945–1950, vol. 10.

B031. Atkinson, R. and Lee, G. **THE RED ARMY IN RETREAT.** Washington Post, Nov. 18, A1,A28–A29; Nov. 19, A1,A28; Nov. 20, A1,A14; Nov 21, A1,A2.

Contents - Soviet Army coming apart at the seams: poverty, ethnic schisms, desertion beset once proud military. Brutality stalks Soviet conscripts. A stubborn fidelity: political officers cling to tradition. The battle to beat swords into shoes: defense plants are forced into production of consumer goods.

B032. Atkinson, S.R. **SOVIET DEFENSE POLICY UNDER GORBACHEV: THE GROWING CIVILIAN INFLUENCE**, Alexandria, VA., Center for Naval Analyses, c1990, 35 pp. (CNA Occasional Paper, Mar. 1990).

Partial contents - National security decision-making before Gorbachev. The rise of the institutchiki. The institutchiki and recent national security decisions.

B033. Balassa, B.A. **PERESTROIKA AND ITS IMPLICATIONS FOR EUROPEAN SOCIALIST COUNTRIES.** Washington, DC (1818 H St., NW, Washington 20433): Development Economics, the World Bank, 1990, 22 pp., 28 cm.

Cover title, Paper presented at the Hungarian–U.S. roundtable held in Budapest, Hungary, Nov. 22–25, 1989, May 1990. Includes bibliographical references (pp. 22). Policy, research, and external affairs working papers; WPS 428. Perestroika.

B034. Barany, Z.D. **NOT A SMOOTH RIDE: SOVIET TROOP WITHDRAWALS FROM HUNGARY.** *Report on Eastern Europe*, Vol. 1, June 15, 1990, pp. 20–28.

Soviet troops are withdrawing from Hungary on or even ahead of schedule. But there are many more issues on which the experts do not see eye to eye.

B035. Barany, Z.D. **A HUNGARIAN DREAM COMES TRUE: SOVIET TROOPS TO LEAVE AFTER 45 YEARS.** *Report on Eastern Europe*, Vol. 1, Mar. 30, 1990, pp. 23–28.

On March 10 a historic agreement between Hungary and the Soviet Union was signed in Moscow on the withdrawal of all Soviet troops from Hungary by June 30, 1991.

B036. Barnet, R.J. **AFTER THE COLD WAR.** *New Yorker*, Vol. 65, Jan. 1, 1990, pp. 65–76.

The long joust we call the Cold War no longer serves the interest of either the United States or the Soviet Union. The institutions of the Cold War will survive and will set limits on the process. The great challenge of the next decades is to make the domestic institutions of nations reflect the political, economic, and ecological realities of the post-Cold War world.

B037. Beichman, A. **THE LONG PRETENSE: SOVIET TREATY DIPLOMACY FROM LENIN TO GORBACHEV.** With a foreword by W.F. Buckley, Jr. New Brunswick, NJ: Transaction Publishers, c1991, xiv, 303 pp., 24 cm.
Includes bibliographical references (pp. 281–292) and index.

B038. Belikov, I. **SOVIET SCHOLARS' DEBATE ON SOCIALIST ORIENTATION IN THE THIRD WORLD.** *Millennium*, Vol. 20, Spring 1991, pp. 23–39.
Following the reforms initiated in 1985 under the course of perestroika, a gradual change began within the overall ideological climate in the Soviet Union. Criticism, very cautious at the beginning, grew and called into question a number of previously sacred official principles and dogmas. The turning point in this process occurred in 1987, when the first elements of real pluralism became distinguishable in both the social sciences and in public opinion. Considers the impact of these changes upon Soviet foreign policy, especially in the Third World.

B039. Bell, P.M.H. (Philip Michael Hitt). 1930–. **JOHN BULL AND THE BEAR: BRITISH PUBLIC OPINION, FOREIGN POLICY, AND THE SOVIET UNION, 1941–1945.** New York, NY: E. Arnold, 1990, p. cm.
Includes bibliographical references and index.

B040. Bernstein, A.H. **SOVIET DEFENSE SPENDING: THE SPARTAN ANALOGY.** *Comparative Strategy*, Vol. 9, No. 9, 1990, pp. 33–65.
This essay was prompted by the comparison between the Soviet Union and ancient Sparta recently made by economists and Sovietologists....The aim of the paper is not so much to support or criticize the analogy as to provide the means for evaluating it.

B041. **BEYOND THE COLD WAR: SUPERPOWERS AT THE CROSSROADS.** Edited by M. Cox, Lanham, MD: University Press of America, 1990, p. cm.
Exxon Education Foundation series on rhetoric and political discourse, v. 14.

B042. **BEYOND THE HOPPO RYODO: JAPANESE–SOVIET–AMERICAN RELATIONS IN THE 1990s.** J.D.C. Jacob, ed. Washington, DC: AEI Press, 1991.

B043. **BEYOND THE COLD WAR: SOVIET AND AMERICAN MEDIA IMAGES.** Edited by E.E. Dennis, G. Gerbner and Y.N. Zassoursky. Newbury Park: Sage, c1991, x, 180 pp., 23 cm.
Includes bibliographical references (p. 170) and index.

B044. **BEYOND SUPERPOWER RIVALRY: LATIN AMERICA AND THE THIRD WORLD.** Edited by J.F. Weeks. New York, NY: New York University Press, c1991.

Proceedings of a conference held in Vienna in late spring of 1989. Includes index.

B045. Black, W.B. and Blashfield, J.F. **RUSSIA AT WAR.** New York, NY: Crestwood House, c1991. World War II 50th Anniversary Series.
Includes index.
Describes Hitler's invasion of Russia in 1941 and the Soviet defense and ultimate victory.

B046. Blan, S. **AFTER AFGHANISTAN: REASSESSING SOVIET CAPABILITIES AND POLICIES FOR POWER PROJECTION.** *Comparative Strategy*, Vol. 9, No. 2, 1990, pp. 117–136.
The withdrawal of Soviet combat troops from Afghanistan as of February 1989 allows us to begin retrospective assessments of that conflict's impact on the elements of Soviet military operations abroad. These are doctrine, strategy, tactics, force structure, command, control, communication, and intelligence (C I).

B047. **BLUEPRINT FOR REARMAMENT - READER.** Edited by S.T. Ross and D.A. Rosenberg, New York, NY: Garland Pub., 1990, 1 v. (various pages), 29 cm.
Includes bibliographical references.

B048. Bluth, C. **NEW THINKING IN SOVIET MILITARY POLICY.** New York, NY: Published in North America for the Royal Institute of International Affairs (by) Council on Foreign Relations Press, c1990, 118 pp., 22 cm. Chatham House Papers.
Includes bibliographical references.

B049. Borovik, A. 1960–. **THE HIDDEN WAR: A RUSSIAN JOURNALIST'S ACCOUNT OF THE SOVIET WAR IN AFGHANISTAN.** New York, NY: Atlantic Monthly Press, c1990, 288 pp. (8) pp. of plates, ill., map, 24 cm.
Translation of: Afghanistan. Originally published: U.S.S.R.: International Relations Publishing House, 1990. A Morgan Entrekin book.

B050. Bowles, W.D. and Arefieva, E.B. **PROPOSALS FOR JOINT U.S.–U.S.S.R. COOPERATION WITH DEVELOPING COUNTRIES: TRIPARTITE PROJECTS.** Washington, Overseas Development Council, 1990. 33 pp.
Partial contents - The feasibility of U.S.–U.S.S.R. cooperation. Potential source of funding, Possible areas of cooperation.

B051. Brands, H.W. **INSIDE THE COLD WAR: LOY HENDERSON AND THE RISE OF THE AMERICAN EMPIRE, 1918–1961.** New York, NY: Oxford University Press, 1991, xiv, 337 pp., 25 cm.
Includes bibliographical references (pp. 315–331) and index.

B052. Breslauer, G.W. **SOVIET STRATEGY IN THE MIDDLE EAST.** With contributions by G. Golan.... et al. Boston: Unwin Hyman, 1990 (Cambridge (England), University Press) xvi, 320 pp., 25 cm.
A book of the Berkeley–Stanford Program in Soviet Studies Includes bibliographical references and index.

B053. Brooks, T.A. **THE SOVIET NAVY IN 1989: A U.S. VIEW.** United States Naval Institute Proceedings, Vol. 116, May 1990, pp. 235–238.

The Soviets in 1989 sent 30 vessels to overseas scrap yards. Most of the 15 submarines....were of the 1950s-vintage Whiskey class. But even as they were ridding themselves of "yard queens," the Soviets were building a newer, leaner, and meaner fleet.

B054. Brown, B. **THE ISLAMIC RENAISSANCE PARTY IN CENTRAL ASIA.** *Report on the U.S.S.R.*, Vol. 3, May 10, 1991, pp. 12–14.

The branches of the all-Union Islamic Renaissance Party in Tafikistan and Uzbekistan have been outlawed by the authorities in those republics, but the party remains the most potent challenger of the Communist political establishment in the two republics.

B055. Brown, B. **THE ALL-UNION REFERENDUM IN CENTRAL ASIA.** *Report on the U.S.S.R.*, Vol. 3, Mar. 29, 1991, pp. 1–5.

Despite attempts by opposition groups in some Central Asian republics to persuade voters to boycott or vote "no" in the all-Union referendum, voting was heavily in favor of continuation of the Union. Republican leaders had predicted this outcome.

B056. Brzezinski, Z. **ZBIGNIEW BRZEZINSKI: GALLOPING PAST CONVENTIONAL WISDOM.** *International Economy*, Vol. 4, Apr.–May, 1990, pp. 51–54.

Interview with Zbigniew Brzezinski discusses the events in Eastern Europe and the Soviet Union, and the direction of U.S. foreign policy.

B057. Bundy, McG. **FROM COLD WAR TOWARD TRUSTING PEACE.** *Foreign Affairs*, Vol. 69, No. 1, 1990, pp. 197–212.

Concludes that as a matter of history we cannot yet say that the cold war is over. But looking ahead from where we are now it is not wrong to say that the last decade of the century bids fair to be a time of steadily stronger peace, both in Europe and in the overall relations between the two great protagonists of the years since 1945.

B058. Bunn, M. **FOUNDATION FOR THE FUTURE, THE ABM TREATY AND NATIONAL SECURITY.** Washington, Arms Control Association, 1990, 222 pp.

Contents - The ABM Treaty: cornerstone of security and arms control. The history of nuclear defense and the ABM Treaty. How the ABM Treaty works. The Strategic Defense Initiative. The Soviet ABM program. The reinterpretation of the ABM Treaty. Soviet compliance with the ABM Treaty. U.S. compliance with the ABM Treaty. Grey-area systems and the ABM Treaty. Nationwide missile defenses or the ABM Treaty? Other options for SDI. Reaffirming the ABM Treaty.

B059. Bunn, M. **FOUNDATION FOR THE FUTURE: THE ABM TREATY AND NATIONAL SECURITY.** Washington, DC: Arms Control Association, c1990, viii, 222 pp., ill, 28 cm.

Includes bibliographical references (pp. 188–217) and index.

B060. Caldwell, L.T. **SOVIET–AMERICAN RELATIONS: THE COLD WAR ENDS.** *Current History*, Vol. 89, Oct. 1990, pp. 305–308,343–346.

The world has changed in one year. The United States and the Soviet Union are still global superpowers, at least in military terms, but reductions in East–West tensions and political change in East Europe have greatly accelerated trends in international affairs away from military power.

B061. Calingaert, D. **SOVIET NUCLEAR POLICY UNDER GORBACHEV: A POLICY OF DISARMAMENT.** New York, NY: Praeger, 1991, x, 180 pp., 23 cm.

Includes bibliographical references (pp. 167–171) and index.

B062. Callaghan, T.A., Jr. **DO WE STILL NEED NATO?** *Journal of Defense and Diplomacy*, Vol. 8, Apr. 1990, pp. 51–54.

The Soviet threat may be non-existent. But Soviet military power remains. Even after the first round of Conventional Forces Europe (CFE) negotiations are completed, Soviet forces will still be stronger than all of NATO's. Thus prudence should be the rule in the Alliance's reaction to events in Eastern Europe.

B063. Campbell, D. **GLOBAL INSCRIPTION: HOW FOREIGN POLICY CONSTITUTES THE UNITED STATES.** *Alternatives*, Vol. 15, Summer 1990, pp. 263–286.

Was the behavior of the Soviet Union the organizing principle for U.S. foreign policy during the Cold War era, or was U.S. foreign policy constituted by dimensions other than external necessity.

B064. Carmody, M.D. **THE CVs ARE NOT ENOUGH.** United States Naval Institute Proceedings, Vol. 116, Jan. 1990, pp. 106–107.

Retired Admiral discusses the Soviet military doctrine as it applies to naval operations and examines U.S. naval options. Soviet strategy employs missile-carrying submarines and long-range aircraft as offensive weapons against U.S. naval forces and sea lines of communication (SLOC)....A glance at a map reveals the vulnerability of sea lanes vital to U.S. and allied forces. Equally disturbing is the Soviets' well-rehearsed tactical coordination between their missile-launching submarines and the long-range aircraft that provides continuous tracking and terminal guidance for missiles.

B065. Chalmers, M. **SOVIET WEAPONS PROCUREMENT IN THE 1980'S: TIME FOR GLASNOST IN THE PENTAGON?** *Defense Analysis*, Vol. 6, Sept. 1990, pp. 255–262.

The U.S. DOD figures on procurement have escaped the detailed outside analysis which has been given to DOD estimates of the Soviet defense budget....Raises a number of questions about the published figures which are in need of a convincing answer.

B066. Chang, G.H. **FRIENDS AND ENEMIES: THE UNITED STATES, CHINA, AND THE SOVIET UNION, 1948–1972.** Stanford, CA: Stanford University, 1990, ix, 383 pp. (16) pp. of plates, ill., 23 cm. Modern America.

Includes bibliographical references (pp. 357–375) and index.

B067. **THE CHANGING U.S.–SOVIET STRATEGIC BALANCE.** *Global Affairs*, Vol. 5, Spring 1990, pp. 5–24.

A record of the proceeding's of a conference on the above theme held in Moscow Jan. 24–26, 1990.

B068. **THE CHANGING WESTERN ANALYSIS OF THE SOVIET THREAT.** Edited by C.-C. Schweitzer, New York, NY: St. Martin's Press, 1990, c1989, p. cm.

North Atlantic Treaty Organization.

B069. Chelminski, R. **KATYN: ANATOMY OF A MASSACRE.** *Reader's Digest*, Vol. 136, May 1990, pp. 69–79.

Based on interviews with sources in the U.S., Great Britain, Poland and the Soviet Union, the author discusses the massacre of Polish soldiers held in Soviet prisoner-of-war camps. Discusses the Soviet responsibility for the event.

B070. Chernoff, F. **START OR FINISH? THE FUTURE OF STRATEGIC ARMS CONTROL AND PROFOUND FORCE REDUCTIONS.** *Defense Analysis*, Vol. 6, Sept. 1990, pp. 235–254.

Where should the American arms control policy be heading? This paper outlines one set of policy objectives and offers a package of proposals designed to achieve them....Weapons deployment and arms control have always been intimately related, their interdependence is now greater than ever....The time to make decisions on at least some of the long-term goals is now, before START is signed.

B071. Chichock, M.A. **THE SOVIET UNION AND YUGOSLAVIA IN THE 1980'S: A RELATIONSHIP IN FLUX.** *Political Science Quarterly*, Vol. 105, Spring 1990, pp. 53–74.

Describes a fundamental alteration that has come to characterize the Soviet-Yugoslav relationship in the Gorbachev era. The author concludes that a nonthreatening transformation took shape that was an early indicator of the change process in the rest of Eastern Europe.

B072. Christians, F.W. **PATHS TO RUSSIA: FROM WAR TO PEACE.** Foreword by H. Schmidt, translation from the German by Joachim Neugroschel, New York, NY: Macmillan, Toronto: Collier Macmillan Canada, New York, NY: Maxwell Macmillan International, c1990, xv, 236 pp., 25 cm.

B073. **CHRONICLE OF A REVOLUTION: A WESTERN–SOVIET INQUIRY INTO PERESTROIKA.** Edited by A. Brumberg, New York, NY: Pantheon Books, c1990, vi, 266 pp., 24 cm.

Includes bibliographical references (pp. 239–253) and index.

B074. Chufrin, G. **THE U.S.S.R. AND ASIA-PACIFIC IN 1990.** *Asian Survey*, Vol. 31, Jan. 1991, pp. 14–20.

Summarizes Soviet policy in the Asian-Pacific region as one of nonconfrontation aimed at changing in the eyes of the Pacific community the traditional image of the Soviet Union as an expansionist country to that of a prospective partner. And although signals sent by Moscow to this effect did not always get an adequate response from the regional countries, this probably was not because the signals were intentionally ignored but because they were either not properly interpreted or simply required time for adjustment to new realities.

B075. Cimbala, S.J. **UNCERTAINTY AND CONTROL: FUTURE SOVIET AND AMERICAN STRATEGY.** New York, NY: St. Martin's Press, 1990, vii, 183 pp., 24 cm.
Includes bibliographical references and index.

B076. Cimbala, S.J. **CONFLICT TERMINATION IN EUROPE: GAMES AGAINST WAR.** New York, NY: Praeger, 1990, xxiv, 268 pp., ill, maps, 25 cm.
Includes bibliographical references (pp. 255–257) and index.

B077. Cimbala, S.J. **SOVIET CONTROL STRATEGY: IMPLICATIONS FOR WESTERN DEFENSE.** New York, NY: St. Martin's Press, 1990, p. cm.
Includes index.

B078. Clark, S.L., 1959– . **THE SOVIET MILITARY FACTOR IN A CHANGING WORLD.** Boulder, CO: Westview Press, 1991.
Includes index.

B079. Clarke, J.C. III. **RUSSIA AND ITALY AGAINST HITLER: THE BOLSHEVIK-FASCIST RAPPROCHEMENT OF THE 1930s.** Foreword by C. Foust. New York, NY: Greenwood Press, 1991, xvii, 218 pp., ill., 25 cm.
Includes bibliographical references (pp. 201–207) and index.

B080. Clarke, D.L. **SOVIET TROOP WITHDRAWALS FROM EASTERN EUROPE.** *Report on Eastern Europe*, Vol. 1, Mar. 30, 1990, pp. 41–47.
After World War II, contingents of the Soviet Army stayed in Eastern Europe as occupiers, as props for the local communist regimes, and as the leading echelons of a potent Soviet offensive capability. The days of a significant Soviet military presence in the region seem numbered.

B081. Clarke, D.L. **THE UNILATERAL ARMS CUTS IN THE WARSAW PACT.** *Report on Eastern Europe*, Vol. 1, No. 5, Feb. 2, 1990, pp. 43–47.
One year after Soviet President Mikhail Gorbachev announced dramatic unilateral cuts in the Soviet armed forces, roughly half of these reduction have taken place....The countries of Eastern Europe quickly followed the Soviet lead, and some have even decided on further reductions. The end of this process is not in sight.

B082. Clarke, D.L. **BUILDING FOR THE FUTURE IN ARMS CONTROL.** *Report on Eastern Europe*, Vol. 1, Jan. 5, 1990, pp. 39–42.
While no major arms control agreements were signed in 1989, enough progress was achieved to hold out the promise of several treaties in 1990. Both NATO and the Warsaw Pact are committed to signing an initial agreement on reducing conventional arms in Europe, and the Presidents of the USA and the U.S.S.R. have told their bureaucracies that they want to see the terms of a strategic arms pact ready for their June summit.

B083. **CLASSIC ISSUES IN SOVIET FOREIGN POLICY: FROM LENIN TO BREZHNEV.** Edited by F.J. Fleron, Jr., E.P. Hoffman and R.F. Laird. New York, NY: Aldine de Gruyter, c1991.

Includes bibliographical references and index.

B084. Clemens, W.C. **CAN RUSSIA CHANGE?: THE U.S.S.R. CONFRONTS GLOBAL INTERDEPENDENCE.** Boston, MA: Unwin Hyman, 1990, xxiv, 384 pp., 24 cm.

Includes bibliographical references and index.

B085. Cobban, H. **THE SUPERPOWERS AND THE SYRIAN-ISRAELI CONFLICT: BEYOND CRISIS MANAGEMENT?** New York, Praeger, 1991, 182 pp. (Washington Papers 149)

Contents - The context of the Syrian-Israeli conflict, 1978–1989. Developments in the conflict. The U.S.-Israeli relationship. The Soviet-Syrian relationship. Beyond crisis management?

B086. **COLD WAR RHETORIC: STRATEGY, METAPHOR AND IDEOLOGY.** M.J. Medhurst....et al. New York, NY: Greenwood Press, 1990, xv, 224 pp., 25 cm.

Includes bibliographical references (p. 209–216) and index. Contributions to the study of mass media and communications, 0732-4456, No. 19.

B087. **CONFIDENTIAL U.S. STATE DEPARTMENT CENTRAL FILES. THE SOVIET UNION (MICROFORM): FOREIGN AFFAIRS, 1955–1959,** decimal numbers 661 and 611.61. Project coordinator, G. Murphy. Bethesda, MD: University Publications of America, 1990, c1989. Microfilm reels.

The documents are from Record Group 59 general records of the Department of State. Accompanied by a printed reel guide, compiled by B.D. Hydrick. Includes index.

B088. **CONFIDENTIAL U.S. STATE DEPARTMENT CENTRAL FILES. THE SOVIET UNION (MICROFORM): INTERNAL AFFAIRS, 1955–1959,** decimal numbers 761, 861, and 961. Project coordinator, G. Murphy. Bethesda, MD: University Publications of America, 1990, c1989. Microfilm reels.

The documents are from Record Group 59, general records of the Department of State. Accompanied by a printed reel guide, compiled by B.D. Hydrick. Includes index.

B089. **CONTEMPORARY ISSUES IN SOVIET FOREIGN POLICY: FROM BREZHNEV TO GORBACHEV.** Edited by F.J. Fleron, Jr., E.P. Hoffman and R.F. Laird. New York, NY: Aldine de Gruyter, c1991.

Includes bibliographical references and index.

B090. Corcoran, E.A. **PERESTROIKA AND THE SOVIET MILITARY: IMPLICATIONS FOR U.S. POLICY.** Washington, Cato Institute, 1990, 35 pp.

Political changes in the Soviet Union and the virtual disintegration of the Warsaw Pact have dramatically decreased the military threat to the West. Contends that systemic problems in the Soviet economy have necessarily led to a fundamental restructuring of the Soviet military posture.

B091. Cordell, L. **SOVIET ATTITUDES TOWARD THE GERMAN DEMOCRATIC REPUBLIC.** *Political Quarterly*, Vol. 61, July–Sept. 1990, pp. 285–298.

Despite the basic congruence of views between the German Democratic Republic (GDR) and the Soviet Union since the former state's foundation in October 1949, the two states have pursued bilateral policies that operate from quite different objective conditions. The pattern of coordination between the two states is such that the results display a clear asymmetry. No one was more keenly aware than the SED of the fact that both German states were economically and politically important to the Soviet Union. As a consequence the U.S.S.R became less anxious about an inter-German rapprochement than in previous years.

B092. Corning, G.P. **THE PHILIPPINE BASES AND U.S. PACIFIC STRATEGY.** *Pacific Affairs*, Vol. 63, Spring 1990, pp. 6–23.

Argues that mutual withdrawal from Cam Ranh Bay and the Philippine bases would have to be part of a larger agreement on naval arms limitation throughout the Pacific. Such an agreement would take time to negotiate but is not unrealistic in view of the dramatic changes within Eastern Europe during 1989. With continued progress toward Sino-Soviet detente and a Cambodian solution, the time is right to relax the superpower rivalry in East Asia.

B093. Covington, S.R. **NATO AND SOVIET SECURITY REFORM.** *Washington Quarterly*, Vol. 14, Winter 1991, pp. 39–50.

This paper will examine the course of Soviet security reform, General Staff thinking about military reform, war prevention, and future military strategy, and their implications for NATO's transformation in the 1990s.

B094. Cox, M. **WHATEVER HAPPENED TO THE "SECOND" COLD WAR? SOVIET–AMERICAN RELATIONS: 1980–1988.** *Review of International Studies*, Vol. 16, 1990, pp. 155–172.

During his eight years in office Ronald Reagan attempted not only to dominate the U.S. political scene but to establish a clear neo-conservative agenda. It is too soon to pass final judgement on the Reagan Presidency, its place in American history. In one area, however, history may judge that Reagan succeeded beyond his wildest dreams: in his management of the U.S.–Soviet relationship....In this essay the author wants to provide a broad survey of U.S.–Soviet relations in the Reagan years and will attempt to do so by seeking to answer some questions.

B095. Critchlow, J. **UZBEKISTAN: WHATEVER HAPPENED TO MARXISM–LENINISM?** *Report on the U.S.S.R.*, Vol. 3, Mar. 22, 1991, pp. 17–20.

Interviews with the Uzbek Komsomol secretary for ideology and the chairman of the philosophy department at the Tashkent Economics Institute suggest that, while Marxism–Leninism is fading from the scene in Uzbekistan, ideology - albeit without Marx - is still viewed as a system of thought control. The secretary is candid about the mistakes of the old ideology, but he talks of the same normative role in society.

B096. Critchlow, J. **CENTRAL ASIA: THE RUSSIAN CONQUEST REVISITED.** *Report on the U.S.S.R.*, Vol. 3, Mar. 8, 1991, pp. 15–18.

Discusses the history of the Russian conquest of Central Asia and discusses how these events planted the seeds for current conflicts in that region.

B097. Crow, S. **"WHO LOST EASTERN EUROPE?"** *Report on the U.S.S.R.*, Vol. 3, Apr. 12, 1991, pp. 1–5.

Contends that while Soviet hard-liners seem determined to prove that the loss of Eastern Europe has done severe damage to Soviet security, more moderate thinkers point to the relaxation of international tensions and the corresponding modification of Soviet security requirements. Gorbachev himself seems to be trying to reconcile the hard-liners to the loss of the Soviet Union's satellites by pointing out that the countries of Eastern Europe are now discovering that they need the U.S.S.R. after all.

B098. Crow, S **ANOTHER CONSERVATIVE ATTACK ON SOVIET FOREIGN POLICY.** *Report on the U.S.S.R.*, Vol. 3, Mar. 8, 1991, pp. 6–7.

Considers recent criticisms from within the conservative wing of the Soviet government on Soviet foreign policy. Analyzes sources and reasons for the criticisms.

B099. Crow, S. **THE SOVIET-JAPANESE SUMMIT: EXPECTATIONS UNFULFILLED.** *Report on the U.S.S.R.*, Apr. 26, 1991, pp. 1–5.

Despite eleventh-hour attempts to resolve delicate issues, the Soviet-Japanese summit failed to yield a breakthrough in relations between the two countries. The refusal of President Gorbachev to compromise on the dispute over the Kurile Islands - the key obstacle to good relations with Japan - can be attributed to the long history of the dispute, the rise of Soviet conservatism, and the pressure of Soviet public opinion. The summit also highlighted the decline of Gorbachev's image as a diplomat.

B100. Crow, S. **MOSCOW LOOKS HARD AT ITS FOREIGN AID PROGRAM.** *Report on the U.S.S.R.*, Vol. 2, Aug. 10, 1990, pp. 8–9.

The U.S.S.R.'s reassessment of its foreign aid policy is a mammoth task, yet it must be accomplished quickly because the Soviet economy is deteriorating. Reassessing the interests of any state is a difficult task, and, in the Soviet Union's case, where the state's foundations are seriously undermined, the reappraisal will be agonizing.

B101. Crozier, B. **THE ENDURING SOVIET GLOBAL THREAT.** *Global Affairs*, Vol. 5, Summer–Fall 1990, pp. 1–18.

The Communist threat will end only when all its power bases have collapsed. Even if the West does not insist on "unconditional surrender," it is not obliged to give the Soviet regime the means to recover from its self-inflicted ills and resume its threat to our collective survival. Communism has collapsed as a doctrine and an inspiration. Whether the same is true of communism as an instrument of Soviet global strategy is more debatable.

B102. **CURRENT SOVIET STRATEGY: DISSENTING VIEWS.** *Global Affairs*, Vol. 2, Spring 1990, whole issue (pp. 1–172).

Contents - Strategies for the 1990s, by D. Quayle. The changing U.S.–Soviet strategic balance. The Soviet threat in the 1990s, by C.S. Gray. The balance of power conflicts of Eurasia, by A.J. Gregor. Malta in retrospect, by V. Bukovsky. Eastern Europe: the revolution in its future, by M. Djilas. Market communism at the brink, by S. Rosefielde. Red star over Afghanistan, by E.D. Krakowski. Moscow's Third World empire, by M. Leighton. The illusion of strategic stability, by M. Ruhle.

B103. Da Cunha, D. **SOVIET NAVAL POWER IN THE PACIFIC.** Boulder, CO: L. Rienner Publishers, 1990, xii, 284 pp. (8) pp. of plates, ill., maps, 23 cm.
Includes bibliographical references (pp. 259–273) and index.

B104. Davison, K.L. **THE GEOPOLITICS OF THE SOVIET WITHDRAWAL FROM AFGHANISTAN.** *Strategic Review*, Vol. 18, Winter 1990, pp. 39–48.
The withdrawal of forces from that battered country cannot be adjudged a strategic setback for Moscow. In fact, Moscow has advanced its objectives not only in Southwest Asia but on a broad international front. Only a patient U.S. policy aimed particularly at Pakistan and Iran can deny those objectives and make the Soviet withdrawal into a true historic defeat.

B105. Dawisha, K. **PERESTROIKA, GLASNOST AND SOVIET FOREIGN POLICY** *Harriman Institute Forum*, Vol. 3, Jan. 1990, pp. 1–8.
Perestroika and glasnost have brought to the surface features of Soviet political culture which have been suppressed for decades. Exploding into the open are ethnic, group, class and national interests....If glasnost has created the environment for numerous societal tendencies to come to the fore, it has been perestroika which has begun to aggregate these tendencies into new channels for foreign policy formulation....Perestroika, therefore, is not only having an impact on foreign policy: Gorbachev is using foreign policy as an instrument to advance perestroika.

B106. Dawisha, K. **EASTERN EUROPE, GORBACHEV, AND REFORM: THE GREAT CHALLENGE.** Cambridge (England), New York, NY: Cambridge University Press, 1990, xv, 319 pp., ill., 24 cm.
Includes bibliographical references and index.

B107. **THE DE-ESCALATION OF NUCLEAR CRISES.** Edited by J.E. Nation. New York, NY: St. Martin's Press, 1991.
Includes index.

B108. DeNevers, R. **THE SOVIET UNION AND EASTERN EUROPE: THE END OF AN ERA.** London, Brassey's, 1990, 95 pp. (Adelphi Papers No. 249).
Contents - Historical context. Soviet policy under Gorbachev. East European reactions: from reform to revolution. After the fall: prospects for the future.

B109. Derring, O.G. **TAJIK OFFICIAL VIEW SOVIET, U.S. DEA COUNTERNARCOTICS COOPERATION.** JPRS Report (Narcotics), Feb. 5, 1991, pp. 25–26.
Translation of an interview with a specialist on drug addiction from Tajikistan, originally appearing in the Tajik newspaper Komsomolets Tadzhikistana, Dec. 19, 1990, 4 pp. Derring, who took part in a Moscow seminar on combatting drug addiction, describes the presentation of the U.S. Drug Enforcement Administration at the meeting.

B110. Desai, P. **PERESTROIKA IN PERSPECTIVE: THE DESIGN AND DILEMMAS OF SOVIET REFORM.** Princeton, NJ: Princeton University Press, c1990, viii, 221 pp., ill., 22 cm. Princeton paperbacks.
Includes bibliographical references (pp 209–211) and index.

B111. Djilas, M. **THE LEGACY OF COMMUNISM IN EASTERN EUROPE: THE FORUM SPEAKS WITH MILOVAN DJILAS.** *Fletcher Forum*, Vol. 15, Winter 1991, pp. 83–92.

B112. Doherty, C.J. **SUPERPOWER RELATIONS: BUSH LIFTS SOVIET CREDIT BAN TO EASE FOOD SHORTAGE.** *Congressional Quarterly Weekly Report*, Vol. 48, Dec. 15, 1990, pp. 4144–4145.

He suspended a 15-year-old ban on extending commercial credits to the Soviets, enabling them to buy up to $1 billion worth of U.S. agricultural goods....In addition to providing agricultural credits, Bush approved sending technical experts to the Soviet Union to help improve the country's troubled food distribution network. A February summit on START (Strategic Arms Reduction Treaty) was also announced.

B113. **DOMESTIC DETERMINANTS OF SOVIET FOREIGN POLICY TOWARDS SOUTH ASIA AND THE MIDDLE EAST.** Edited by Hafeez Malik, New York: St. Martin's Press, 1990, xiii, 332 pp., 25 cm.

Papers presented at a seminar held Oct. 6–8, 1988, at Villanova University. Includes bibliographical references and index.

B114. Dorrance, J.C. **THE SOVIET UNION AND THE PACIFIC ISLANDS: AN AMERICAN ASSESSMENT AND PROPOSED WESTERN STRATEGY.** Canberra, Research School of Pacific Studies, Australian National University, 1990, 227 pp. (Working Paper No. 207).

Any future Soviet political successes, as in the past, will in some measure flow from the activities of regional surrogates or of others who independently pursue objectives congruent with Moscow's. Nevertheless, there can be little doubt that the Soviet diplomatic, political and economic presence will expand modestly.

B115. Dorrance, J.C. **THE SOVIET UNION AND THE PACIFIC ISLANDS: A CURRENT ASSESSMENT.** *Asian Survey*, Vol. 30, Sept. 1990, pp. 908–925.

The Soviet Union, despite internal and foreign policy reforms, will remain the West's most formidable political competitor. Traditional Western security interests and concerns in the pacific islands will thus remain relevant. Soviet regional activities continue to require monitoring.

B116. Downs, G.W. and Rocke, D.M. **TACIT BARGAINING, ARMS RACES, AND ARMS CONTROL.** Ann Arbor, MI: University of Michigan Press, c1990, x, 242 pp., ill., 23 cm.

Includes bibliographical references (pp. 223–233) and index.

B117. Drew, S.N. et al. **THE FUTURE OF NATO: FACING AN UNRELIABLE ENEMY IN AN UNCERTAIN ENVIRONMENT.** New York, NY: Praeger, 1991.

Includes bibliographical references and index.

B118. Dunay, P. **MILITARY DOCTRINE: CHANGE IN THE EAST?** New York, NY: Institute for East–West Security Studies, 1990, ii, 85 pp., 23 cm. Occasional paper series, 15.

Includes bibliographical references.

B119. Duncan, W.R. (Walter Raymond), and McGiffert C. 1936–. **MOSCOW AND THE THIRD WORLD UNDER GORBACHEV.** Ekedahl, Boulder, CO: Westview Press, 1990, xvi, 260 pp., maps, 24 cm.
Includes bibliographical references (pp. 241–243) and index.

B120. **THE DYNAMICS OF SOVIET DEFENSE POLICY.** Edited by B. Parrott, Washington, DC: Wilson Center Press, c1990, viii, 388 p., map, 23 cm.
Includes bibliographical references and index.

B121. Dzhus, A.M. **SOVIET WINGS: MODERN MILITARY SOVIET AIRCRAFT.** Edited by J.W.R. Taylor. London (England): Greenhill Books; Novato, CA: Presidio Press, 1991.
Includes bibliographical references and index.

B122. **EAST–WEST TRADE AND THE ATLANTIC ALLIANCE.** Edited by D.A. Baldwin and H.V. Milner, Houndmills, Basingstoke, Hampshire, Macmillan, 1990, xi, 227 pp., ill., 23 cm.
Includes bibliographical references and index.

B123. **EAST–WEST RELATIONS IN THE 1990S: THE NAVAL DIMENSION.** Edited by J. Pay and G. Till, New York, NY: St. Martin's Press, 1990, xv, 316 pp., ill., maps, 24 cm. Studies in contemporary maritime policy and strategy series.
Includes bibliographical references and index.

B124. **ECONOMIC REFORMS AND WELFARE SYSTEMS IN THE USSR, POLAND, AND HUNGARY: SOCIAL CONTRACT IN TRANSFORMATION.** Edited by J. Adam. New York, NY: St. Martin's Press, 1991.
Includes index.

B125. Eliason, L.R., 1936– . **PERESTROIKA OF THE RUSSIAN SOUL: RELIGIOUS RENAISSANCE IN THE SOVIET UNION.** Jefferson, NC: McFarland and Co., c1991, x, 150 pp., 23 cm.
Includes bibliographical references (pp. 141–145) and index.

B126. Emadi, H. **STATE, REVOLUTION, AND SUPERPOWERS IN AFGHANISTAN.** New York: Praeger, 1990, xvii, 156 pp., 22 cm.
Includes bibliographical references (pp. 135–147) and index.

B127. Ember, L.R. **CHEMICAL WEAPONS DISPOSAL: DAUNTING CHALLENGES STILL AHEAD.** *Chemical and Engineering News*, Vol. 68, Aug. 13, 1990, pp. 9–19.
U.S./Soviet agreement to dispose of the bulk of their chemical arsenals by the year 2002 faces hurdles of unperfected technology, environmental concerns, and unrealistic schedules.

B128. Eshel, D. **SOVIET AIRBORNE FORCES.** *Military Technology*, Vol. 14, July 1990, pp. 50–51,54.
The Soviet Army has a three-level concept for airborne operations....The Soviets have drawn their conclusions from experiences during the 2nd World

War....This has led to impressive advances in the concept of airborne operations, placing the Soviets second to none in this field.

B129. **EVALUATING THE AIR OFFENSIVE: THE WSEG I STUDY.** Edited by S.T. Ross and D.A. Rosenberg, New York: Garland Pub., 1990, iv, (various pagings), ill., 29 cm.

America's plans for war against the Soviet Union, 1945–1950, vol. 13.

B130. **THE FADING THREAT: SOVIET CONVENTIONAL MILITARY POWER IN DECLINE:** Report of the Defense Policy Panel of the Committee on Armed Service, House of Representatives, 101st Congress, 2nd session, Washington, DC: U.S. G.P.O.

At head of title: 101st Congress, 2nd session. Committee print.

B131. Fairbanks, C.H., Jr. **GORBACHEV'S GLOBAL DOUGHNUT: THE EMPIRE WITH A HOLE IN THE MIDDLE.** *National Interest*, No. 19, Spring 1990, pp. 21–33.

Examines the reasons why the Soviet Union has abandoned the communist regimes of Eastern Europe while still showing a commitment to shoring up threatened communist regimes in the Third World. Discusses possible U.S. responses to Soviet policy in regional conflicts.

B132. Fane, D. **AFTER AFGHANISTAN: THE DECLINE OF SOVIET MILITARY PRESTIGE.** *Washington Quarterly*, Vol. 13, Spring 1990, pp. 5–16.

Mikhail Gorbachev's glasnost set the stage for a social revolution about the Soviet military....Today, beyond the headlines about Soviet force cuts and budgetary constraints lies a larger reality: the unprecedented loss of influence and prestige by Soviet military and the accelerating demilitarization of Soviet society. This essay describes this demilitarization.

B133. Feffer, J. **BEYOND DETENTE: SOVIET FOREIGN POLICY AND U.S. OPTIONS.** New York, NY: Noonday Press, 1990, xvii, 237 pp., maps, 21 cm.

A report prepared for the American Friends Service Committee. Includes bibliographical references and index.

B134. Feinberg, R.E. **ECONOMIC REFORM IN THREE GIANTS: U.S. FOREIGN POLICY AND THE U.S.S.R., CHINA, AND INDIA,** New Brunswick, N.J., Transaction Books, 1990, 247 pp. (U.S.-Third World Policy Perspectives No. 14).

Three of the largest and strategically most important underdeveloped nations in the world - the Soviet Union, China, and India - are simultaneously in the throes of historic changes. Economic reform in the Giants clearly has profound consequences for their own political systems - and for the lives of the 2.2 billion people (nearly half the world's population) living in their societies. The reform in the Giants are also prompting dramatic changes in the international political and economic order. Concludes implications for the U.S.

B135. Feinbergt, E.L. **THE PHYSICIST AND THE SOVIET CITIZEN.** *Nature*, Vol. 344, Mar. 1, 1990, pp. 11–14.

Profiles Soviet dissident scientist Andrei Sakharov and his campaigns for disarmament and human rights.

B136. Feiveson, H.A. and VonHippel, F.N. **BEYOND START: HOW TO MAKE MUCH DEEPER CUTS.** *International Security*, Vol. 15, Summer 1990, pp. 154–180.

If the U.S. and Soviet governments decided, in a post-START strategic-arms reduction agreement, to accept the infeasibility of counterforce missions requiring thousands of warheads, it would be possible for them to agree on very much smaller strategic forces. To keep the strategic forces as large as is envisioned in the START agreement would be both provocative and clearly unnecessary in view of the changed situation in Eastern Europe and the Soviet Union.

B137. Fiddick, T.C., 1939–. **RUSSIA'S RETREAT FROM POLAND, 1920: FROM PERMANENT REVOLUTION TO PEACEFUL COEXISTENCE.** Houndmills, Basingstoke, Hampshire: macmillan, 1990, xiv, 348 pp., maps, 23 cm.

Includes bibliographical references (pp. 328–336) and index.

B138. Fieldhouse, R. **CRUISE MISSILE COMPROMISE SURFACING.** Bulletin of the atomic scientists, June 1990, pp. 21–24.

The Soviets wanted strict controls and the Americans wanted no controls on sea-launched cruise missiles. But the impasse that has blocked START has apparently been broken.

B139. Fitzgerald, M.C. **SOVIET ARMED FORCES AFTER THE GULF WAR: DEMISE OF THE DEFENSIVE DOCTRINE?** *Report on the U.S.S.R.*, Vol. 3, Apr. 19, 1991, pp. 1–4.

The war in the Persian Gulf gave the Soviet military the opportunity to observe the operation of modern weapons, whose technological superiority was convincingly demonstrated. As a result, Soviet military experts have begun to argue that the experience of the Gulf war necessitates the urgent reform of Soviet military doctrine.

B140. Flowerree, C.C. **IN TENDING ARMS CONTROL AGREEMENTS.** *Washington Quarterly*, Vol. 13, Winter 1990, pp. 199–214.

The discussion that follows will touch on several aspects of the after-life of arms control treaties: arrangements for overseeing the proper functioning of agreements, problems and deficiencies in these arrangements and some suggestions for possible changes and improvements.

B141. **THE FOREIGN POLICY AND DIPLOMATIC ACTIVITY OF THE U.S.S.R..** International Affairs (Moscow), Jan. 1990, pp. 5–111.

Contents - Perestroika in Soviet foreign policy: response to the challenge of the times. The Program for comprehensive security in action. The U.S.S.R. in the UN and other international organizations. International scientific and technological and cultural cooperation. The U.S.S.R.'s bilateral relations. The Soviet Union and the non-aligned movement. Restructuring the diplomatic service. Foreign policy and Soviet public opinion. The diplomatic service within the rule-of-law state system. The U.S.S.R. supreme Soviet and the U.S.S.R. foreign ministry.

B142. Foye, S. **THE SOVIET OFFICER CORPS AND GORBACHEV'S CRACKDOWN.** *Report on the U.S.S.R.*, Vol. 3, Feb. 1, 1991, pp. 29–30.

As Soviet security forces and army units slowly tighten their stranglehold on the pro-independence movements in the Baltic republics, observers inside and outside the Soviet Union have speculated on the extent to which the Soviet officer corps supports Moscow's current policy of repression.

B143. Foye, S. **THE HIGH COMMAND CONFRONTS "NEW POLITICAL THINKING" AT HOME AND ABROAD.** *Report on the U.S.S.R.*, Vol. 3, Mar. 29, 1991, pp. 24–27.

The Soviet High Command has generally been united in its criticism of Gorbachev's reform policies both at home and in the diplomatic sphere. Gorbachev's turn to the right has, however, brought the generals increasingly into the political arena, a process that seems likely to challenge unanimity within their ranks. An analysis of recent articles and speeches by the defense minister and the chief of the General Staff indicates that such a splintering may indeed have begun.

B144. Foye, S. **FROM DEFENDING THE EMPIRE TO SAVING THE UNION.** *Report on the U.S.S.R.*, Vol. 3, Jan. 4, 1991, pp. 10–12.

The Twenty-Eighth Party Congress appeared to be a turning point of sorts in Gorbachev's relations with the military leadership. It represented the high point of criticism by the generals of Gorbachev's peace initiatives with the West - an attack that was successfully beaten off by Gorbachev, his foreign minister, Eduard Shevardnadze, and other architects of the "new thinking." Since then, the High Command, as a whole, appears to have grudgingly accepted Gorbachev's arms control agreements and restructured European security system.

B145. Foye, S. **CRACKDOWN ORDERED TO ENFORCE MILITARY DRAFT.** *Report on the U.S.S.R.*, Vol. 3, Jan. 18, 1991, pp. 7–9.

The defense Ministry claimed that widespread draft resistance was threatening Soviet defense capabilities and instructed by the airborne troops, to aid commissariats in rounding up draftees for military service.

B146. Foye, S. **OVERSIGHT COMMITTEE REJECTS CPSU CONTROL OVER ARMED FORCES.** *Report on the U.S.S.R.*, Vol. 3, Apr. 19, 1991, pp. 4–6.

In an announcement on April 3, the U.S.S.R. Committee for Constitutional Compliance ruled that army regulations subordinating military commanders to Party bodies were unconstitutional. This potentially significant decision comes in the middle of a growing political battle for control of the armed forces.

B147. Freedman, R.O. **MOSCOW AND THE MIDDLE EAST: SOVIET POLICY SINCE THE INVASION OF AFGHANISTAN.** Cambridge (England), New York, NY: Cambridge University Press, 1991, xii, 426 pp., 24 cm.

Includes bibliographical references (pp. 399–415) and index.

B148. Freedman, R.O. **SOVIET POLICY TOWARD ISRAEL UNDER GORBACHEV.** New York, Praeger, 1991, 141 pp. (Washington Papers 150).

Contents - Efforts to improve relations with Israel, 1985–1986. Soviet-Israeli relations, 1987–1988: a new beginning. Soviet-Israeli relations, 1989–1990: toward a new relationship. Conclusion.

B149. Fuller, G.E. **THE EMERGENCE OF CENTRAL ASIA.** Foreign Policy, No. 78, Spring 1990, pp. 49–67.

The concept of "Central Asia" is in profound flux, promising to have effects as far away as the Arab world and the Indian subcontinent....As brutal as much of Soviet history has been to the Soviet Muslim republics, they have benefited from considerable economic, political, and social development. They may enter into the broader Muslim world as more mature....However, the smaller possibility also exists that the Soviet Muslim states, once on their own could be drawn toward a radical Islamic expression.

B150. **FUNDAMENTALS OF MILITARY ECONOMIC KNOWLEDGE.** (Washington) Foreign Broadcast Information Service, 1991, 105 pp. JPRS Report (Soviet Union: Military Affairs); JPRS-UMA-91-003 L, 10 April 1991)

Partial contents - Military economic knowledge and its place in the system of knowledge on war. The interrelationship of war and economics, peculiarities of the economic support for modern war. The role of labor resources in the economic support of a war. Economic preparation of the country for defense. Management of the military economy.

B151. Furtado, F.J. **U.S. AND SOVIET LAND-ATTACK SLCM PROGRAMS: IMPLICATIONS FOR STRATEGIC STABILITY.** Ottawa, Operational Research and Analysis Establishment, 1990, 47 pp. (ORAE Memorandum No. 129).

Assesses the impact of sea-launched cruise missiles on strategic stability. It reviews current American and Soviet SLCM programs, and each country's perspective on the importance of SLCMs.

B152. Gacek, C.M. **AREAS FOR U.S.-SOVIET COOPERATION AT THE UNITED NATIONS.** Washington, Heritage Foundation, 1991, 12 pp. (Backgrounder No. 831).

The United Nations used to be a main Cold War ideological battleground between the United States and the Soviet Union. But now the ideological struggle between Washington and Moscow has abated....This fundamental change in relations between the two nations raises the possibility of selected cooperation by the world's two great powers.

B153. Gaddis, J.L. **THE UNITED STATES AND THE END OF THE COLD WAR: IMPLICATIONS, RECONSIDERATIONS, PROVOCATIONS.** New York, NY: Oxford University Press, 1991.

Includes index.

B154. Gaffney, F. Jr. **SOVIET MILITARY RELIEF ACT.** Washington Times, June 5, 1990, F1,F4.

Discusses recent legislation introduced in Congress to reduce the U.S. defense budget and delete funds for sophisticated American weapon systems and other legislation easing trade restrictions to the Soviets. Contends that the "primary beneficiary" to this combination of legislation would not be American exporters - as this bill's sponsors intend. Instead, it would be the

Soviet defense sector and those of other, potentially hostile powers. consequently, perhaps a more apt title for this bill would be "The Soviet Military Relief Act of 1990."

B155. Ganjoo, Satish, 1956–. **SOVIET AFGHAN RELATIONS.** Delhi: Akashdeep Pub. House, 1990, xiii, 155 pp., 22 cm.

Includes bibliographical references (pp. 145–151).

B156. Garfinkle, A. **STARTING OVER.** National Interest, No. 29, Summer 1990, pp. 71–76.

Ever since the Soviet concession on SDI at Jackson Hole, Wyoming in mid-September 1989, expectations for a reasonably quick completion of a START Treaty have run very high. Judging from the pace of negotiations so far in 1990, these expectations are justified.

B157. Garthoff, R.L. **DETERRENCE AND THE REVOLUTION IN SOVIET MILITARY DOCTRINE.** Washington, DC: Brookings Institution, c1990, x, 209 pp., 24 cm.

Includes bibliographical references and index.

B158. Garthoff, R.L. **ESTIMATING SOVIET MILITARY FORCE LEVELS: SOME LIGHT FROM THE PAST.** *International Security*, Vol. 14, Spring, 1990, pp. 93–116.

Reflects on and assesses past Soviet announcements of military force reductions. This article presents an inside view of how that estimate was prepared, together with some additional observations on subsequent estimates of Soviet force levels.

B159. Garthoff, R.L. **CHANGING REALITIES, CHANGING PERCEPTIONS: DETERRENCE AND U.S. SECURITY AFTER THE COLD WAR.** *Brookings Review*, Vol. 8, Fall 1990, pp. 13–20.

The transformation of the political situation in the Soviet Union and Europe cannot fail to have major implications for U.S. policy and strategy. Deterrence of nuclear war and of possible aggressive Soviet moves remains an American policy objective.

B160. Garthoff, R.L. **THE MEDITERRANEAN SUMMIT.** *Mediterranean Quarterly*, Vol. 1, Spring 1990, pp. 14–24.

The significance of the Mediterranean summit cannot be fully determined until developments still in play more clearly delineate its aftermath. It is, however, quite clear that it was an important stepping stone in the path of evolving.

B161. Gati, C. **THE BLOC THAT FAILED: SOVIET–EAST EUROPEAN RELATIONS IN TRANSITION.** Bloomington: Indiana University Press, c1990, xiv, 226 pp., 21 cm. A Midland book, MB561.

Published in association with the Center for Strategic and International Studies, Washington, DC. Includes bibliographical references (pp. 220–222) and index.

B162. Gebhardt, J.F. 1948–. **THE PETSAMO-KIRKENES OPERATION: SOVIET BREAKTHROUGH AND PURSUIT IN THE ARCTIC, OCTOBER 1944.** Fort

Leavenworth, KS: Combat Studies Institute, U.S. Army Command and General Staff College, Washington, DC: For sale by the Supt. of Docs., U.S. G.P.O., 1990, xvi, 182 pp., ill., 25 cm.

Includes bibliographical references (pp. 171–182).

B163. Gerrits, A. **THE FAILURE OF AUTHORITARIAN CHANGE: REFORM, OPPOSITION, AND GEO-POLITICS IN POLAND IN THE 1980S.** Aldershot, Brookfield, VT: Dartmouth, c1990, ix, 260 pp., 23 cm.

Qs Publications - P. 1 of cover. Includes bibliographical references.

B164. Gideon, J.P. **BEYOND GLASNOST: SOVIET SPACE AND STRATEGIC PROGRAMS FOR THE 1990S.** Alexandria, VA, Center for Intelligence Studies, 1990, 7 pp. (Special Report, Vol. 1, No. 2).

While many of Gorbachev's declarations appear promising and some have indeed led to reductions in conventional forces, the United States has seen little or no slowing in Soviet strategic force modernization.

B165. Glantz, D.M. **SOVIET MILITARY OPERATIONAL ART: IN PURSUIT OF DEEP BATTLE.** With a foreword by C.E. Vuono. London (England), Portland, OR: F. Cass, 1991, xxiv, 295 pp., ill., 24 cm.

Includes bibliographical references (pp. 267–289) and index.

B166. Glantz, D.M. **THE ROLE OF INTELLIGENCE IN SOVIET MILITARY STRATEGY IN WORLD WAR II.** Novato, CA: Presidio, c1990, x, 262 pp., ill., maps, 24 cm.

Includes bibliographical references (pp. 227–245) and index.

B167. Glantz, D.M. **SOVIET MILITARY INTELLIGENCE IN WAR.** London, England, Portland, OR: Frank Cass, 1990, xv, 422 pp., ill., maps, 23 cm.

Includes bibliographical references (pp. 386–413) and index. Cass series on Soviet military theory and practice, 3.

B168. Godevilla, A. **THE ABUSE OF ARMS CONTROL.** *Global Affairs*, Vol. 5, Summer–Fall 1990, pp. 36–46.

Like their predecessors, the agreements-in-principle reached in and around the Washington summit of 1990 make sense only if one assumes that the party with which they were made is totally benevolent and would not dream of cheating or of using the situation created by the agreements to win a war, argues the author.

B169. Goel, M.S. (Mahatma Sharan), 1953–. **INDO–U.S.S.R. TRADE AND ECONOMIC RELATIONS.** New Delhi: Deep and Deep Publications, c1990, 372 pp., 22 cm.

Includes bibliographical references (pp. 361–367).

B170. Golan, G. **GORBACHEV'S "NEW THINKING" ON TERRORISM.** Foreword by W. Laqueur. New York: Praeger, 1990, xviii, 117 pp., 24 cm.

Published with the Center for Strategic and International Studies, Washington, D.C. Includes bibliographical references (pp. 105–112) and index.

B171. Golan, G. **SOVIET POLICIES IN THE MIDDLE EAST: FROM WORLD WAR TWO TO GORBACHEV.** Cambridge (England), New York, NY: Cambridge University Press, 1990, viii, 319 pp., map, 24 cm, Cambridge Soviet Union paperbacks; 2.

Includes bibliographical references (pp. 291–309) and index.

B172. Goldstein, J.S. 1952– and Freeman, J.R. **THREE-WAY STREET: STRATEGIC RECIPROCITY IN WORLD POLITICS.** Chicago, IL: University of Chicago Press, 1990, xiii, 239 pp., ill., 24 cm.

Includes bibliographical references (pp. 219–233) and index.

B173. Goldstein, J.S., Freeman, J.R. **U.S.-SOVIET-CHINESE RELATIONS: ROUTINE, RECIPROCITY, OR RATIONAL EXPECTATIONS?** *American Political Science Review*, Vol. 85, Mar. 1991, pp. 17–35.

The behaviors of the United States, the Soviet Union, and China are a relatively stable mix of bureaucratic routine and reciprocity. The results also indicate complex, asymmetrical connections among U.S.-Soviet, U.S.-Chinese, and Soviet-Chinese relations, consistent with the notion of a strategic triangle.

B174. Goodman, M.A., 1938– . **GORBACHEV'S RETREAT: THE THIRD WORLD.** New York, NY: Praeger, 1991.

Includes bibliographical references and index.

B175. Goodman, L.M. and Hoff, L.A. **OMNICIDE: THE NUCLEAR DILEMMA.** New York, NY: Praeger, 1990, xx, 153 pp., 23 cm.

Includes bibliographical references (pp. 139–143) and indexes. Nuclear disarmament.

B176. Gorbachev, M.S. **PERESTROIKA AND SOVIET–AMERICAN RELATIONS.** Translated from the Russian by APN Publishers, Madison, CT: Sphinx Press, 1990, p. cm.

B177. **GORBACHEV AND HIS GENERALS: THE REFORM OF SOVIET MILITARY DOCTRINE.** Edited by W.C. Green and T. Karasik, Boulder, CO: Westview Press, 1990, viii, 239 pp., 22 cm.

Includes bibliographical references and index.

B178. **GORBACHEV AND EUROPE.** Edited by V. Harle and J. Iivonen, London: Printer Publishers, 1990, xi, 213 pp., ill., 24 cm.

Includes bibliographical references and index.

B179. **GORBACHEV AND EUROPE.** Edited by V. Harle and J. Iivonen. New York, NY: St. Martin's Press, 1990, xi, 213 pp., ill., 24 cm.

Based on work of TAPRI Workshop in "The Soviet Union and Europe," which met twice, in Tampere on 26–29 February 1988, and in Geneva on 2–4 December 1988 -Pref. Includes bibliographical references and index.

B180. **GORBACHEV'S NEW THINKING AND THIRD WORLD CONFLICTS.** Edited by Jiri Valenta and Frank Cibulka. New Brunswick, N.J., Transaction Publ., c1990, 352 pp.

Partial contents - Gorbachev's "new thinking" and Third World regional conflicts conceptualized. Regional focus: the conflict in south Asia. Regional focus: the conflict in Central America. Superpowers and regional conflicts: American policies and future options.

B181. Gray, C.S. **DESTINATION UNKNOWN: FROM SALT TO START.** *Strategic Review*, Vol. 19, Spring 1991, pp. 32–43.

The promises of the SALT-START process remain, to date, unfulfilled. The most consistent feature of the SALT-START enterprise has been an uncertainty of purpose....While not necessarily a disaster for Western security, the SALT process did not serve the purposes that the U.S. government has established for arms control. We should not expect any more from START, argues the author.

B182. Gray, C.S. **THE SOVIET THREAT IN THE 1990S.** *Global Affairs*, Vol. 5, Spring 1990, pp. 25–44.

Whether perestroika succeeds or fails, and whether or not a rather authoritarian presidential system of government succeeds the reign of the CPSU. Russian geography, history, culture, and armament renders it a permanent threat to the balance of power in Eurasia.

B183. Gray, C.S. **DOES VERIFICATION REALLY MATTER?: FACING POLITICAL FACTS ABOUT ARMS CONTROL NON-COMPLIANCE.** *Strategic Review*, Vol. 18, Spring 1990, pp. 32–42.

No democracy in the Twentieth Century has designed, let alone implemented, a sanctions policy to cope with arms control non-compliance. Long experience tells us that a Western democracy cannot design, agree upon, and apply sanctions for non-compliance. The current (CFE and START) debate about arms control verification continues to ignore, or perhaps be ignorant of, this central point.

B184. Graziani, G. **GORBACHEV'S ECONOMIC STRATEGY IN THE THIRD WORLD.** Foreword by E.H. Preeg, New York, NY: Praeger, 1990, xx, 116 pp., 25 cm.

Published with the Center for Strategic and International Studies, Washington, DC. Includes bibliographical references (pp. 101–109) and index.

B185. **GREAT POWER RELATIONS IN ARGENTINA, CHILE, AND ANTARCTICA.** Edited by M.A. Morris, New York, NY: St. Martin's Press, 1990, x, 210 pp., maps, 23 cm.

Includes bibliographical references and index.

B186. Greenfield, M. **THE THRILL IS GONE.** *Newsweek*, Vol. 115, June 11, 1990, 72 pp.

Contends that the high-risk drama of summits past reflected their rarity and unpredictability. This way's better.

B187. Greiner, B. **THE CUBAN MISSILE CRISIS.** *Diplomatic History*, Vol. 14, Spring 1990, pp. 205–221,223–229,231–239,241–247,249–256.

Contents - The Cuban missile crisis reconsidered, by B. Greiner. Commentary: evaluating and using historical hearsay, by R.L. Garthoff. Commentary: reconsidering Khrushchev's gambit - defining the Soviet Union and Cuba, by B.J. Bernstein. commentary: new light on the Cuban missile crisis?, by M. Trachtenberg. Commentary: the defense of Cuba theme and the missile crisis. by T.G. Paterson.

B188. Grey, R.D., Jennisch, L.A. and Tyler, A.S. **SOVIET PUBLIC OPINION AND THE GORBACHEV REFORMS.** *Slavic Review*, Vol. 49, Summer 1990, pp. 261–271.

The Soviet Interview Project gathered data from 2,793 former citizens of the Soviet Union who had emigrated to the United States between 1979 and 1982.

B189. Gross, N. **YOUTH AND THE ARMY IN THE U.S.S.R. IN THE 1980'S.** *Soviet Studies*, Vol. 42, July 1990, pp. 481–498.

This paper examines the problem of youth and the army in the Soviet Union during the past decade, drawing on new facts revealed in candid press discussion in the era of glasnost'....Discusses the role of army life in motivating young men to perform military service or to pursue military careers. The changing social and political values of young Soviet people and their relationship to army service and the choice of military occupations.

B190. Grove, E. **MARITIME STRATEGY AND EUROPEAN SECURITY.** London, Washington, DC: Brassey's (UK), 1990, xxiii, 168 pp. (17) pp. of plates, ill., 24 cm.

Includes bibliographical references (pp. 161–164) and index.

B191. Guertner, G.L. **DETERRENCE AND DEFENSE IN A POST-NUCLEAR WORLD.** Houndmills, Basingstoke, Hampshire: Macmillan, 1990, xvi, 177 pp., ill., 23 cm.

Includes bibliographical references and index.

B192. Guertner, G.L. **DETERRENCE AND DEFENSE IN A POST-NUCLEAR WORLD.** New York, NY: St. Martin's Press, 1990, xvi, 177 pp., ill., 23 cm. Includes bibliographical references and index.

B193. Hadji, S.B. **OVERVIEW OF INTELLECTUAL PROPERTY RIGHTS IN EASTERN EUROPE AND THE U.S.S.R..** *International Quarterly*, Vol. 2, July 1990, pp. 1–30.

Partial contents - Laws and treaties. Patents. Industrial designs. Trademarks, Copyrights. International treaties.

B194. Hahn, W.F. **NATO AND GERMANY.** *Global Affairs*, Vol. 5, Winter 1990, pp. 1–18.

Mikhail Gorbachev is using the "liberalized" satellites as pawns to make inroads into the European Community. His disarmament offensive is aimed at preempting any potential security cast for the EC. Recent events raise fundamental questions about whether the Cold War is really over or is a power struggle being waged by other expedients than war.

B195. Hall, R.C.M. **SOVIET MILITARY ART IN A TIME OF CHANGE: COMMAND AND CONTROL OF THE FUTURE BATTLEFIELD.** London (England), Washington, DC: Brassey's (UK), 1991.

Includes bibliographical references and index.

B196. Halperin, M.H. and Woods, J.M. **ENDING THE COLD WAR AT HOME.** Foreign Policy, No. 81, Winter 1990–91, pp. 128–143.

The postwar confrontation between the two leading nuclear powers that was dubbed the "Cold War" produced other distortions of the democratic process that endure today as well....Perhaps the most entrenched legacy of the Cold War is a carefully structured system of government information controls - a system steeped in secrecy: secret agencies, secret budgets, secret documents....This pervasive threat....was said to justify extraordinary measures unprecedented in peacetime, including restrictions on liberty at home.

B197. Hart, G., 1936– . **RUSSIA SHAKES THE WORLD: THE SECOND RUSSIAN REVOLUTION AND ITS IMPACT ON THE WEST.** New York, NY: Cornelia and Michael Bessie Books, c1991.

Includes index.

B198. Haslam, J. **THE SOVIET UNION AND THE POLITICS OF NUCLEAR WEAPONS IN EUROPE, 1969–87.** Ithaca, NY: Cornell University Press, 1990, xv, 227 pp., 22 cm.

Includes index.

B199. Hawkes, N. 1952– **GLASNOST AND PERESTROIKA.** Vero Beach, FL: Rourke Enterprises, 1990, 48 pp., ill. (some col.), maps, 26 cm. World issues.

Includes index. Examines the meaning of Glasnost and Perestroika in the context of current Soviet history and describes the social and economic changes that have taken place within the Soviet Union and in the newly-independent countries of Eastern Europe.

B200 Hazan, B. 1942–. **GORBACHEV AND HIS ENEMIES: THE STRUGGLE FOR PERESTROIKA.** Boulder, CO: Westview Press, 1990, viii, 335 pp., 24 cm.

Includes bibliographical references and index.

B201. **HEGEMONIC RIVALRY: FROM THUCYDIDES TO THE NUCLEAR AGE.** Edited by R.N. Lebow and B.S. Strauss. Boulder, CO: Westview Press, 1991, xii, 295 pp., 23 cm.

Product of a conference in June 1988....in Cadenabbia, Italy. Acknowledgments.

Includes bibliographical references and index.

B202. Heitman, S. **THE RIGHT TO LEAVE: THE NEW SOVIET DRAFT LAW ON EMIGRATION.** Koln: Bundesinstitut fur Ostwissenschaftliche und Internationale Studien, c1990, iii, 53 pp., 30 cm. Berichte des Bundesinstituts fur Ostwissenschaftliche und Internationale Studien, 26-1990.

Summary in German. Includes bibliographical references.

B203. **HENRY S. ROWEN ON U.S.–JAPAN DEFENSE RELATIONS IN A NEW GLOBAL ORDER.** *Japan Economic Survey*, Vol. 14, Aug. 1990, pp. 6–10.

The reform movement in Eastern Europe and recent improvements in U.S.–Soviet relations have raised questions on both sides of the Pacific about the impact of these developments on East Asian society. In a recent conversation with JES editor Barbara Wanner, Henry S. Rowen, assistant secretary of defense for international security affairs, examines how the transition to a new global order will affect U.S.–Japan defense cooperation.

B204. Hilton, S.E., 1940– . **BRAZIL AND THE SOVIET CHALLENGE, 1917–1947.** Austin, TX: University of Texas Press, c1991, xvi, 287 pp., map, 27 cm.

Includes bibliographical references (pp. 261–271) and index.

B205. Hines, J.G., Mahoney, D. **DEFENSE AND COUNTEROFFENSIVE UNDER THE NEW SOVIET MILITARY DOCTRINE.** Santa Monica, Calif., Rand Corporation, 1991, 125. pp. (Rand Corporation. R-3982-USDP)

Contents - Nature of military art discussions, 1988–1989. Changes in military doctrine: 1987. Party elaboration of military doctrine: 1988. Framework for analysis of Soviet operational concepts. Reserves and second echelons in defense. Fire assets for defense. Positional and maneuver forms in defense. Counteroffensive: where defensive doctrine ends. Conclusion.

B206. Hines, K.L. and Springer, S.E. **THE SOVIET ARMY TO THE YEAR 2000.** *Journal of Soviet Military Studies*, Vol. 3, June 1990, pp. 221–253.

This article examines the media discussions of alternative military structures and the views of the primary military and political policy makes during the Gorbachev era. The discussion conclude with some assessments on the probable structure of the Soviet Army through the year 2000 and offers some tentative prospects for military force development into the early twenty-first century.

B207. Hoan, B. **SOVIET ECONOMIC AID TO VIETNAM.** *Contemporary Southeast Asia*, Vol. 12, Mar. 1991, pp. 360–376.

This is a review and description of two books in Vietnamese that provide a rare glimpse of Soviet economic aid to Vietnam. One is an official document while the other is a translation of a Russian book but both contain frank and unexpectedly objective information and assessments of various aspects of the Soviet-Vietnamese economic linkage.

B208. Holden, G. **NEW THINKING: SOVIET REFORM POLICIES AND CONVENTIONAL DISARMAMENT.** London, Winchester, MA: Pluto Press with the Transnational Institute, 1990, p. cm.

Includes bibliographical references.

B209. Holden, G. **THE END OF AN ALLIANCE: SOVIET POLICY AND THE WARSAW PACT, 1989–90.** Frankfurt am Main: Peace Research Institute Frankfurt, 1990, 36 pp., 30 cm.

Includes bibliographical references (pp. 31–36).

B210. Holden, G. **SOVIET MILITARY REFORM: CONVENTIONAL DISARMAMENT AND THE CRISIS OF MILITARISED SOCIALISM.** London (England): Pluto Press with the Transnational Institute (TNI); Concord, MA: Distributed in the U.S.A. by Paul and Co., 1991.

Includes bibliographical references and index.

B211. Holmes, K.R. **BUSH LOST HIS WAY AT THE WASHINGTON SUMMIT.** Washington, Heritage Foundation, 1990, 2 pp. (Executive Memorandum, No. 267).

Argues that the summits between Bush and Gorbachev have followed an unfortunate pattern. As also happened at the Malta summit last December 2–3, Gorbachev came to the Washington meeting asking for payment for good behavior. This pattern made sense at Malta. It was the first summit meeting since the fall of the Berlin Wall in November 1989....There was no need to grant the Soviets further concessions at the Washington summit because Gorbachev had done nothing to earn them.

B212. Holmes, K.R. **THE NEW SOVIET CHALLENGE: EVALUATING MALTA AND ANTICIPATING THE JUNE SUMMIT.** Washington, Heritage Foundation, 1990, 10 pp. (Heritage Lectures 235).

Director of Foreign Policy and Defense Studies for the Heritage Foundation spoke on Jan. 8, 1990. Contends that if the Malta Summit decided nothing, it did set the course of U.S.–Soviet relations for the coming year. Another summit is to be held next June. Arms control negotiations are to be accelerated for the purpose of signing agreements at that summit. And Bush made a series of economic concessions to Gorbachev, presumably as payment for his acquiescence to changes in Eastern Europe.

B213. Holzman, F.D. **HOW THE CIA DISTORTED THE TRUTH ABOUT SOVIET MILITARY SPENDING.** *Challenge*, Vol. 33, Mar.–Apr. 1990, pp. 27–31,34–36.

Inaccurate CIA reports led officials in two administrations to conclude that a military buildup was needed. But, instead of outspending the United States in ME (military expenditures), the Soviets appear to have spent less than we.

B214. Homet, R.S. 1932–. **THE NEW REALISM: A FRESH BEGINNING IN U.S.–SOVIET RELATIONS.** New York, NY: Harper Collins Publishers, c1990, xvi, 316 pp., ill., 24 cm.

A Cornelia and Michael Bessie book. Includes bibliographical references (pp. 285–290) and index.

B215. Horelick, A.L. **U.S.–SOVIET RELATIONS: THRESHOLD OF A NEW ERA.** *Foreign Affairs*, Vol. 69, No. 1, 1990, pp. 51–69.

As the United States and the Soviet Union reach the threshold of a new era in their relations, their roles in shaping the post-cold war world will be different from those played in managing the East–West conflict....Both will have to adapt their policies and behavior....In making this adjustment, the United States can draw on its own democratic institutions and traditions....For the Soviet Union, this will be an entirely new experience for which the history of its foreign relations....have poorly prepared it.

B216. Horensma, P., 1955– . **THE SOVIET ARCTIC.** London (England), New York, NY: Routledge, 1991.

Includes bibliographical references and index.

B217. Hough, J.F. **GORBACHEV'S ENDGAME.** *World Policy Journal*, Vol. 7, Fall 1990, pp. 639–672.

If Gorbachev is going to remain in power until at least 1995, it is incumbent upon the United States to deal with him until and unless the next election produces a new national leader....Under the circumstances, to speak of supporting Yeltsin against Gorbachev is not just a mistake but madness.

B218. Hough, J.F. 1935–. **RUSSIA AND THE WEST: GORBACHEV AND THE POLITICS OF REFORM.** New York, NY: Touchstone, 1990, 286 pp., 22 cm.
Includes bibliographical references (pp. 257–274) and index.

B219. Hull, A.W. **THE MASSING OF FORCES AND MEANS - A KEY SOVIET OPERATIONAL CONCEPT.** *Jane's Soviet Intelligence Review*, Vol. 3, Mar. 1991, pp. 104–109.
Discusses the Soviet military principle of massing forces and means. Demonstrates why massing of forces is likely to remain central to Soviet military operational behavior. Comments on the impact this will have on the Soviet response to the Strategic Defense Initiative.

B220. Huntington, T. **SOVIET BOOSTER.** *Air and Space*, Vol. 5, Mar. 1991, pp. 90–95.
Space Commerce Corporation, founded by Art Dula, tries to market Soviet space services in the U.S. including arranging for U.S. satellites to be launched aboard Soviet boosters. But U.S. export policy classifies satellites and boosters as munitions and bans their export to the Soviet Union. Dula is looking for ways to open a window to allow for joint commercialization projects.

B221. Hyland, W., 1929– . **THE COLD WAR: FIFTY YEARS OF CONFLICT.** New York, NY: Times Books, 1991.
Previously published: The Cold War is Over.
Includes bibliographical references and index.

B222. **THE IMPOVERISHED SUPERPOWER: PERESTROIKA AND THE SOVIET MILITARY BURDEN.** Edited by H.S. Rowen and C. Wolf, Jr. San Francisco, CA.: ICS Press, Lanhan, MD: Distributed to the trade by National Book Network, c1990, xiv, 372 pp., ill., 24 cm.
Includes bibliographical references (pp. 287–353) and index.

B223. **IN SEARCH OF CIVIL SOCIETY: INDEPENDENT PEACE MOVEMENTS IN THE SOVIET BLOC.** Edited by V. Tismaneanu, New York, NY: routledge, 1990, x, 193 pp., 24 cm.
A Foreign Policy Research Institute book - P. (ii). Includes bibliographical references and index.

B224. **INTERNATIONAL LAW.** Contributors, D.I. Feldman....R.A. Mullerson (managing editor)....G.A. Tunkin (i.e., G.I. Tunkin) (managing editor). Moscow: Progress Publishers; Chicago, IL: Imported by Imported Publications, c1990, 294 (1) pp., 20 cm.
Translated from Russian. Title on verso t.p.: Mezhdunarodnoe pravo. Includes bibliographical references (pp. 293–295).

B225. **INTERNATIONAL JOINT VENTURES: SOVIET AND WESTERN PERSPECTIVES.** Edited by A.B. Sherr et al. New York, NY: Quorum Books, c1991.
A project of the Center for Foreign Policy Development at Brown University, the Institute for World Economy and International Relations of the U.S.S.R. Academy of Sciences, and the All-Union Research Institute of

Foreign Economic Relations, State Foreign Economic Relations Committee, of the U.S.S.R. Council of Ministers.

Includes bibliographical references and index.

B226. **IS THE CASE OF RAOUL WALLENBERG CLOSED?** International Affalrs (Moscow) No. 1, 1990, pp. 234–238.

Conversation between Valentin Nikiforov, Deputy Minister of Foreign Affairs of the U.S.S.R., Vladimir Pirozhkov, Deputy Chairman of the U.S.S.R. State Security Committee, Raoul Wallenberg's relatives and the leadership of the Raoul Wallenberg Association.

B227. Ivanov, V. 1957–. **THE PHILOSOPHY OF SURVIVAL.** Translated from the Russian by V. Schneierson, Moscow: Progress Publishers, c1990, 151 pp., 20 cm.

Translation of: Voina, mir i progress chelovechestva. Includes bibliographical references.

B228. Jacobs, G. **EVOLUTION OF THE SOVIET AIRCRAFT CARRIER DOCTRINE.** *Jane's Soviet Intelligence Review*, Vol. 2, May 1990, pp. 194–198.

Aircraft carrier Tbilisi culminates a half-century of evolutionary development of Soviet attack aircraft carrier advocacy and doctrinal debates concerning the role of carrier-based aviation.

B229. Jacobsen, C.G. **DRAMATIC CHANGE IN SOVIET DEFENSE DECISION-MAKING.** *Bulletin of Peace Proposals*, Vol. 21, June 1990, pp. 115–119.

The end of the 1980s saw sweeping change in Soviet defense decision-making. Defense procurement, deployment, strategy and, information all used to be a jealously-guarded military preserve. Now, however, new civilian legislative bodies are acquiring unheard-of-powers of oversight, challenge and advice borrowing openly from U.S. practice.

B230. Jalonen, O.-P. **SOVIET MILITARY DOCTRINE: STABILITY OR CHANGE?** *Current Research on Peace and Violence*, Vol. 13, No. 1, 1990, pp. 17–28.

It is the purpose of this article to try to evaluate whether or not the late 80's change can be considered as a unique phenomenon or whether such reforms have occurred earlier.

B231. James, D. **"PRINCE" OR PAWN?** *World and I*, Vol. 6, Apr. 1991, pp. 404–411.

Reviews the recent biography of Castro by George Anne Geyer and discusses Castro's rise to power and relationship with the Soviet Union.

B232. Jelavich, B., 1923– . **RUSSIAN'S BALKAN ENTANGLEMENTS, 1806–1914.** Cambridge (England), New York, NY: Cambridge University Press, 1991.

Includes bibliographical references.

B233. **JEWS IN EASTERN POLAND AND THE USSR, 1939–46.** Edited by A. Polonsky and N. Davies. New York, NY: St. Martin's Press, 1991.

Seven of the chapters were first presented at the International Conference on the History and Culture of Polish Jews held in Jerusalem in Feb. 1988. Includes index.

B234. Johnston, R.H., 1937– . **SOVIET FOREIGN POLICY, 1918–1945: A GUIDE TO RESEARCH AND RESEARCH MATERIALS.** Wilmington, DE: Scholarly Resources, 1991, xi, 236 pp., 23 cm.
Includes index.

B235. Joseph, P. **POLITICAL CHANGES AFTER THE COLD WAR.** *Dissent*, Vol. 37, Spring 1990, pp. 145–148.
While critical questions surround the future of Eastern Europe and the Soviet Union, there is another set of questions in the background: the implications of these changes for American politics.

B236. Kadish, S., 1959– . **BOLSHEVIKS AND BRITISH JEWS: THE ANGLO-JEWISH COMMUNITY, BRITAIN, AND THE RUSSIAN REVOLUTION.** London (England), Portland, OR: F. Cass, 1991.
Includes bibliographical references and index.

B237. Karatnycky, A. **THE EMPIRE STRIKES OUT.** *American Spectator*, Vol. 24, Feb. 1991, pp. 20–25.
In the final analysis, about the only thing that seems certain is that there will not be and cannot be what the Bush Administration seems to want - a democratic Soviet Union. A transition to full democracy will mean that many of the U.S.S.R.'s constituent republics will likely split off. And those that choose to remain are likely to join what is in essence a loose confederation based on economic treaties and mutual defense pacts. The Soviet Union can survive only through a crackdown and mass repression - as an empire maintained at the barrel of a gun.

B238. Karp, A. **THE UNITED STATES AND THE SOVIET UNION AND THE CONTROL OF BALLISTIC MISSILE PROLIFERATION TO THE MIDDLE EAST.** New York, NY: Institute for East–West Security Studies, 1989 (i.e., 1990) 32 pp., 23 cm. Public policy papers.
Includes bibliographical references (pp. 32).

B239. Karsh, E. **SOVIET POLICY TOWARDS SYRIA SINCE 1970.** New York, NY: St. Martin's Press, 1991, ix, 235 pp., 23 cm.
Includes bibliographical references and index.

B240. Kartchner, K.M., 1956– . **NEGOTIATING START: THE QUEST FOR STABILITY AND THE MAKING OF THE STRATEGIC ARMS REDUCTION TREATY.** With a foreword by E. Rowny. New Brunswick, NJ: Transaction Publishers, c1991.
Includes bibliographical references and index.

B241. Kaslow, A. **REDEFINING RELATIONS WITH THE KREMLIN; DEALING WITH THE SOVIETS.** *Europe*, No. 304, Apr. 1991, pp. 6–8.
In these days of post-cold war planning, Western confidence in the East's reduced security threats has been checked by the Soviet Union's instability and its potential to disrupt reforms elsewhere in the region.

B242. Katz, M.N. **THE DECLINE OF SOVIET POWER: IMPLICATIONS FOR INTERNATIONAL RELATIONS.** *Survival*, Vol. 32, Jan.–Feb. 1990, pp. 15–28.

The decline of Soviet power will not necessarily herald the dawn of a new, peaceful era in international relations. Instead, conflict will continue at a very great cost....This article will examine just what this "very great cost" might be in Europe, Central Asia, the Far East and the Third World. While the problems related to what was previously regarded as the primary Soviet threat will diminish, other serious security problems will arise.

B243. Katz, M.N. **BEYOND THE REAGAN DOCTRINE: REASSESSING U.S. POLICY TOWARD REGIONAL CONFLICTS.** *Washington Quarterly*, Vol. 14, Winter 1991, pp. 169–179.

How exactly should U.S. foreign policy deal with lingering vestiges of the past and new problems of international security in an era of improved Soviet-U.S. relations?

B244. Kaufmann, W.W. **GLASNOST, PERESTROIKA, AND U.S. DEFENSE SPENDING.** Washington, DC: Brookings Institution, c1990, x, 52 (35) pp., 23 cm.

Includes bibliographical references.

B245. Kauppi, M.V. **MOSCOW AND THE CONGO.** *Problems of Communism*, Vol. 39, Mar.–Apr. 1990, pp. 42–60.

Relations between the Soviet Union and the People's Republic of the Congo are neither unique nor extraordinarily important in their own right. Yet study of this relationship can contribute in important ways to a fuller, more balanced understanding of Soviet policy toward Sub-Saharan Africa....This article argues that Soviet-Congolese relations reveal a pattern very similar to that of Moscow's relations with other African states of socialist orientation.

B246. Kay, M.A. **THE YUGOSLAV GOVERNMENT-IN-EXILE AND THE PROBLEMS OF RESTORATION.** *East European Quarterly*, Vol. 25, Mar. 1991, pp. 1–19.

Britain's own declining influence and status within the Big Three prevented her from fulfilling her obligations to the Yugoslav exiles.

B247. Keeble, C. **BRITAIN AND THE SOVIET UNION, 1917–1989.** New York, NY: St. Martin's Press, 1990, xiv, 387 pp. (16) pp. of plates, ill., 23 cm

Includes bibliographical references (pp. 357–274).

B248. Kennan, G.F., 1904– . **MEASURES SHORT OF WAR: THE GEORGE F. KENNAN LECTURES AT THE NATIONAL WAR COLLEGE, 1946–47.** Edited by G.D. Harlow and G.C. Maerz. Washington, DC: National Defense University Press. Sold by Supt. of Docs., U.S. G.P.O., 1991.

Includes index.

B249. Kessler, R. **ESCAPE FROM THE CIA: HOW THE CIA WON AND LOST THE MOST IMPORTANT KGB SPY EVER TO DEFECT TO THE U.S.** New York, NY: Pocket Books, c1991, viii, 210 pp., ill., 24 cm.

B250. Kessler, R. **THE SPY IN THE RUSSIAN CLUB: HOW GLENN SOUTHER STOLE AMERICA'S NUCLEAR WAR PLANS AND ESCAPED TO MOSCOW.** New York, Charles Scribner's Sons, 1990, 275 pp.

Recounts the case of Navy photographer Glen Souther, who became a Soviet spy and defected to Moscow, where he committed suicide in 1989. The author states that, while assigned to the Navy's Fleet Intelligence Center for Europe and the Atlantic, Souther "had access to all of America's nuclear war plans," specifically the Single Integrated Operations Plan, or SIOP.

B251. Kiezun, W. **MANAGEMENT IN SOCIALIST COUNTRIES: U.S.S.R. AND CENTRAL EUROPE.** Berlin (Germany), New York, NY: Aldeline de Gruyter, 1991.

Includes bibliographical references and indexes.

B252. Kirkey, C. **THE NATO ALLIANCE AND THE INF TREATY.** *Armed Forces and Society*, Vol. 16, Winter, 1990, pp. 287–305.

The INF Treaty of December 1987 has focused renewed attention on the central military and political issues that lie at the heart of NATO. Defenders of the treaty claim that the agreement between the United States and the Soviet Union is clearly in the Alliance's interest. On the other hand, critics of the treaty perceive fundamental weaknesses. Weaknesses that may interfere with NATO's objectives....An examination of these arguments suggests that, on balance, the assertions made by the proponents of the treaty are marginally more persuasive.

B253. Kirkpatrick, J.J. **BEYOND THE COLD WAR.** *Foreign Affairs*, Vol. 69, No. 1, 1990, pp. 1–16.

If things develop in Eastern Europe as expected, Europeans will have new burdens to assume. Americans will have old burdens to relinquish. We will need to learn to be a power, not a superpower.

B254. Kline, M. **CASTRO AND "NEW THINKING" IN LATIN AMERICA.** *Journal of Inter-American Studies and World Affairs*, Vol. 32, Spring 1990, pp. 83–118.

This article will start with (1) an overview of Cuban Latin American foreign policy since the 1970s; then proceed to (2) an interpretation of Soviet "new thinking;" and finally (3) argue that this particular interpretation of "new thinking" is consistent with, and not contradictory to, Castro's foreign policy.

B255. Kokoshin, A.A. **THE NEW SOVIET MILITARY DOCTRINE: POLITICAL, STRATEGIC, AND ECONOMIC DIMENSIONS.** *Mediterranean Quarterly*, Vol. 1, Winter 1990, pp. 37–49.

Soviet military doctrine developed as a systematic approach to the character of a possible future war, to war preparations for the country and its armed forces, and to the modalities of waging war. Two major components could be distinguished in this doctrine, one of them sociopolitical in nature and the other focused on technical military matters.

B256. Kolasky, J. **PARTNERS IN TYRANNY: THE NAZI-SOVIET NONAGGRESSION PACT, AUGUST 23, 1939.** Toronto: Mackenzie Institute, c1990, xvi, 158 pp., 19 cm.

Includes bibliographical references (pp. 150–152) and index.

B257. Kortunov, S. **START II AND BEYOND.** *Bulletin of the Atomic Scientists*, Vol. 46, Oct. 1990, pp. 21–24.

An influential Soviet arms control official believes the next phase of negotiations will bring a major reorganization of nuclear forces, as well as drastic reductions.

B258. Kosach, G.G. **NEW SOVIET THINKING ON THE MIDDLE EAST.** *Middle East Report*, Vol. 21, Mar.–Apr. 1991, pp. 37–38.

Examines current Soviet policy in the Middle East. Considers such issues as Soviet attitudes toward the Arab-Israeli conflict, history of Soviet involvement in the Middle East and other issues and trends.

B259. Kozyrev, A.V. **THE NEW SOVIET ATTITUDE TOWARD THE UNITED NATIONS.** *Washington Quarterly*, Vol. 13, Summer 1990, pp. 41–53.

Profound transformations in Soviet society are linked inseparably to revolutionary changes in the foreign policy of the Soviet Union....These sea changes are manifested most evidently in the fundamental shift in the Soviet attitude regarding the United Nations.

B260. Kraemer, S.F. **THE KRASNOYARSK SAGA.** *Strategic Review*, Vol. 18, Winter 1990, pp. 25–38.

Soviet Foreign Minister Shevardnadze's admission that the giant radar at Krasnoyarsk represents a breach of the ABM Treaty climaxed a long and somber story....The story is not over: the Krasnoyarsk radar may yet play a part in the end-game of hastened negotiations toward the conclusion of a START Treaty.

B261. Lacayo, R. **A HURRY-UP SUMMIT.** *Time*, Vol. 135, Apr. 16, 1990, pp. 26–28.

Despite Lithuania and strategic-arms talks that have hit some snags, the Bush–Gorbachev meeting is pushed up to May 30.

B262. LaFeber, W. **AMERICA, RUSSIA, AND THE COLD WAR, 1945–1990.** New York, NY: McGraw-Hill, c1991.

Rev. ed. of: America, Russia, and the Cold War, 1945–1984. 5th ed., c1985. Includes bibliographical references.

B263. Laidi, Z. **THE SUPERPOWERS AND AFRICA: THE CONSTRAINTS OF A RIVALRY, 1960–1990.** Translated by P. Baudoin, Chicago, IL: University of Chicago Press, c1990, xxv, 232 pp., map, 24 cm.

Translation of: Les contraintes du'une rivalite. Includes bibliographical references (pp. 203–226) and index.

B264. Laird, R.F., 1946– . **THE SOVIETS, WEST GERMANY, AND EUROPEAN SECURITY.** Boulder, CO: Westview Press, 1991.

B265. Laqueur, W. 1921–. **RUSSIA AND GERMANY: A CENTURY OF CONFLICT.** With a new preface and introduction by the author. New Brunswick, NJ: Transaction Publishers, c1990, v, 377 pp., maps, 23 cm.

Cover title: Russia and Germany., originally published: Boston: Little, Brown, 1965. Includes bibliographical references (pp. 327–341) and index.

B266. Lavalle, E.M. **COLLECTIVE SECURITY AND THE SUPERPOWERS: TRENDS OF SIGNIFICANCE FOR THE PERSIAN GULF STATES.** *Current Research on Peace and Violence,* Vol. 13, No. 1, 1990, pp. 29–38.

A review of recent approaches to security and peace-keeping issues arising out of regional conflicts provides evidence of changes which will prove significant to the Persian Gulf States and other regional configurations of states. The new approach stresses consensus and collaboration with a pragmatic approach to the resolution of peace and security issues emanating from regional conflicts. The new approach is one of conflict management driven by the domestic and global interests of the two superpowers and increasingly articulated through the United Nations. In the United Nations Security Council the new approach is followed and participated in by the other permanent members.

B267. **LEARNING IN U.S. AND SOVIET FOREIGN POLICY.** Edited by G.W. Breslauer and P.E. Tetlock. Boulder, CO: Westview Press, 1991.

Includes index.

B268. Ledeen, M.A., 1941– . **SUPERPOWER DILEMMAS: THE U.S. AND THE U.S.S.R. AT CENTURY'S END.** New Brunswick, NJ: Transaction Publishers, c1991.

Rev. ed. of: Grave New World, 1985.

Includes bibliographical references and index.

B269. Lee, T.V., Searle-White, J. **PRISONERS DILEMMA MEETS GLASNOST: A COMPARATIVE ADVANTAGE SOLUTION TO THE UNITED STATES PRISON CRISIS.** *Cornell International Law Journal,* Vol. 24, Winter 1991, pp. 25–56.

Where can we find a place with substantial space, expertise in running prisons, and a desperate need for U.S. dollars, a combination that would make it the perfect place to expand American prison capacity? The answer is obvious: the Soviet Union. A joint project, in which the U.S. Bureau of Prisons built and maintained new prison facilities in the U.S.S.R.: with the assistance of Soviet personnel, would alleviate domestic problems of both countries. Such an undertaking would also build on the emerging spirit of open-mindedness and superpower cooperation.

B270. Leighton, M.K. **SOVIET PROPAGANDA AS A FOREIGN POLICY TOOL.** New York, NY: Freedom House, 1991, 190 pp., 24 cm. Focus on issues, No. 12.

Includes bibliographical references (pp. 171–185) and index.

B271. Leighton, M. **MOSCOW'S THIRD WORLD EMPIRE.** *Global Affairs,* Vol. 5, Spring 1990, pp. 133–156.

B272. Lemiski, K. **POLISH POLITICAL ACTIVISM IN THE U.S.S.R..** *Report on the U.S.S.R.,* Vol. 2, Sept 7, 1990, pp. 13–18.

One effect of perestroika and glasnost has been the assertion of demands for rights and political representation by ethnic minorities whose existence was hardly recognized before, among them the Polish population of Belorussia, Lithuania, and Ukraine.

B273. Lepingwell, J. **NEW SOVIET REVELATIONS ABOUT KAL-007.** *Report on the U.S.S.R.*, Vol. 3, Apr. 26, 1991, pp. 9–15.

The Soviet government newspaper Izvestia has published a series of remarkable articles about how Korean Air Lines flight 007 came to be shot down in September, 1983. The series shed light on one of the most critical events in US-Soviet relations of the past decade and resolves a number of questions concerning the incident.

B274. Lepingwell, J.W.R. **SOVIET EARLY WARNING RADARS DEBATED.** *Report on the U.S.S.R.*, Vol. 2, Aug. 17, 1990, pp. 11–15.

Two public debates have arisen over the future of the Soviet Union's ballistic missile early earning system. The U.S.S.R. Ministry of Defense is finding its authority challenged by the residents of Mukachevo who are concerned about the environmental effects of an early warning radar being built nearby, and the issue of the Krasnoyarsk radar station has been reopened in the popular press. These debates illuminate the changing nature of Soviet defense decision-making.

B275. Levin, B.M. and Levin, M.B. **WHY DO THEY DRINK?** *Soviet Review*, Vol. 31, Mar.–Apr. 1990, pp. 80–96.

Soviet authors analyze survey responses as to why students drink.

B276. Levine, A.J. **THE SOVIET UNION, THE COMMUNIST MOVEMENT AND THE WORLD: PRELUDE TO THE COLD WAR, 1917–1941.** New York, NY: Praeger, 1990, 189 pp., 22 cm.

Includes bibliographical references (pp. 175–182) and index.

B277. Levine, R.A. **STILL THE ARMS DEBATE.** Aldershot, Hants: Dartmouth Pub. Co., Brookfield, VT: Gower Pub. Co., c1990, xiii, 453 pp., ill., 23 cm.

Includes bibliographical references (pp. 415–437) and index.

B278. Lockwood, D. **VERIFYING START: FROM SATELLITES TO SUSPECT SITES.** *Arms Control Today*, Vol. 20, Oct. 1990, pp. 13–19.

Combination of national technical means of verification and the inspections and cooperative measures now being negotiated will give the United States an excellent capability to monitor Soviet compliance with START.

B279. Lockwood, D. **MOSCOW SUMMIT, START SIGNING POSTPONED.** *Arms Control Today*, Vol. 21, Mar. 1991, pp. 25,28.

On January 28, only two weeks before the scheduled Moscow summit at which the United States and the Soviet Union expected to sign a historic Strategic Arms Reduction Talks (START) treaty, Secretary of State James Baker announced that the meeting would have to be postponed to "a later date in the first half of this year." Details reasons for the delays, including the Gulf War, the Baltic situation, and unresolved arms control issues.

B280. Lopatin, V. **THE ARMY AND THE ECONOMY: ECONOMIC ASPECTS OF SOVIET MILITARY REFORM.** *Global Affairs*, Vol. 6, Winter 1991, pp. 1–22.

Our goal is modest: to formulate the problem, to examine it more broadly and more rigorously, and to define possible approaches to the solution.

B281. Lowenthal, M.M. **THE NEW SOVIET LEGISLATURE: COMMITTEE ON DEFENSE AND STATE SECURITY.** Report of the committee on Armed Services, House of Representatives, 101st Congress, 2nd session. Washington, DC: U.S. G.P.O.

At head of title: 101st Congress, 2nd session. committee print.

B282. Lucas, M.R. **THE WESTERN ALLIANCE AFTER INF: REDEFINING U.S. POLICY TOWARD EUROPE AND THE SOVIET UNION.** Boulder, Colo., Lynne Rienner Publishers, 1990, 266 pp.

Partial contents - The political and military context of the INF Treaty. The economic and technological challenge of post-INF Europe. The challenge of detente and pan-Europeanization for the future of the Western Alliance.

B283. Luttwak, E.N. **THE SHAPE OF THINGS TO COME.** *Commentary*, Vol. 89, June 1990, pp. 17–25.

With the waning of the Soviet–American conflict, we now have to ask ourselves what are likely to be the new antagonisms that could shape world politics through the end of the millennium and beyond. More specifically, we have to look at four large possibilities.

B284. Lynch, A. **DOES GORBACHEV MATTER ANYMORE?** *Foreign Affairs*, Vol. 69, Summer 1990, pp. 19–29.

Argues that, as important as Gorbachev has been in effecting the recent break through the East–West relations, it is less certain that he will prove as important in the future. Asserts that many of the changes in international relations that Gorbachev has set in motion are irreversible and that while it is preferable to the West that Gorbachev remain at the helm of the Soviet state, the irreducible American interest in a plural distribution of geopolitical power in Europe is now assured, independent of events in Moscow.

B285. Lynch, A. **THE CONTINUING IMPORTANCE OF IDEOLOGY IN SOVIET FOREIGN POLICY.** *Harriman Institute Forum*, Vol. 3, July 1990, pp. 1–8.

The collapse of communist authority throughout the region, clearly reflects a decline in the level and character of ideologically driven hostility in Soviet foreign policy and East–West relations as a whole.

B286. Ma'aroof, M.K. **AFGHANISTAN AND SUPER POWERS.** New Delhi: Commonwealth Publishers, 1990, viii, 347 pp., 22 cm.

Includes bibliographical references (pp. 320–342).

B287. Macdonald, H. 1947–. **THE SOVIET CHALLENGE AND THE STRUCTURE OF EUROPEAN SECURITY.** Aldershot, Hants, England: E. Elgar, Brookfield, VT, U.S.A.: Gower Pub. Co., c1990, ix, 318 pp., 23 cm.

Includes bibliographical references (pp. 289–313) and index.

B288. Mack, A. and O'Hare M. **MOSCOW–TOKYO AND THE NORTHERN TERRITORIES DISPUTES.** *Asian Survey*, Vol. 30, Apr. 1990, pp. 380–394.

The most serious barrier today to a major improvement in relations between Tokyo and Moscow is the long-standing and bitter dispute over a number of small islands lying between the northern Japanese island of Hokkaido and the U.S.S.R.'s Kamchatka Peninsula. The territories in question - Etorofu, Kunashiri, Shikotan and the Habomai Islands - are claimed by both the Japanese and the Soviets, but have been occupied by the latter since the end of World War II.

B289. Makarov, S.O. 1848–1904. **DISCUSSION OF QUESTIONS IN NAVAL TACTICS.** Translated from the Russian by J.B. Bernadou, with an introduction and notes by R.B. Bathurst. Annapolis, MD: Naval Institute Press, c1990, xxxvi, 306 pp., ill., 22 cm.

Translation of: Razsuzhdeniia po voprosam morskoi taktiki, "This translation was originally published in 1898 by the Office of Naval Intelligence as part of its General Information Series" - Verso of t.p., Includes bibliographical references and index.

B290. **MANAGING MILITARY OPERATIONS IN CRISIS: A CONFERENCE REPORT.** C.P. Niblack, ed. Santa Monica, CA: Rand Corp., 1991.

Documents the results of the Conference on Military Operations and Crisis Management, held Jan. 1990 in Santa Monica, CA. Prepared for the Carnegie Corporation. R-4038-CC. Dec. 1990.

Includes bibliographical references.

B291. Manes, C.W. **AMERICA WITHOUT THE COLD WAR.** Foreign Policy, No. 78, Spring 1990, pp. 3–25.

Western leaders regard the growing democratization of Eastern Europe as a vindication of Western policy....Consider(s) in detail the consequences for American foreign policy of these profound changes (and) the very different paths the country might follow in a post-Cold War world.

B292. Manthorpe, W.H.J. **THE SOVIET NAVY 1989: A SOVIET VIEW.** *United States Naval Institute Proceedings*, Vol. 116, May 1990, pp. 232–234.

The Soviet Navy was more insular in 1989 - both in operations and in debate. Most Soviet warships....spent lots of time in port or close to home. Military publications concentrated on training, combat readiness, and morale.

B293. Mark, C.R. **THE MIDDLE EAST: CHANGING ALIGNMENTS, ENDURING DISPUTES.** *CRS Review*, Vol. 12, Mar.–Apr. 1991, pp. 20–21.

The U.S. role in liberating Kuwait from Iraqi occupation in 1991 is viewed favorably by most Middle Eastern states, but such good will cannot be expected to last indefinitely. Evidence of regional political changes, such as the Arab League votes to oppose Iraq or the rise of pricing moderates within OPEC, may be temporary. Includes sidebar, Soviet oil and gas, by J.P. Hardt and P. Kaiser.

B294. Martin, D.R. and Gibbs, S. **SOVIET REFUGEES: THE CONTINUING DILEMMA.** GAO Journal, No. 9, Summer 1990, pp. 24–28.

As the Soviet Union finally lets its people go, the United States has to deal with the numbers.

B295. Mathews, T. and Bogert, C. **YELTSIN'S CHALLENGE.** *Newsweek*, Vol. 115, June 11, 1990, pp. 20,22,24–25.

Back from the political dead, a scrappy iconoclast puts a scare into Mikhail Gorbachev and confronts President Bush with an awkward dilemma.

B296. Mauer, M. **AMERICANS BEHIND BARS: A COMPARISON OF INTERNATIONAL RATES OF INCARCERATION.** Washington, Sentencing Project, 1991, 20 pp.

Compares and contrasts the rate of incarceration in the U.S. with those of South Africa and the Soviet Union. The United States now has the world's highest known rate of incarceration, with 426 prisoners per 100,000 population. South Africa is second in the world with a rate of 333 per 100,000, and the Soviet Union third with 268 per 100,000 population. Black males in the United States are incarcerated at a rate four times that of Black males in South Africa, 3,109 per 100,000 compared to 729 per 100,000.

B297. Mazarr, M.J., 1965– . **START AND THE FUTURE OF DETERRENCE.** New York, NY: St. Martin's Press, 1991, viii, 257 pp., 23 cm.

Includes bibliographical references (pp. 221–251) and index.

B298. MccGwire, M. **PERESTROIKA AND SOVIET NATIONAL SECURITY.** Washington, DC: Brookings Institution, c1991, xi, 481 pp., 24 cm.

Includes bibliographical references and index.

B299. McCormick, G.H. **STRANGER THAN FICTION: SOVIET SUBMARINE OPERATIONS IN SWEDISH WATERS.** Santa Monica, CA: Rand Corporation, 1990, xiii, 72 pp., ill., maps, 23 cm.

A Project of Air Force report prepared for the United States Air Force, January 1990, R-3776-AF, Rand library collection - Label on cover. Includes bibliographical references (pp. 69–72).

B300. McDaniel, T. **AUTOCRACY, MODERNIZATION, AND REVOLUTION IN RUSSIA AND IRAN.** Princeton, NJ: Princeton University press, c1991, 239 pp., 25 cm.

Includes bibliographical references (pp. 233–235) and index.

B301. McDonald, H. **CENTRAL ASIA.** *Far Eastern Economic Review*, Vol. 148, May 24, 1990, pp. 27–28,30,32,34.

Contents - Tremors in Tartary. Fallout from glasnost. Piety and patriotism.

B302. McDougall, D. 1945–. **SOVIET-AMERICAN RELATIONS SINCE THE 1940S.** Melbourne, New York, NY: Edward Arnold, 1990, vi, 182 pp. ill, 21 cm.

Includes bibliographical references (pp. 169–174) and index.

B303. McGrath, P. **HOW TO HELP GORBACHEV.** *Newsweek*, Vol. 117, June 17, 1991, pp. 34–35,38–39.

Discusses Soviet President Gorbachev's request for massive Western aid and the debate in the West over the conditions for and the efficaciousness of such aid

B304. McMichael, S.R., 1951– . **STUMBLING BEAR: SOVIET MILITARY PERFORMANCE IN AFGHANISTAN.** London (England), Washington, DC: Brassey's, 1991.

B305. Melancon, M. 1940–. **THE SOCIALIST REVOLUTIONARIES AND THE RUSSIAN ANTI-WAR MOVEMENT, 1914–1917.** Columbus, OH: Ohio State University Press, c1990, xii, 368 pp., ports, 24 cm.

Includes bibliographical references (pp. 337–356) and index.

B306. **MEMO 2: SOVIETS EXAMINE FOREIGN POLICY FOR A NEW DECADE.** Edited by S. Hirsch, Washington, DC: Bureau of National Affairs, 1991, xii, 322 pp., 23 cm.

Translated from Russian. produced through collaboration with the Institut mirovoi ekonomiki i mezhdunarodnykh otnoshenii and editors of Mirovaia eknomika i mezhdunarodnye otnosheniia. Includes bibliographical references.

B307. Menges, C.C. **NATO AND GEOPOLITICS.** *Global Affairs*, Vol. 5, Summer–Fall 1990, pp. 74–93.

The Soviet Union is conducting a double global strategy: normalization in some regions, including Europe; and, continuing indirect aggression in other regions. An appropriate counterstrategy includes, informing the world about the facts of indirect aggression, withholding and terminating economic aid of all types to the Soviet Union and its accomplice regimes....helping anti-Communist armed resistance movements succeed, and encouraging political liberalization and transitions to democracy.

B308. Menon, R. **GORBACHEV'S JAPAN POLICY.** *Survival*, Vol. 33, Mar.–Apr. 1991, pp. 158–172.

It is an opportune time to ponder some of the problems that must be resolved for a fundamental transformation in Soviet-Japanese relations....In Soviet-Japanese relations so far lies the unresolved territorial dispute and Japan's scepticism that the changes wrought by Gorbachev will fundamentally lessen the Soviet threat.

B309. Menos, D. 1924–. **THE SUPERPOWERS AND NUCLEAR ARMS CONTROL: RHETORIC AND REALITY.** New York, NY: Praeger, 1990, xiv, 179 pp., 25 cm.

Includes bibliographical references (pp. 165–171) and index.

B310. Michel, T. **GLASNOST AND SOVIET MUSLIMS.** *America*, Vol. 163, Oct 13, 1990, pp. 241–246.

It is unlikely that Central Asian Muslims will be satisfied with their present limited goals of the opening of mosques, schools and religious instruction.

B311. **MILITARY HISTORY SYMPOSIUM (U.S.) (12TH: 1986: UNITED STATES AIR FORCE ACADEMY).** Transformation in Russian and Soviet military history: proceedings of the Twelfth Military History Symposium, United States Air Force Academy, 1–3 October 1986. Edited by C.W. Reddel. Washington, DC: United States Air Force Academy, Office of Air Force History, United States Air force, 1990, xxii, 405 pp., ill., 23 cm.

B312. Min, B.O. Nelson, D.N. and Zhong, Y. **FOREIGN POLICY PRAGMATISM AND DOMESTIC REFORM: LINKAGES IN THE U.S.S.R. AND CHINA.** *Journal of Asian and African Affairs*, Vol. 2, July 1990, pp. 29–68.

Through a comparison of Soviet and Chinese foreign policies towards the Third World, this study empirically examines the changing emphases or priorities in these states' international relations and,....assess(es) the congruence of domestic socio-economic or political reforms with such new foreign policy directions.

B313. Mlynar, Z. **CAN GORBACHEV CHANGE THE SOVIET UNION? THE INTERNATIONAL DIMENSIONS OF POLITICAL REFORM.** Translated by M. Sling and R. Tosek, Boulder, CO: Westview Press, 1990, viii, 184 pp., 23 cm.

Translation of: Was kann Gorbatschow andern? Includes bibliographical references and index.

B314. Moffitt, L. **NEW DIMENSIONS FOR PERESTROIKA.** *World and I*, Vol. 5, June 1990, pp. 98–101.

Assesses the implications of the Apr. 1990 meeting in Moscow of Mikhail Gorbachev with controversial Korean evangelist Sun Myung Moon. With crises facing the Soviet Union from all levels and all segments of society, Gorbachev considers the spiritual dimension of Soviet reform.

B315. Moodie, M. 1948–. **CONVENTIONAL ARMS CONTROL AND DEFENSE ACQUISITION: CATCHING THE CABOOSE?** Foreword by G. A. Carver, remarks by Representative D. McCurdy and Senator T.E. Wirth, Washington, DC: Center for Strategic and International Studies, c1990, xvi, 48 p., 23 cm.

Includes bibliographical references (pp. 47–48).

B316. Morrison, D.C. **RED RETRENCHMENT.** *National Journal*, Vol. 22, Apr. 28, 1990, pp. 1056.

With the creation in late-1988 of a 43-member Defense and State Security Committee of the Supreme Soviet, the Soviet military also faces a new obstacle with which its American counterpart has long had to grapple: legislative oversight.

B317. Mortimer, E. **ALAS, POOR GORBY.** Financial Times, May 29, 1990, 19 pp.

The special build-up given to a U.S.–Soviet summit is a kind of courtesy, just as it was a courtesy to go on treating Britain and France as notionally equal "great powers" in the 1950s.

B318. Murray, B. **CAN SPACE EXPLORATION SURVIVE THE END OF THE COLD WAR?** *Space Policy*, Vol. 7, Feb. 1991, pp. 23–34.

Maintains that early space exploration was driven by the rivalry between the U.S. and the U.S.S.R., but with the end of the Cold War the superpowers are turning to domestic issues. Sees international cooperation as a means of sustaining space exploration.

B319. **MUTUAL SECURITY: A NEW APPROACH TO SOVIET-AMERICAN RELATIONS.** Edited by R. Smoke and A. Kotunov. With prefaces by C. Vance and G. Arbatov. New York, NY: St. Martin's Press, c1991, xxvii, 403 pp., 25 cm.

A joint study by the Center for Foreign Policy Development at Brown University and the Institute for the U.S.A. and Canada of the Soviet Academy of Sciences.

Includes bibliographical references and index.

B320. **MUTUAL PERCEPTIONS OF LONG-RANGE GOALS: CAN THE UNITED STATES AND THE SOVIET UNION COOPERATE?** Edited by K. Gottstein. Boulder, CO: Westview Press; Frankfurt (West Germany): Campus Verlag, 1991.
Includes bibliographical references and index.

B321. Myers, D.B. 1944–. **NEW SOVIET THINKING AND U.S. NUCLEAR POLICY.** Philadelphia: Temple University Press, 1990, xvii, 295, pp., 24 cm.
Includes bibliographical references (pp. 265–292).

B322. **NEGOTIATING ARMS CONTROL: MISSED OPPORTUNITIES AND LIMITED SUCCESSES.** Edited by K.W. Thompson. Lanham, MD: University Press of America; Charlottesville, VA: Miller Center, University of Virginia, c1991, xii, 142 pp., 23 cm.

B323. **NEITHER EAST NOR WEST: IRAN, THE SOVIET UNION, AND THE UNITED STATES.** Edited by N.R. Keddie and M.J. Gasiorowski. New Have, CT: Yale University Press, c1990, ix, 295 pp., 24 cm.
Based on a conference held at U.C.L.A. in April 1988. Includes bibliographical references and index.

B324. Nel, P. **THE CHANGING CONTENT OF SOVIET POLICY TOWARDS SOUTH AFRICA.** Koln: Bundesinstitut fur Ostwissenschaftliche und Internationale Studien, c1990, 58 pp., 30 cm. Berichte des Bundesinstituts fur Ostwissenschaftliche und Internationale Studien, 16-1990.

B325. Nelan, B.W. **KOHL WINS HIS WAY; COVER STORIES.** *Time*, Vol. 136, July 30, 1990, pp. 24–29.
Discusses the negotiations between Gorbachev and Kohl regarding German unification.

B326. Nelson, D. **KEEP AN EYE ON TURKEY.** National Interest, No. 19, Spring 1990, pp. 117–121.
Warns that in dramatically changing circumstances, it would be dangerous to assume that the force of history alone will determine the future relations between Turkey and the Soviet Union....Changes in the U.S.S.R., the pragmatism of Ankara's centrist civilian leadership, and other more imminent security issues confronting Turkey may be propelling relations between the two countries into uncharted waters - and more important for the United States, causing serious concern about the fate of NATO's cornerstone southern flank.

B327. Neupokoyev, F.K. **THE AIR DEFENSE BATTLE.** Soviet Union Military Affairs, June 8, 1990, whole issue (pp. 1–209) (JPRS-UMA-90-007-L).
Partial contents - Enemy offensive air weapons. Air defense. Foundations of surface-to-air missile (AA artillery) position defense. Developing and making the battle plan. Planning and organization of combat actions. Combat support. The conduct of the air defense battle. For official use only.

B328. Newby, L. **SINO-SOVIET RAPPROCHEMENT AND ITS IMPLICATIONS FOR CHINA'S FOREIGN POLICY.** In RUSI and Brassey's Defense Yearbook 1990. London, Brassey's Defense Publishers, 1990, pp. 377–394.

China's avowed aim to hold a position of equidistance between the Soviet Union and the United States an unashamed bid to play a heightened role in international affairs....The aim of this article is to examine the main factors motivating China's Soviet policy, and the implications of China's policy of equidistance for regional powers and the global balance of power.

B329. Nincic, M. **U.S. SOVIET POLICY AND THE ELECTORAL CONNECTION.** *World Politics*, Vol. 42, Apr. 1990, pp. 370–396.

Examine(s) the possibility that United States attitudes toward the Soviet Union are not only....determined by that country's capacities and behavior, but that they are substantially shaped by domestic political rhythms within the United States and, in particular, by the electoral cycle.

B330. Nixon, R. **SHOULD WE HELP GORBACHEV?** *American Spectator*, Vol. 23, Mar. 1990, pp. 18–21.

The former President explains his current opposition to U.S. assistance to Gorbachev's U.S.S.R. concludes that "I do not question Gorbachev's sincerity. He is profoundly sincere in wanting to rescue the Soviet system from a terminal illness. He has been bold and courageous in adopting policies at home and abroad that serve that purpose. We should help Gorbachev - but only if his reforms go far enough to have a change to succeed and if as a result the Soviet Union becomes less oppressive at home and less aggressive abroad.

B331. O'Hanlon, M. **U.S. COSTS OF VERIFICATION AND COMPLIANCE UNDER PENDING ARMS TREATIES.** Washington, Congressional Budget Office, 1990, 69 pp.

New types of verification procedures have been introduced recently, giving a prominent role to various types of on-site inspections....There have been concerns, however, that such measures could prove costly. This study....addresses the costs of verification and compliance of five pending arms control accords.

B332. O'Neill, W.L. **A BETTER WORLD: STALINISM AND THE AMERICAN INTELLECTUALS.** A new introduction by the author. New Brunswick, NJ: Transaction Publishers, c1990, 447 pp., 23 cm.

Reprint. Originally published: New York: Simon and Schuster, c1982, Includes index.

B333. Oberdorfer, D. **THE TURN: FROM THE COLD WAR TO A NEW ERA, 1983–1990: THE UNITED STATES AND THE SOVIET UNION.** New York, NY: Poseidon Press, c1991.

Includes bibliographical references and index.

B334. Odom, W.E. **THE SOVIET MILITARY IN TRANSITION.** *Problems of Communism*, Vol. 39, May–June 1990, pp. 51–71.

Mikhail Gorbachev has introduced major changes in Soviet foreign policy, military strategy and doctrine, manpower policies, military research and procurement, and military organization. Stressing cooperation in solving global problems instead of competition between political systems, he has reversed the offensive bias in Soviet strategy and force structure and attempted to reduce the military drain on the weakened Soviet economy. The challenge of ethnic unrest and separatism, however, may force Gorbachev into heavy reliance on the very military force that he is attempting to reduce.

B335. **ON DISARMAMENT: THE ROLE OF CONVENTIONAL ARMS CONTROL IN NATIONAL SECURITY STRATEGY.** Edited by R.A. Hallenbeck and D.E. Shaver. Foreword by W.F. Burns. New York, NY: Praeger, 1991, xiii, 229 pp., ill., 25 cm.

Includes bibliographical references (pp. 217–222) and index.

B336. **THE OTHER SIDE OF THE TABLE: THE SOVIET APPROACH TO ARMS CONTROL.** Edited by M. Mandelbam, New York, NY: Council on Foreign Relations Press, c1990, vi, 209 pp., 23 cm.

Includes bibliographical references.

B337. Parrish, M. **SOVIET SECURITY AND INTELLIGENCE ORGANIZATION, 1917–1990: A COMPENDIUM: BIOGRAPHICAL DICTIONARY AND REVIEW OF LITERATURE IN ENGLISH.** With an introduction by R. Conquest. Westport, CT: Meckler, c1991.

Includes bibliographical references.

B338. Patman, R.G. **THE SOVIET UNION IN THE HORN OF AFRICA: THE DIPLOMACY OF INTERVENTION AND DISENGAGEMENT.** Cambridge (England), New York, NY: Cambridge University Press, 1990, xvii, 411 pp., ill., 24 cm.

Revision of the author's thesis (Ph.D.) - University of Southampton, 1986. Includes bibliographical references (pp. 375–396) and index.

B339. Payne, D.W. **FIDEL CASTRO VERSUS PERESTROIKA.** *Report on the U.S.S.R.*, Vol. 2, Jan 12, 1990, pp. 6–10.

The most severe strain on Castro is presented by Mikhail Gorbachev's steadfast pursuit of perestroika, which Castro rejects for Cuba, and the collapse of Communist governments in Eastern Europe....Neither Gorbachev nor Castro wants a major shift in the long-standing Soviet–Cuban relationship....Castro is not at the end of his rope, but....his alternatives are constrained both at home and abroad.

B340. Pehe, J. **THE ECOLOGICAL DAMAGE CAUSED BY SOVIET TROOPS.** *Report on Eastern Europe*, Vol. 1, Aug. 3, 1990, pp. 28–31.

Since early march 1990, when the Soviet Union began withdrawing the troops it had been stationed in Czechoslovakia since 1968, the Czechoslovak public has gradually become aware of the extensive ecological damage that the troops have caused. The Czechoslovak government has insisted that the clean-up of the polluted sites be paid for by the Soviet Union, but the Soviets have disputed these claims.

B341. **PERESTROIKA AND EAST–WEST ECONOMIC RELATIONS: PROSPECTS FOR THE 1990'S.** Edited by M. Kraus and R.D. Liebowitz, New York, NY: New York University Press, c1990, x, 356 pp., 24 cm.

Based on a conference held at Middlebury College in September 1988, and cosponsored by the Geonomics Institute for International Economic Advancement and ISKAN. Includes bibliographical references and index.

B342. **PERESTROIKA AND INTERNATIONAL LAW: CURRENT ANGLO-SOVIET APPROACHES TO INTERNATIONAL LAW.** Edited by A. Carty and G. Danilenko, New York, NY: St. Martin's Press, 1990, ix, 231 pp., 23 cm.

Includes bibliographical references and index.

B343. **PERESTROIKA AND INTERNATIONAL LAW.** Edited by W.E. Butler, Dordrecht, Boston, MA: Nijhoff, Norwell, MA., U.S.A. Sold and distributed in the U.S.A. and Canada by Kluwer Academic Publishers, c1990, vi, 330 pp., 25 cm.

Papers from the III Anglo–Soviet Symposium on Public International Law held at University College, London, on 20–22 March 1989 under the auspices of the Centre for the Study of Socialist Legal Systems, University College, London, and the Soviet Association of International Law. Includes bibliographical references (pp. 313–328).

B344. **PERESTROIKA, SOVIET DOMESTIC AND FOREIGN POLICIES.** Edited by T. Hasegawa and A. Pravda. London: Royal Institute of International Affairs, Lond, Newbury Park: Sage Publications, 1990, xii, 276 pp., 23 cm.

Includes bibliographical references and index.

B345. Perkins, R. Jr. **THE ABCs OF THE SOVIET–AMERICAN NUCLEAR ARMS RACE.** Pacific Grove, CA: Brooks/Cole, c1991, xiv, 241 pp., ill., map, 23 cm.

Includes bibliographical references and index.

B346. Perle, R. **AMERICA'S AGENDA SHOULD BE GORBACHEV'S TOO.** Washington Post, May 30, 1990, A21.

Former Assistant Secretary of Defense in the Reagan administration contends that the most helpful thing President Bush can do for President Gorbachev this week is to insist on the American agenda at the summit.

B347. Pfaltzgraff, R.L. Jr. **CRISIS IN THE BALTICS: U.S. POLICY OPTIONS.** *World and I*, Vol. 6, Apr. 1991, pp. 50–57.

A clearly defined U.S. strategy demands that we jettison the policy of strengthening Gorbachev against forces said to be more reactionary.

B348. Pilon, R. **WILL THE WORLDWIDE LIBERAL REVOLUTION BYPASS AMERICA THROUGH JUDICIAL RESTRAINT?** *Cato Policy Report*, Vol, 12, Mar. –Apr. 1990, pp. 1,10–14.

Analyzes the recent developments in the U.S.S.R. and Eastern Europe changing their governments from decentralization to democratization to liberalization. The author argues that unlike these countries, through judicial restraint, the United States is abandoning its liberal stance of protecting individual rights in support of special interests. He contends that it is the special interest that the peoples of the socialist world are attempting to overturn.

B349. Pisar, S. **DEALING WITH RUSSIA: WEAPONS OF PEACE.** New York, NY: Scribner; Toronto (Canada): Maxwell Macmillan Canada; New York, NY: Maxwell Macmillan International, c1991.
A Robert Stewart book.
Includes bibliographical references and index.

B350. **PLAN FROLIC AND AMERICAN RESOURCES.** Edited by S.T. Ross and D.A. Rosenberg, New York, NY: Garland Pub., 1990, 1 v. (various pagings), 29 cm.
America's plans for war against the Soviet Union, 1945–1950, Vol. 6.

B351. Polmar, N. and Robinson, R. **WHAT LURKS IN THE SOVIET NAVY?** *U.S. Naval Institute Proceedings*, Vol. 116, Feb. 1990, pp. 43–51.
Since the 1962 Cuban Missile Crisis, U.S. military analysts and critics have considered the Soviet Navy a defensive force. But today, even with the current thaw in relations, Soviet submarines remain an offensive threat.

B352. Porter, B.D. **RED ARMIES IN CRISIS.** Washington, DC: Center for Strategic and International Studies, 1991.
Includes bibliographical references.

B353. Prins, G. **THE ROLE OF SUPERPOWER SUMMITRY: RECESSIONAL.** *Political Quarterly*, Vol. 61, July–Sept. 1990, pp. 263–277.
Summitry over matters of war and peace in the superpower age grew from origins in wholly exceptional circumstances and then passed through three distinct phases> How did this come about?....In what ways, if any, is the Summit a viable instrument for the future? This essay will address these questions.

B354. Pritchard, C.G. **SOVIET BOMBER FORCES BOOSTED BY DISARMAMENT?** *International Defense Review*, Vol. 23, Aug. 1990, pp. 837–840.
Regarding bombers, agreement was reached on two important issues at the June summit: U.S. and Soviet long-range strategic bombers will be counted as equivalent to 10 and 12 nuclear warheads. The Soviet Backfire bomber will be defined as an "intermediate range" it will be excluded from START reductions.

B355. Pry, P.V. **THE STRATEGIC NUCLEAR BALANCE.** New York, NY: C. Russak, 1990, 2 v., ill., 24 cm.
Includes bibliographical references and indexes.

B356. **PSYCHOLOGICAL OPERATIONS AND POLITICAL WARFARE IN LONG-TERM STRATEGIC PLANNING.** Edited by J. Radvanyi, New York, NY: Praeger, 1990, vi, 157 pp., 25 cm.
Includes bibliographical references (pp. 145–150) and index.

B357. Pucher, J. **CAPITALISM, SOCIALISM, AND URBAN TRANSPORTATION: POLICIES AND TRAVEL BEHAVIOR IN THE EAST AND WEST.** *Journal of the American Planning Association*, Vol. 56, Summer 1990, pp. 278–296.
Urban transportation systems in the Soviet Union, Europe, and North America are very different. The dominance of public transport in the Soviet

Union contrasts strikingly with the almost exclusive reliance on the automobile in the United States. European countries lie between these two extremes....Socialist governments strongly supported public transport. By contrast, the more market-oriented a country's economy, the ore it has neglected public transport, and instead subsidized highway construction, auto use, and suburbanization.

B358. Putintsev, A.D. **U.S.S.R., PERESTROIKA.** Written and compiled by A. Putintsev. Moscow: Novosti Press Agency Pub. House, 1990, 1 v. (unpaged), ill. (some col.), 22 cm.

Title on p. (2) of cover: SSSR perestroika.

B359. Rabkin, R. **IMPLICATIONS OF THE GORBACHEV ERA FOR CUBAN SOCIALISM.** *Studies in Comparative Communism*, Vol. 23, Spring 1990, pp. 23–46.

Argues that Castro's rejection of Gorbachev style reforms is based on the implications of the reforms for three aspects of the Soviet-Cuban relationship: the economic, the strategic, and the ideological. The reduction of East–West tensions means a decline in Cuba's value as a strategic ally and correspondingly undermines the rational for favored economic treatment by the Soviet Union. Also argues that Gorbachev's endorsement of pluralism has led to a loss of ideological clarity and....subtly legitimizes a more critical attitude toward questions of leadership inside Cuba itself.

B360. Rachwald, A.R. **IN SEARCH OF POLAND: THE SUPERPOWERS' RESPONSE TO SOLIDARITY, 1980–1989.** Stanford, CA: Hoover Institution Press, c1990, xii, 149 pp., 24 cm. Hoover Press publication, 396.

Includes bibliographical references (pp. 139–142) and index.

B361. Radu, M. and Klinghoffer, A.J. **THE DYNAMICS OF SOVIET POLICY IN SUB-SAHARAN AFRICA.** New York, NY: Holmes and Meier, 1990, p. cm.

Includes index.

B362. Raeff, M. **RUSSIA ABROAD: A CULTURAL HISTORY OF THE RUSSIAN EMIGRATION, 1919–1939.** New York, NY: Oxford University Press, 1990, viii, 239 pp., 25 cm.

Includes bibliographical references (pp. 199–220) and indexes.

B363. Ranger, R. and Zakheim, D.S. **ARMS CONTROL DEMANDS COMPLIANCE.** *Orbis*, Vol. 34, Spring 1990, pp. 211–225.

Signing the agreement is merely the first step in a long-term process that included verification (determining whether the agreement was being implemented) and enforcing compliance (punishing violations).

B364. **REFORGING EUROPEAN SECURITY: FROM CONFRONTATION TO COOPERATION.** Edited by K. Gottfried and P. Bracken, with contributions by J. Dean et al., Boulder, CO: Westview Press, c1990, xii, 266 pp., maps, 23 cm.

Includes bibliographical references and index.

B365. Reisch, A. **HUNGARY: THE HARD TASK OF SETTING RELATIONS WITH THE U.S.S.R. ON A NEW FOOTING.** *Report on Eastern Europe,* Vol. 2, May 24, 1991, pp. 6–23.

For the past five months, Hungarian and Soviet negotiators have gone through three rounds of talks over the draft of a new comprehensive interstate treaty needed to replace a treaty signed in 1967....The unsettled financial aspect of the continuing Soviet troop withdrawal from Hungary and the virtual collapse of bilateral trade in the framework of the Council for Mutual Economic Assistance, have made the treaty negotiations more arduous than expected.

B366. Reisch, A. **HUNGARY AND UKRAINE AGREE TO UPGRADE BILATERAL RELATIONS.** *Report on Eastern Europe,* Vol. 1, Nov. 2, 1990, pp. 6–12.

Hungarian President Arpad Goncz's three-day official visit to Ukraine in late September set the stage for a major upgrading of Ukrainian–Hungarian relations in the political, economic, and cultural fields, with full diplomatic relations as the long-term goal. Another beneficiary of this development is the Magyar ethnic minority in the Transcarpathian Oblast of Ukraine.

B367. **REMEMBERING WAR: A U.S.–SOVIET DIALOGUE.** Compiled by H. Keyssar, V. Pozner, New York, NY: Oxford University Press, 1990, xx, 254 pp., ill., map, 26 cm.

Based on the May 7, 1985 television broadcast, Remembering war.

B368. Renner, M.G. **IS THE SOVIET UNION PREPARED FOR PEACE?** *World Watch,* Vol. 3, Sept.–Oct. 1990, pp. 11–17,19.

Cuts in military spending could help save the nation's economy, but the transition to a peacetime footing may not be as easy as it seems.

B369. **RESHAPING EUROPE: STRATEGIES FOR A POST-COLD WAR EUROPE.** Edited by K.R. Holmes and J.P. Kosminsky. Washington, Heritage Foundation, 1990, 210 pp.

Contents - The new political landscape of Europe, by D. Seay. A new American role in Europe's balance of power, by J.P. Kosminsky. Beyond 1992: Protecting America's economic interests in post-Cold War Europe, by R.D. Utt and W.D. Eggers. Orchestrating retreat: Moscow and the changing Europe in 1990s, by L. Aron. conclusion, by J.P. Kosminsky.

B370. Richter, F., Echterling, J. **MILITARY REFORM DEVELOPS IN THE SOVIET UNION.** *Aussenpolitik,* Vol. 42, No. 1, 1991, pp. 48–57.

The process of change inside the Soviet Union is bound to even affect....the armed forces. Efforts envisaging military reform have been initiated which, if successful, will have also far-reaching international implications....Examine this development with reference to the relevant Soviet sources.

B371. **THE RISE OF THE NEW EUROPE.** *U.S. News and World Report,* Vol. 108, Feb. 26, 1990, pp. 28–29.

From the rubble of the old order, a new Germany is emerging, and the Continent is being radically reshaped.

B372. Ro'i, Y. **THE STRUGGLE FOR SOVIET JEWISH EMIGRATION, 1948–1967.** Cambridge (England), New York, NY: Cambridge University Press, 1991, xvii, 458 pp., 24 cm.

Includes bibliographical references (pp. 429–435) and index.

B373. Robinson, W.H. **PARLIAMENTARY DEVELOPMENT IN CENTRAL EUROPE AND THE U.S.S.R.** *CRS Review*, Vol. 12, Mar.–Apr. 1991, pp. 30–32.

Recent developments in Central Europe and the Soviet Union have created opportunities for Congress to contribute to the development of democratic institutions. Congress has asked the Library of Congress to work as its agent in some of these efforts. During the coming months, articles in the CRS Review will explore these developments in greater depth.

B374. Rosefielde, S. **SOVIET DEFENSE SPENDING: THE CONTRIBUTION OF THE NEW ACCOUNTANCY.** *Soviet Studies*, Vol. 42, Jan. 1, 1990, pp. 59–80.

Western defense analysts have long relied on three kinds of information to measure the scale of Soviet military spending: official defense budgetary statistics, other accounting data, and intelligence assessments. We now know with considerable certainty that military activities absorb a larger share of gross national product than the government has hitherto chosen to admit officially. Gorbachev affirms that the true figure is 9% of Soviet GNP, rather than 2% as previously claimed. Two innovative studies by Peter Wiles and Dmitri Steinberg using new accountancy methods find that Soviet defense spending is probably much higher than Gorbachev's latest figure suggests. This essay critically evaluates Wiles' and Steinberg's contributions.

B375. Rosten, K.A. **SOVIET-U.S. JOINT VENTURES: PIONEERS ON A NEW FRONTIER.** *California Management Review*, Vol. 33, Winter 1991, pp. 88–108.

Surveys a number of operating Soviet-U.S. joint ventures to pinpoint issues that were difficult to resolve during the cause of initial negotiations and to identify hurdles that joint ventures needed to overcome before beginning operations.

B376. Rourke, J.T. 1945–. **MAKING FOREIGN POLICY: UNITED STATES, SOVIET UNION, CHINA.** Pacific Grove, CA: Brooks/Cole Pub. Co., c1990, xiv, 274 pp., ill., 23 cm.

Includes bibliographical.

B377. Rowen, H.S., Wolf, C., Jr. and Tayler, J. **THE SOVIET UNION AS MILITARY GIANT AND ECONOMIC WEAKLING.** Stanford, CA: Hoover Institution, Stanford University, 1990, 19 pp., 23 cm

Includes bibliographical references (pp. 18–19). Essays in public policy, No. 18.

B378. Rowny, E.L. **ARMS CONTROL AND THE FUTURE OF U.S.-SOVIET RELATIONS.** *Strategic Review*, Vol. 19, Winter 1991, pp. 17–25.

For the past forty years, the goals and means of arms control were shaped by the Cold War....Now that the Cold War is over, arms control in the 1990s must adapt to the changes in the U.S. and Soviet relations.

B379. Rozman, G. **JAPAN'S RESPONSE TO THE GORBACHEV ERA, 1985–1991: A RISING SUPERPOWER VIEWS A DECLINING ONE.** Princeton, NJ: Princeton University Press, 1991.

Includes bibliographical references and index.

B380. Rubinstein, A.Z. **SOVIET CLIENT-STATES: FROM EMPIRE TO COMMONWEALTH?** *Orbis*, Vol. 35, Winter 1991, pp. 69–78.

The New Thinking he (Gorbachev) has applied to Eastern Europe and the Third World reveals a determination, not to abandon five decades of Soviet foreign-policy gains, but to advance Soviet interests at the same time that he addresses his urgent domestic problems....This restructuring requires an appropriate response from Washington: with regard to Europe, it means that, whatever America's new role there, it must not allow Moscow unilateral advantage on the continent; with regard to the Third World, it means recognizing that the Soviet-American competition continues, albeit by political rather than military means.

B381. Rubinstein, A.Z. **SOVIET FOREIGN POLICY SINCE WORLD WAR II: IMPERIAL AND GLOBAL.** New York, NY: Harper Collins, 1991.

Includes bibliographical references and index.

B382. Rubinstein, A.Z. **MOSCOW'S THIRD WORLD STRATEGY.** Princeton, NJ: Princeton University Press, c1990, xi, 329 pp., 24 cm.

Includes bibliographical references (pp. 313–320) and index.

B383. Rumer, E.B., 1958– . **THE END OF A MONOLITH: THE POLITICS OF MILITARY REFORM IN THE SOVIET ARMED FORCES.** Santa Monica, CA: Rand Corp., 1991, xiii, 44 pp., 23 cm.

Prepared for the Under Secretary of Defense for Policy. August 1990. R-3993-USDP.

Includes bibliographical references.

B384. **RUSI AND BRASSEY'S DEFENSE YEARBOOK, 1990.** London, Brassey's, 1990, 501 pp.

Partial contents - Into the 21st century. Western Europe and the Atlantic Alliance. Technology and defense procurement. The Soviet Union and Eastern Europe. The Middle East. The Pacific Basis and Africa. Signposts.

B385. Sakharov, A., 1921– . **MOSCOW AND BEYOND, 1986–1989.** Translated by A. Bouis. New York, NY: Knopf, 1991, xvii, 168 pp., (16) pp. of plates, ill., 25 cm.

Translation of: Gor kii, Moskva, dalee vezde. Includes index.

B386. Sanders, S.W. **LIVING OFF THE WEST: GORBACHEV'S SECRET AGENDA AND WHY IT WILL FAIL.** Lanham, MD: Madison Books. Distributed by National Book Network, c1990, xiii, 249 pp., 24 cm.

Includes bibliographical references (pp. 209–227) and index.

B387. Saperstein, A.M. **THE "LONG PEACE".** *Journal of Conflict Resolution*, Vol. 35, Mar. 1991, pp. 68–79.

One of the reasons advanced for the absence of a major war between the two superpowers during the forty-five years of their enmity since World War

II is that the world system in which they functioned was essentially bipolar and hence, presumably, inherently more stable than previous multipolar worlds.

B388. Sapir, J. **THE SOVIET MILITARY SYSTEM.** Translated by D. Macey. Cambridge (England): Polity Press, 1991. 362 pp., ill., 24 cm.
Translation of: Le Systeme Militaire Sovietique.
Includes bibliographical references (pp. 312–339) and index.

B389. Sato, T., Momose, T. and Williams, D. **THE GORBACHEV REVOLUTION AND JAPAN.** *Tokyo Business Today*, Vol. 58, Mar. 1990, pp. 26–31.
Examines Japanese economic relations with the Soviet Union and Eastern Europe. Provides a brief overview of Japan's trade with and investment in the Soviet bloc countries. Describes the mounting skepticism among Japanese business interests over the market potential of Eastern Europe and the Soviet Union.

B390. Sauerwein, B. and Plugge, M. **NEW SOVIET MILITARY DOCTRINE: THE VOROSHILOV ACADEMY'S INTERPRETATION.** *International Defense Review*, Vol. 23, Jan. 1990, p. 21
The Soviet's modern military doctrine is a result of "new thinking" in terms of foreign policy, war, defense and national security. The priority of human values had preempted the change in 1987: Whereas the previous doctrine focussed on a potential war and the conduct of war, the key tenet now is the prevention of war.

B391. Saul, N.E. **DISTANT FRIENDS: THE UNITED STATES AND RUSSIA, 1763–1867.** Lawrence, KS: University Press of Kansas, c1991, xvi, 448 pp., ill., ports, 24 cm.
Includes bibliographical references (pp. 407–430) and index.

B392. **SAY THE RIGHT THING.** *New Republic*, Vol. 202, June 11, 1990, pp. 7–10.
Presents talking points for the 1990 Bush–Gorbachev Summit.

B393. Schifrin, M. **SHALOM, COMRADE.** *Forbes*, Vol. 147, May 27, 1991, pp. 106–108.
Discusses problems facing Soviet Jews who immigrate to Israel.

B394. Schoenfeld, G. **LOOSE CANNON: THE SCARY STATE OF SOVIET NUKES.** *New Republic*, Vol. 204, Mar. 11, 1991, pp. 16–18.
As nationalism tears apart the Soviet Union, the chance that is could split into fifteen or more states - some of them armed with nuclear weapons - is scary enough. But even if Moscow keeps its hand on the button, there's plenty of reason for concern. Chernobyl, and the jitters of the Red Army officials, suggest that the world's largest stockpile of nuclear arms is no longer in particularly safe hands.

B395. Schofield, C. **INSIDE THE SOVIET MILITARY.** Photographs by L. Yakutin. Preface by D. Yazov. Forward by C. Donnelly. New York, NY: Abbeville Press, 1991.
Includes index.

B396. Seay, D. **AN AMERICAN RESPONSE TO THE BALKAN REVOLUTIONS.** Washington, Heritage Foundation, 1991, 20 pp. (Backgrounder No. 820)

The U.S. policy of opposing the breakup of Yugoslavia is a relic of the Cold War, when an unstable Yugoslavia would have been a tempting target for Moscow, Seay says. Now, he says, Yugoslavia's national unity is of little strategic importance to the West. There is little to be gained by supporting efforts to keep the country together by force.

B397. Seay, D. **HOW AMERICA CAN HELP BALTIC INDEPENDENCE.** Washington, Heritage Foundation, 1990, 17 pp. (Backgrounder No. 762).

The United States should formally recognize the independent government of Lithuania, include the Baltic states in the U.S. foreign aid bill for Eastern Europe, and warn Mikhail Gorbachev that U.S.–Soviet relations will suffer if Moscow uses force to quell the Baltic independence movements.

B398. Seay, D. **PROMOTING THE PEACEFUL DECOLONIZATION OF THE SOVIET UNION.** Washington Heritage Foundation, 1990, 19 pp.

The Soviet Union is undergoing a process of "decolonization" as the long-oppressed subject nationalities demand their freedom. With vital interests at stake, the United States and the West must use their influence to help ensure that this process occurs peacefully, says Seay.

B399. **SECURITY IMPLICATIONS OF SDI: WILL WE BE MORE SECURE IN 2010?** Edited by J. Simon, with an introduction by F.C. Ikle, Washington, DC: National Defense University Press, 1990, xiii, 251 pp., ill, 23 cm.

....evolved from a conference held in 1986 sponsored by the Mobilization Concepts Development Center, Institute for National Strategic Studies, national Defense University; the Strategic Studies Institute of the U.S. Army War College; and the American Enterprise Institute - Acknowl. Includes bibliographical references and index.

B400. Segal, G. 1953–. **THE SOVIET UNION AND THE PACIFIC.** London: Royal Institute of International Affairs, Boston, MA: Unwin Hyman, 1990, 236 pp., ill., 22 cm.

Includes bibliographical references (pp 201–227) and index.

B401. Segal, G. **NORTHEAST ASIA: ALL ABOARD THE DETENTE TRAIN?** *World Today*, Vol. 46, Mar. 1990, pp. 49–53.

The Soviet Union and China warmed up for their normalization of relations in 1989....North Korea has made some noises but there has been no significant progress so far (and) Soviet–Japanese relations, has lagged behind the pace of the improved political climate elsewhere in Northeast Asia.

B402. Shao, W. **CHINA'S RELATIONS WITH THE SUPERPOWERS: STRATEGIC SHIFTS AND IMPLICATIONS.** *survival*, Vol. 32, Mar.–Apr. 1990, pp. 157–172.

This article examines a number of policy issues in China's relations with the U.S. and the U.S.S.R. The key questions are....the American sanctions imposed on China....the Sino-Soviet rapprochement.

B403. Sharp, J.M.O. **CONTINUITY AND CHANGE IN SOVIET ARMS CONTROL POLICY.** *Journal of Soviet Military Studies*, Vol. 3, Mar. 1990, pp. 1–31.

This essay begins with an overview of Soviet Arms control diplomacy from 1945 through 1985, then assesses the degree of continuity and change in the Gorbachev approach.

B404. Sherr, J., 1951– . **SOVIET POWER, THE CONTINUING CHALLENGE.** New York, NY: St. Martin's Press, 1991, xxxiii, 283 pp., 23 cm.
Includes bibliographical references (pp. 272–278) and index.

B405. Shevardnadze, E.A. **A NEW WORLD VISION: SOVIET FOREIGN POLICY IN THE AGE OF PERESTROIKA.** Translated by C. Cosman, C. Fitzpatrick and P. Goldberg. New York, NY: Pantheon Books, 1991.
Translation from the Russian.

B406. Shipley, P. **HOSTILE ACTION: THE KGB AND SECRET SOVIET OPERATIONS IN BRITAIN.** New York, St. Martin's Press, 1990, c1989, ix, 224 pp., 25 cm.
Includes bibliographical references (pp. 212–217) and index.

B407. Shlapentokh, V. **SOVIET INTELLECTUALS AND POLITICAL POWER: THE POST-STALIN ERA.** Princeton, NJ: Princeton University Press, c1990, xiv, 330 pp., 24 cm.
Includes bibliographical references (pp. 287–311) and indexes.

B408. Shul gin, V.V. (Vasilii Vital evich), 1878–. **DAYS OF RUSSIAN REVOLUTION: MEMOIRS FROM THE RIGHT, 1905–1917.** Edited, translated, and with an introduction by B.F. Adams. Gulf Breeze, FL: Academic International Press, 1990, xx, 251, pp, ill., maps, 23 cm. The Russian series, Vol. 38.
Includes bibliographical references (pp. 2112–244) and index.

B409. Shuman, M., Harvey, H. and Arbess, D.J. **ALTERNATIVE SECURITY: BEYOND THE CONTROLLED ARMS RACE.** New York, NY: Hill and Wang, 1990, p. cm.

B410. Simon, R.J. **THE U.S. SHOULD WELCOME SOVIET JEWS.** *World* and I, Vol. 5, Jan 1990, pp. 218–223.
Refusal to allow all Soviet Jews who wish to leave the U.S.S.R. to enter the United States would be a moral failure and a practical mistake.

B411. Simonyan, R.G. and Grishin, S.V. **TACTICAL RECONNAISSANCE: A SOVIET VIEW,** (Washington, G.P.O., 1990) 199 pp. (Soviet Military Thought No. 23).
Published under the auspices of the United States Air Force. Translation of Razvedka v boiu, 1980.

B412. **SINO-SOVIET RELATIONS AFTER THE SUMMIT:** A workshop sponsored by the Senate Foreign Relations Committee and the Congressional Research Service - May 15, 1989.
Prepared for the Subcommittee on East Asian and Pacific Affairs of the Committee on Foreign Relations, United States Senate, by the Congressional Research Service, Library of Congress, Washington, DC: U.S. G.P.O.

At head of title: Committee print. 101st Congress, 2nd session, House of Representatives.

B413. Smoke, R. **THINK ABOUT NUCLEAR ARMS CONTROL: UNDERSTANDING THE ARMS RACE.** New York, NY: Walker, 1991.
Includes bibliographical references and index.
Discusses the nuclear arms race, its historical background, technological ramifications, and impact on contemporary life.

B414. Smolansky, O.M. **THE U.S.S.R. AND IRAQ: THE SOVIET QUEST FOR INFLUENCE.** With B.M. Smolansky. Durham, NC: Duke University Press, 1991.
Includes bibliographical references and index.

B415. Sobell, V. 1948–. **THE CMEA IN CRISIS: TOWARD A NEW EUROPEAN ORDER?** Foreword by J. Prybyla. New York, NY: Praeger, 1990, xiv, 104 pp., 24 cm.
Published with the Center for Strategic and International Studies, Washington, DC. Includes bibliographical references (pp. 83–100) and index.

B416. Sodaro, M.J. **MOSCOW, GERMANY, AND THE WEST FROM KHRUSHCHEV TO GORBACHEV.** Ithaca, NY: Cornell University Press, 1990, xiv, 423 pp., 25 cm.
Includes bibliographical references and index.

B417. **SOLDIERS AND THE SOVIET STATE: CIVIL-MILITARY RELATIONS FROM BREZHNEV TO GORBACHEV.** Edited by T.J. Colton and T. Gustafson. Princeton, NJ: Princeton University Press, c1990, xiii, 370 pp., 25 cm.
A research study of the Center for Strategic and International Studies. Includes bibliographical references and index.

B418. **THE SOURCES OF SOVIET NAVAL CONDUCT.** Edited by P.S. Gillette, W.C. Frank, Jr., foreword by R.J. Kurth. Lexington, MA: Lexington Books, c1990, xiv, 295 pp., 24 cm.
Includes bibliographical references.

B419. **SOVIET FOREIGN ECONOMIC POLICY AND INTERNATIONAL SECURITY.** Edited by E. Stubbs. Armonk, NY: M.E. Sharpe, c1991.
Includes revisions of papers presented at a conference sponsored by the Center for Foreign Policy Development at Brown University held in Dec. 1988.
Includes bibliographical references and index.

B420. **SOVIET STRATEGY AND THE NEW MILITARY THINKING.** Edited by D. Leebaert and T. Dickinson. Cambridge (England), New York, NY: Cambridge University press, 1991.
Includes index.

B421. **SOVIET FOREIGN POLICY: CLASSIC AND CONTEMPORARY ISSUES.** Edited by F.J. Fleron, Jr., E.P. Hoffman and R.F. Laird. New York, NY: Aldine de Gruyter, c1991.

Includes bibliographical references and index.

B422. **SOVIET STRATEGIC AND SPACE PROGRAMS.** Washington, U.S. Dept. of Defense, 1990, 24 pp.

B423. **SOVIET UNION.**

Treaty between the United States of America and the Union of Soviet Socialist Republics on the Limitation of Underground Nuclear Tests and the Treaty between the United States and the Union of Soviet Socialist Republics on Underground Nuclear Explosions for Peaceful Purposes: texts of treaties and protocols. Washington, DC: U.S. Arms Control and Disarmament Agency, 1990, 99 pp., 23 cm.

B424. **SOVIET DOCUMENTS ON THE USE OF WAR EXPERIENCE.** Translated by H.S. Orenstein. With an introduction by D.M. Glantz. London (England), Portland, OR: Frank Cass, c1991, 2 vols.

Translated from the Russian.

Includes bibliographical references.

B425. **SOVIET AIR POWER: PROSPECTS FOR THE FUTURE: PERESTROIKA AND THE SOVIET AIR FORCES.** Edited by E.S. Williams. London: Tri-Service Press, 1990, xviii, 247 pp., ill., 23 cm.

Includes bibliographical references and index.

B426. **SOVIET DIPLOMACY AND NEGOTIATING BEHAVIOR - 1988–90: GORBACHEV-REAGAN-BUSH MEETINGS AT THE SUMMIT.** Vol. III, Washington, G.P.O., 1991, 478 pp.

At head of title: Special studies series on foreign affairs issues. Study prepared by the Senior Specialists Section, Office of Research Coordination, Congressional Research Service, Library of Congress.

B427. **SOVIET REQUIREMENTS FOR WESTERN TECHNOLOGY: A FORECASTING METHODOLOGY.** (S.l.) Technology Transfer Assessment Center, Central Intelligence Agency (1991?), 2 volumes.

Presents a proof-of-concept for a methodology which demonstrates how the Soviets use Western technology in future military systems, and forecasts Soviet requirements for Western technology....The paper provides a brief overview of the Soviet process for identifying Western technologies required for development and production of future weapon systems. The methodology, which simulates this process, is presented with a detailed case study of its application in the area of microelectronics.

B428. **THE SOVIET MILITARY.** Prepared by the American Forces Information Service. (Washington?) Current News Analysis and Research Service, 1990, 65 pop. (U.S. Dept. of Defense. Current News, special edition, no. 1851 (May 1990)).

A collection of newspaper articles and editorials.

B429. **SOVIET NATIONAL SECURITY POLICY UNDER PERESTROIKA.** Edited by G.E. Hudson, Boston, MA: Unwin Hyman, 1990, xv, 343 pp., 24 cm.

Book began as a Mershon Center faculty seminar at Ohio State University between Dec. 1986 and Oct. 1987. Includes bibliographical and index. Mershon Center series on international security and foreign policy, v. 4.

B430. **THE SOVIET SYSTEM IN CRISIS: A READER OF WESTERN AND SOVIET VIEWS.** Edited by A. Dallin and G.W. Lapidus. Boulder, CO: Westview Press, 1991.

Includes bibliographical references.

B431. **THE SOVIET TAKEOVER OF THE POLISH EASTERN PROVINCES, 1939–1941.** Edited by K. Sword. New York, NY: St. Martin's Press, 1991.

Result of a conference held at the School of Slavonic and East European Studies, University of London, in April 1989. Pref. Includes index.

B432. **SOVIET UNION: MILITARY AFFAIRS.** Washington, Joint Publications Research Service, 1990, 68 pp. (JPRS-UMAS-90-010, Apr. 25, 1990).

Partial contents - Military-political issues. Military science. Warsaw Pact. Armed forces. Ground forces.

B433. **SOVIET "REASONABLE SUFFICIENCY" AND NORWEGIAN SECURITY.** Edited by R. Tamnes, Oslo: Institutt for Forsvarsstudier, 1990, 94 pp., ill. (some col.), 21 cm. Forsvarsstudier, 0333-2470, 5/1990.

Includes bibliographical references.

B434. **SOVIETS EXPAND COASTAL AND ANTI-LANDING DEFENSE.** *International Defense Review*, Vol. 23, July 1990, pp. 731–734.

As a result of the military erosion of the Warsaw Pact, the Soviet forward defense zone in Eastern Europe is shrinking. Nationalist separatism makes it necessary to provide maritime flank protection for the U.S.S.R. proper.

B435. **SOVIET–AMERICAN CONFLICT RESOLUTION IN THE THIRD WORLD: OPPORTUNITIES AND OBSTACLES.** M.N. Katz, ed. Washington, DC: United States Institute of Peace, 1991.

Includes bibliographical references.

B436. **SOVIET–AMERICAN RELATIONS AFTER THE COLD WAR.** Edited by R. Jervis and S. Bialer. Durham, NC: Duke University Press, c1991, vi, 356 pp., 23 cm.

Includes bibliographical references (pp. 315–350) and index.

B437. **SOVIET–BRITISH RELATIONS SINCE THE 1970S.** Edited by A. Pravda and P.J.S. Duncan. Cambridge (England), New York, NY: Cambridge University Press, 1990, xii, 263 pp., 24 cm.

Published in association with the Royal Institute of International Affairs. Includes bibliographical references and index.

B438. **THE SOVIET–EAST EUROPEAN RELATIONSHIP IN THE GORBACHEV ERA: THE PROSPECTS FOR ADAPTATION.** Edited by A. Braun. Boulder, CO: Westview Press, 1990, xi, 249, pp., 23 cm.

Includes bibliographical references (pp. 231–242).

B439. Sowjetunion, 1988–1989. English. **THE SOVIET UNION, 1988–1989. PERESTROIKA IN CRISIS?** Edited by the Federal Institute for Soviet and International Studies, Boulder, CO: Westview Press, 1990, xv, 410 pp., 23 cm.

Translation of: Sowjetunion, 1988–1989. Includes bibliographical references and index.

B440. Spangler, S.E. **FORCE AND ACCOMMODATION IN WORLD POLITICS.** Maxwell Air Force Base, AL: Air University Press; Washington, DC: For sale by the Supt. of Docs., U.S. G.P.O., 1991.

June 1991.

Includes bibliographical references and index.

B441. Staar, R.F., 1923– . **FOREIGN POLICIES OF THE SOVIET UNION.** Stanford, CA: Hoover Institution Press, Stanford, University, c1991, xxxi, 351 pp., ill., 23 cm.

Includes bibliographical references (pp. 319–338) and index.

B442. Stanfield, R.L. **O ISRAEL!** *National Journal*, Vol. 22, June 23, 1990, pp. 1520–1524.

Though they may be upset with Israel's government, American Jews are also energized by the new Soviet Exodus and signs of Eastern European anti-Semitism.

B443. Steininger, R. 1942–. **THE GERMAN QUESTION: THE STALIN NOTE OF 1952 AND THE PROBLEM OF REUNIFICATION.** Translated by J.T. Hedges. Edited by M. Cioc, New York, NY: Columbia University Press, c1990, xvii, 186 pp., 24 cm.

Translation of: Eine vertane Chance. Includes bibliographical references (pp. 159–182) and index.

B444. Steward, D. **SATELLITE SLEUTHS.** *Air and Space*, Vol. 5, June–July 1990, pp. 26–30,32–34.

Describes the Kettering Group, an informal network of people who monitor the Soviet space program. Despite the low rent approach to space science, the Kettering Group is the Western world's most authoritative source of public information about the Soviet space program.

B445. Stewart, G. 1949–. **THE SOVIET UNION.** New York, NY: Crestwood House, Toronto: Collier Macmillan Canada, c1990, 48 pp., ill. (chiefly col.), 23 cm. Places in the news.

Includes index. Examines the Soviet Union's changing political scene, status as a superpower, and relationship with the United States.

B446. Stoessinger, J.G. **NATIONS IN DARKNESS - CHINA, RUSSIA, AND AMERICA.** New York, NY: McGraw-Hill, c1990, p. cm.

Includes bibliographical references.

B447. Stoll, R.J. **U.S. NATIONAL SECURITY POLICY AND THE SOVIET UNION: PERSISTENT REGULARITIES AND EXTREME CONTINGENCIES.** Columbia, S.C., University of South Carolina, 1990, 263 pp. (Studies in International Relations).

Contents - The use of force in the post-World War II era. The utility of force in the nuclear era. Congress, the general public, and national security policy. Organization, leadership, and military policy. Strategic nuclear weapons policies. The prospects for fighting a limited strategic war. Arms control and strategic stability. The United States, NATO, and burden sharing. The conventional balance in Europe: an optimistic assessment? Alternative scenarios for a Warsaw pact blitzkrieg.

B448. Strassner, R. **DIVIDED CAMBODIA IN THE ERA OF SINO-SOVIET DETENTE - THE PARIS CONFERENCE AND ITS BACKGROUND.** Asien, No. 34, Jan. 1990, pp. 55–68.

Describe(s) the development of the Cambodian question in the era of Sino-Soviet detente and in particular the events of the Paris–Cambodia Conference in August 1989.

B449. **THE STRATEGIC ENVIRONMENT.** Edited by S.T. Ross and D.A. Rosenberg. New York, NY: Garland Pub., 1990, 1 v. (various paper), ill., 29 cm.

Includes bibliographical references.

B450. **STRATEGIC POWER: U.S.A./U.S.S.R.** Edited by C.G. Jacobsen....et al. New York, NY: St. Martin's Press, 1990, xxiii, 519 pp., 25 cm.

Includes bibliographical references and index.

B451. **STRATEGIC ARMS REDUCTIONS: BACKGROUND AND NEGOTIATING HISTORY.** Washington, Arms Control Association, 1990, 17 pp. (Background Paper, August 1990).

B452. Suggs, R.C. (Robert Carl), 1932–. **GLASNOST, PERESTROIKA, AND THE SOVIET THREAT.** Washington, DC (220 National Press Bldg., Washington 20045): USIC Educational Foundation, c1990, 25 pp., 28 cm.

Includes bibliographical references (pp. 21–25).

B453. **THE SUMMIT.** *Time*, Vol. 135, June 4, 1990, pp. 25–34,38–41,44–45.

Series of articles examines issue for consideration at the May 31–June 3, 1990 Bush–Gorbachev Summit. Includes an interview with Gorbachev.

B454. **SUPERPOWER POLITICS: CHANGE IN THE UNITED STATES AND THE SOVIET UNION.** Edited by M. Pugh and P. Williams, Manchester, UK, New York, NY: Manchester University Press, New York, NY,: Distributed exclusively in the U.S.A. and Canada by St. Martin's Press, c1990, xi, 208 pp., 21 cm.

Some of the chapters are revised versions of papers delivered at a residential course organized by the Defense Studies Unit of the Politics Department, University of Southampton - Pref. Includes bibliographical references (pp. 197–200) and index.

B455. **SUPERPOWER MARITIME STRATEGY IN THE PACIFIC.** Edited by F.C. Langdon and D.A. Ross, London, New York, NY: Routledge, 1990, p. cm.

Includes bibliographical references.

B456. **SUPERPOWERS AND CLIENT STATES IN THE MIDDLE EAST: THE IMBALANCE OF INFLUENCE.** Edited by M. Efrat and J. Bercovitch. London (England), New York, NY: Routledge, 1991.
Includes bibliographical references and index.

B457. Szayna, T.S., 1960– . **THE ETHNIC FACTOR IN THE SOVIET ARMED FORCES: THE MUSLIM DIMENSION.** Santa Monica, CA: Rand Corp., 1991.
Prepared for the United States Army, March 1991. R-4002-A.

B458. Szulc, T. **CAN CASTRO LAST?** *New York Review of Books*, Vol. 37, May 31, 1990, pp. 12–15.
The imminent threat, as Castro perceives it, is that the Soviet Union, with its decomposing economy and national administration, will be incapable of providing Cuba with an uninterrupted rhythm of deliveries of fuel and grain, and this would be a mortal blow to Cuba.

B459. Tarr, D.W. **NUCLEAR DETERRENCE AND INTERNATIONAL SECURITY: ALTERNATIVE NUCLEAR REGIMES.** New York, NY: Longman, 1991, x, 229 pp., 23 cm.
Includes bibliographical references (pp. 215–222) and index.

B460. Tausky, C. **PERESTROIKA IN THE U.S.S.R. AND CHINA: MOTIVATIONAL LESSONS.** *Work and Occupations*, Vol. 18, Feb. 1991, pp. 94–108.
Review of the Soviet and Chinese pre-reform economic designs indicates that the misuse of resources was prompted by unconditional state support of enterprises coupled with guaranteed employment and flawed incentive criteria. Perestroika plans in both countries were directly aimed at undoing these relationships. Leaders' expectations of soaring inflation and mounting unemployment, however, have put the restructuring plans on hold. It seems that Soviet and Chinese citizens want the gains of reform without the pains, but neither nation's economy is likely to fulfill that wish.

B461. Taylor, A.R. **THE SUPERPOWERS AND THE MIDDLE EAST.** Syracuse, NY: Syracuse University Press, 1991.
Includes bibliographical references and index.

B462. Tedstrom, J. **WESTERN AID TO THE U.S.S.R.: A COMMENTARY.** *Report on the U.S.S.R.*, Vol. 2, Aug. 10, 1990, pp. 1–2.
Suggests that the West could aid the Soviet Union in several ways. First, the West could continue to build on improved political relations, which have begun to reduce the burden of defense. Second, Western countries could continue to relax trade restrictions so that more productive Western technology works its way into Soviet industry....Third, there is a great shortage of many types of medicines and medical equipment that Western countries could increase the level of technical assistance in any number of areas.

B463. **THREE SOVIET SCENARIOS: YOU PICK.** *International Economy*, Vol. 5, Jan.–Feb. 1991, pp. 52–55.
We asked several Soviet experts to rate the scenario considered most likely over the next one to three years. Experts were allowed to briefly modify, or to outline another scenario. In addition, participants were asked to

characterize Western policies appropriate to the scenario considered most likely. The participants include: Helmut Sonnenfeldt, Senator Bill Bradley, Paul H. Nitze, Peter Reddaway, Carl A. Linden, Heinrich Vogel, Horst Teltschik, Harald Malmgren.

B464. Timmermann, H. **THE DECLINE OF COMMUNISM AND ITS CONSEQUENCES FOR EAST-WEST RELATIONS: AN OVERVIEW.** *Issues and Studies*, Vol. 27, Jan. 1991, pp. 70–83.

Examines the main reasons for the decline and loss of authority of communism in the Soviet Union and Eastern Europe, including: the uncompetitiveness of the command economies; the crisis of political legitimacy; and the weakening of the Soviet communist party. Discusses the repercussions of these changes on the international scene and outlines the tasks now faced by western policy-makers.

B465. Timofeyev, P. **AFGHANISTAN-U.S.S.R.-WEST EUROPE DRUG TRAFFICKING CONDUIT EXAMINED.** JPRS Report (Narcotics), Apr. 8, 1991, pp. 44–46.

Translation of an article, datelined Kabul, originally appearing in the Moscow newspaper Sovetskaya Rossiya, Mar. 20, 1991, 5 pp.

B466. Tolz, V. **NEW INFORMATION ABOUT THE DEPORTATION OF ETHNIC GROUPS UNDER STALIN.** *Report on the U.S.S.R.*, Vol. 3, Apr. 26, 1991, pp. 16–20.

During World War II, the Soviet Germans, ethnic groups from the Northern Caucasus, the Crimea, and Georgia, and also the Kalmyks were deported from their homelands to Kazakhstan and Central Asia, where they were subjected to harsh treatment in so-called special settlements. Despite their public rehabilitation after Stalin's death, these peoples did not have their rights fully restored. Recently, the Soviet press has started to discuss the sensitive issue of Stalin's deportations and to publish archive material that sheds new light on this crime of the regime.

B467. Torrey, B.B. and Kingkade, W.W. **POPULATION DYNAMICS OF THE UNITED STATES AND THE SOVIET UNION.** *Science*, Vol. 247, Mar. 30, 1990, pp. 1548–1552.

Population growth in the United States and the Soviet Union is slowing. Since the 1970s, labor force growth in both countries is slowing even more than population growth, and both countries are aging. Economic effects of slowing growth can be compensated for by increased participation in the labor force and increased productivity and by adjustments in the military forces. Economic flexibility and policy choices will determine how successfully the trends to slower population growth will be accommodated.

B468. **THE TRANSFORMATION OF SOCIALISM: PERESTROIKA AND REFORM IN THE SOVIET UNION AND CHINA.** Edited by M. Gurtov, Boulder, CO: Westview Press, 1990, x, 258 pp., ill., 23 cm.

Resulted from a unique conference that was held at Portland State University in Portland, OR, on February 9–12, 1989 - P. vii. Includes bibliographical references and index.

B469. Travis, F.F. **GEORGE KENNAN AND THE AMERICAN-RUSSIAN RELATIONSHIP, 1865–1924.** Athens: Ohio University Press, 1990, xix, 433 pp., ill., 24 cm.

Includes bibliographical references (pp. 385–423).

B470. Trofimenko, H. **THE END OF THE COLD WAR, NOT HISTORY.** *Washington Quarterly*, Vol. 13, Spring 1990, pp. 21–35.

The Malta meeting gave strong impetus to the diplomatic machines of both countries to go full-steam ahead in resolving the items on the now-expanded Soviet–American agenda.

B471. Trout, B.T. **NAVAL ARMS CONTROL IN CONTEMPORARY SOVIET POLICY: THE CHALLENGE OF CONTROLLING NAVIES.** *Defense Analysis*, Vol. 7, Mar. 1991, pp. 63–79.

At Soviet insistence, the issues of naval arms control have assumed greater prominence in contemporary US-Soviet security negotiations....These efforts indicate a clear Soviet intent to alter the architecture of the maritime balance with the United States through negotiated naval arms limitations.

B472. Tucker, J.B. **BACK TO THE FUTURE: THE OPEN SKIES TALKS.** *Arms Control Today*, Vol. 20, Oct. 1990, pp. 20–24.

Eisenhower's 1955 "Open Skies" initiative, the proposal for reciprocal reconnaissance flights over the United States, the Soviet Union, and their European allies remains mired in disputes....If an Open Skies agreement is to be reached in one more round, both the Western countries and the Soviet Union will need to compromise.

B473. Tumarkin, N. **THE GREAT PATRIOTIC WAR AS MYTH AND MEMORY.** *Atlantic Monthly*, Vol. 267, June 1991, pp. 26,28,37,40,42,44.

In Soviet eyes the Second World War is being transformed from heroic farce to grotesque tragedy.

B474. **U.S. CENTRAL INTELLIGENCE AGENCY.** Directorate of Intelligence. Measuring Soviet GNP: problems and solutions; a conference report. Washington, U.S. Central Intelligence Agency, 1990, 195 pp. SOV 90-10038, September 1990.

Partial contents - Alternative methods of valuing Soviet gross national product, by J.S. Pitzer. Estimating the impact of foreign trade on Soviet GNP, by L. Kurtzweg. On improving the measurement of health and education services, by A. Lane. Inflation in Soviet investment and capital stock data, by R.L. Kellogg. Measuring total factor productivity in the Soviet case, by J.W. Kendrick. Official Soviet gross national product accounting, by B. Kostinsky and M. Belkindas.

B475. **U.S. CONGRESS COMMISSION ON SECURITY AND COOPERATION IN EUROPE.** Implementation of the Helsinki Accords. Hearing, 101st Congress, 1st session, Oct. 19, 1989, Washington, G.P.O., 1990, 73 pp. CSCE 101-1-9.

What official U.S. policy is toward the independence movements sweeping through the Baltic States.

B476. **U.S. CONGRESS. COMMISSION ON SECURITY AND COOPERATION IN EUROPE.** Implementation of the Helsinki Accords. Hearing, 101st Congress, 2nd session, Mar. 7, 1990, Washington, G.P.O., 1990, 165. p.

Today's hearings will look at the dramatic consequences of the Soviet Government's decision to relax its emigration policies as well as the impact of glasnost on Jewish life within the Soviet Union.

B477. **U.S. CONGRESS. COMMISSION ON SECURITY AND COOPERATION IN EUROPE.** Implementation of the Helsinki Accords. Hearing, 101st Congress, 1st session, Nov. 28, 1989, Washington, G.P.O., 1990, 26 pp. CSCE 101-1-11.

B478. **U.S. CONGRESS. COMMISSION ON SECURITY AND COOPERATION IN EUROPE.** Implementation of the Helsinki Accords. Hearing, 101st Congress, 2nd session, May 3, 1990, Washington, G.P.O., 1990, 73 pp. CSCE 101-2-17.

The current situation in Afghanistan....why the Soviet Union is continuing to spend significant amounts of money and resources to assist the Kabul Government.

B479. **U.S. CONGRESS. COMMISSION ON SECURITY AND COOPERATION IN EUROPE. IMPLEMENTATION OF THE HELSINKI ACCORDS.** Hearing, 102nd Congress, 1st Session. Feb. 6, 1991. Washington, G.P.O., 1991, 77 pp.

The U.S.S.R. in crisis: State of the Union. CSCE 102-1-3.

B480. **U.S. CONGRESS. COMMISSION ON SECURITY AND COOPERATION IN EUROPE. IMPLEMENTATION OF THE HELSINKI ACCORDS.** Hearing, 102nd Congress, 1st Session. Jan. 2, 1991. Washington, G.P.O., 1991, 124 pp.

CSCE 102-1-2. Soviet crackdown in the Baltic States. The present situation in Lithuania and Latvia, as well as Estonia tangentially.

B481. **U.S. CONGRESS. COMMISSION ON SECURITY AND COOPERATION IN EUROPE.**

Implementation of the Helsinki accords: hearing before the Commission on Security and Cooperation in Europe, 101st Congress, 1st session, the new and improved Supreme Soviet and the institutionalization of human rights reform, November 28, 1989, Washington, DC: U.S. G.P.O.

B482. **U.S. CONGRESS. COMMISSION ON SECURITY AND COOPERATION IN EUROPE.**

Implementation of the Helsinki accords: hearing before the Commission on Security and Cooperation in Europe, 101st Congress, 1st session, the Baltic question, October 19, 1989, Washington, DC: U.s. G.P.O.

B483. **U.S. CONGRESS. COMMISSION ON SECURITY AND COOPERATION IN EUROPE.**

Implementation of the Helsinki accords: hearing before the Commission on Security and Cooperation in Europe, 101st Congress, 2nd session, status report on Soviet Jewry, March 7, 1990, Washington, DC: U.S. G.P.O.

B484. **U.S. CONGRESS. HOUSE. COMMITTEE ON ARMED SERVICES.**

Soviet Union's unilateral force reduction and withdrawal: hearing before the Committee on Armed Services, House of Representatives, 101st Congress, 1st session, hearing held September 15, 1989, Washington, DC: U.S. G.P.O.

B485. **U.S. CONGRESS. HOUSE. COMMITTEE ON ARMED SERVICES.** The new Soviet legislature: Committee on Defense and State Security; report. Washington, G.P.O., 1990, 26. p. At head of title 101st Congress, 2nd session print, no. 8.

The Armed Services Committee of the House of Representatives is developing an active and fruitful relationship with its approximate counterpart, the Defense and State Security Committee on the Supreme Soviet, the standing national legislature of the Soviet Union.

B486. **U.S. CONGRESS. HOUSE. COMMITTEE ON ARMED SERVICES.** Soviet Union's unilateral force reduction and withdrawal. Hearing, 101st Congress, 1st session, Sept. 15, 1989, Washington, G.P.O., 1990, 60 p. At head of title: H.A.S.C. no. 101-37.

Examination of the unilateral force reductions announced by Mr. Gorbachev December 7, 1988.

B487. **U.S. CONGRESS. HOUSE. COMMITTEE ON ARMED SERVICES.** Defense Policy Panel. Prospects of U.S./Soviet relations with emphasis on conventional arms control. Hearing, 101st Congress, 1st session, May 9, 1989, Washington, G.P.O., 1990, 34 pp. At head of title: H.A.S.C. no. 101-29.

Mr. Gorbachev is talking about dramatic revisions in the Soviet military. He has announced a significant unilateral cut and has tabled a conventional arms control proposal that could, if agreed to, lead to deep reductions in Soviet forces.

B488. **U.S. CONGRESS. HOUSE. COMMITTEE ON ARMED SERVICES.** Defense Policy Panel. The fading threat: Soviet conventional military power in decline; report. Washington, G.P.O., 1990, 310 pp. (Citation 110 S. Ct. 2668). At head of title: 101st Congress, 2nd session, print no. 11.

This report will bring the defense Policy panel's work on the changing Soviet threat up to date. It will address the two most critical threat issues that underlie the debate over the U.S. defense budget: how significant are the changes - many completed, but some underway and a few on the horizon - in the Soviet threat? How reversible are these changes?

B489. **U.S. CONGRESS. HOUSE. COMMITTEE ON FOREIGN AFFAIRS.**

First post-cold war superpower summit, May 1990: hearing before the Committee on Foreign Affairs, House of Representatives, 101st Congress, 2nd session, June 13, 1990, Washington, DC: U.S. G.P.O.

B490. **U.S. CONGRESS. HOUSE. COMMITTEE ON FOREIGN AFFAIRS.** Subcommittee on Europe and the Middle East.

United States policy toward Afghanistan: hearing before the Subcommittees on Europe and the Middle East and Asian and Pacific Affairs of the Committee on Foreign Affairs, House of Representatives, 101st Congress, 2nd session, March 7, 1990, Washington, DC: U.S. G.P.O.

B491. **U.S. CONGRESS. HOUSE. COMMITTEE ON FOREIGN AFFAIRS.**

International Plutonium Control Act - H.R. 2403: hearing before the Committee on Foreign Affairs and its Subcommittee on Arms Control, International Security, and Science, House of Representatives, 101st Congress, 1st session, June 20, 1989, Washington, DC: U.S. G.P.O.

B492. **U.S. CONGRESS. HOUSE. COMMITTEE ON FOREIGN AFFAIRS.** Subcommittee on Europe and the Middle East.

Developments in Europe, July 1989: hearing before the Subcommittee on Europe and the Middle East of the Committee on Foreign Affairs, House of Representatives, 101st Congress, 1st session, July 26, 1989, Washington, DC: U.S. G.P.O.

B493. **U.S. CONGRESS. HOUSE. COMMITTEE ON FOREIGN AFFAIRS.** Subcommittee on Europe and the Middle East. Developments in Europe, October 1990. Hearing, 101st Congress, 2nd Session. Oct. 9, 1990. Washington, G.P.O., 1991, 109 pp.

The implications of the unification of Germany; the future role of NATO, European views on the Persian Gulf crisis; European burdensharing support in the Gulf crisis; the major accomplishments of the Helsinki summit; issues in U.S. Soviet relations; developments in Eastern Europe; and the status of arms control negotiations.

B494. **U.S. CONGRESS. HOUSE. COMMITTEE ON FOREIGN AFFAIRS. CHALLENGES FOR NATO AND DEVELOPMENTS IN EAST-WEST RELATIONS.** Hearing, 101st Congress, 1st Session. June 22, 1989. Washington, G.P.O., 1991, 27 pp.

Burdensharing, short-range nuclear force modernization, Europe 1992, and Soviet politics in Europe. Witness: Hon. James A. Baker, III, Secretary of State.

B495. **U.S. CONGRESS. HOUSE. COMMITTEE ON FOREIGN AFFAIRS.** Subcommittee on Europe and the Middle East. Recent developments in the Baltics. Hearing before the Subcommittees on Europe and the Middle East and on Human rights and International Organizations of the Committee on Foreign Affairs, House of Representatives, 102nd Congress, 1st Session. Jan. 23, 1991. Washington, G.P.O., 1991, 47 pp.

The current situation in Lithuania, Latvia and Estonia; United States policies toward the Baltics; Implications of developments in the Baltics for U.S.-Soviet relations; and the implications of developments in the Baltics for the future of Soviet reforms.

B496. **U.S. CONGRESS. HOUSE. COMMITTEE ON FOREIGN AFFAIRS.** Subcommittee on Arms Control, International Security and Science. Roundtable discussion on United States-Soviet relations and the future of arms control. Hearing before the Subcommittees on Arms Control, International Security and Science, and on Europe and the Middle East of the Committee on Foreign Affairs, House of Representatives, 101st Congress, 1st Session. Nov. 15, 1989. Washington, G.P.O., 1991, 31 pp.

B497. **U.S. CONGRESS. HOUSE. COMMITTEE ON FOREIGN AFFAIRS.**543 Subcommittee on Europe and the Middle East. Developments in Europe, March 1989. Hearing, 101st Congress, 2nd session, Mar. 22, 1990, Washington, G.P.O., 1990, 132 pp.

B498. **U.S. CONGRESS. HOUSE. COMMITTEE ON FOREIGN AFFAIRS.** Subcommittee on Arms Control, International Security and Science. United

States–Soviet relations: 1990, Hearing, 101st Congress, 2nd session, Feb. 21–June 12, 1990, Washington, G.P.O., 1990, 226 pp.

The status of Soviet economic reform and the implications of these reforms for U.S.–Soviet economic relations....How far and how fast the Soviet Union will go in the direction of a market-oriented economy.

B499. **U.S. CONGRESS. HOUSE. COMMITTEE ON FOREIGN AFFAIRS.** Subcommittee on Europe and the Middle East. Processing of Soviet refugees. Joint hearing before the Subcommittee on Europe and the Middle East of the Committee on Foreign Affairs and the Subcommittee on Immigration, Refugees, and International Law of the Committee on the Judiciary, House of Representatives, 101st Congress, 1st session, Sept. 14, 1989, Washington, G.P.O., 221 pp. Serial No. 54.

There has been a large increase this year in the number of Soviet applicants who seek refugee status and admission to the United States. A further large increase in applicants is expected in 1990.

B500. **U.S. CONGRESS. HOUSE. COMMITTEE ON FOREIGN AFFAIRS.** Subcommittee on Human Rights and International Organizations. Pace of democratic reforms and status of human rights in Eastern Europe and the Soviet Union. Hearing, 101st Congress, Oct. 4, 1989–June 13, 1990, Washington, G.P.O., 1990, 297 pp.

The focus of the hearing will be on the Soviet satellite states of Poland, Hungary, East Germany, Czechoslovakia, Bulgaria and Romania.

B501. **U.S. CONGRESS. HOUSE. COMMITTEE ON FOREIGN AFFAIRS.** Subcommittee on Arms Control, International Security and Science. Status of U.S. arms control policy. Hearings before the Committee on Foreign Affairs and the Subcommittees on Arms Control, International Security and Science and on Europe and the Middle East, House of Representatives. 101st Congress, 2nd session, Mar. 1–21, 1990, Washington, G.P.O., 1990, 289 pp.

We have got to lock up three arms control agreements, sometime in the near future. We have a lot of changes that have taken place, but we only have one agreement that is actually locked up which is the INF. It may be possible to have seven or eight major agreements this year.

B502. **U.S. CONGRESS. HOUSE. COMMITTEE ON FOREIGN AFFAIRS.** First Post-Cold War Superpower Summit, May 1990, Hearing, 101st Congress, 2nd session, June 13, 1990, Washington, G.P.O., 1990, 96, pp.

B503. **U.S. CONGRESS. HOUSE. COMMITTEE ON WAYS AND MEANS.** Hearing, 101st Congress, 2nd session, Jan. 24 –Apr. 18, 1990, Washington, G.P.O., 1990, 765 pp. Serial No 101-105.

U.S. trade relationships with the Soviet Union and Eastern Europe, the implications of Europe 1992 on American direct investment, and foreign investment in the United States.

B504. **U.S. CONGRESS. SENATE. COMMITTEE ON ARMED SERVICES.** Threat assessment, military strategy, and operational requirements: hearings before the Committee on Armed Services, United States Senate, 101st Congress, 2nd session, December 12, 1989, January 23–26, 30, February 2, 6–8, 21, 22, March 7, 1990, Washington, DC: U.S. G.P.O.

B505. **U.S. CONGRESS. SENATE. COMMITTEE ON FOREIGN RELATIONS.** Threshold Test Ban and Peaceful Nuclear Explosion treaties with the U.S.S.R.: hearings before the Committee on Foreign Relations, United States Senate, 101st Congress, 2nd session, July 17, 31, and September 13, 1990. Washington, DC: U.S. G.P.O.

B506. **U.S. CONGRESS. SENATE. COMMITTEE ON FOREIGN RELATIONS.** Subcommittee on East Asian and Pacific Affairs. Sino-Soviet relations after the Summit; a workshop sponsored by the Senate Foreign Relations Committee and the Congressional Research Service - May 15, 1989, Washington, G.P.O., 1990, 150 pp. (Print, Senate, 101st Congress, 2nd session, committee print, S. Prt. 101-83).

Contents - The Sino-Soviet relationship in the context of changing global relations. Sino-Soviet relations and the Asia regional perspective. The military implications of Sino-Soviet relations. The economic implications of Sino-Soviet relations.

B507. **U.S. CONGRESS. SENATE. COMMITTEE ON FOREIGN RELATIONS. ESTIMATING THE SIZE AND GROWTH OF THE SOVIET ECONOMY.** Hearing, 101st Congress, 2nd Session. July 16, 1990. Washington, G.P.O., 1991, 258 pp. (Hearing, Senate, 101st Congress, 2nd Session, S. Hrg. 101-1112)

Includes reprint of a study by W.T. Lee, Trends in Soviet military outlays and economic priorities, 1970–1988.

B508. **U.S. CONGRESS. SENATE. COMMITTEE ON FOREIGN RELATIONS.** Subcommittee on European Affairs. Soviet disunion: creating a nationalities policy. Hearing, 101st Congress, 2nd session, July 24, 1990, Washington, G.P.O., 1990, 65 pp. (Hearing, Senate, 101st Congress, 2nd session, S. Hrg. 101-887).

The possibility of the breakup of the Soviet Union as we know it. Includes statements by Z. Brzezinski, P.A. Goble and J.H. Billington.

B509. **U.S. CONGRESS. SENATE. COMMITTEE ON FOREIGN RELATIONS. TREATY ON THE FINAL SETTLEMENT WITH RESPECT TO GERMANY.** Hearing, 101st Congress, 2nd Session. Sept. 28, 1990. Washington, G.P.O., 1991, 50 pp. (Hearing, Senate, 101st Congress, 2nd Session, S. Hrg. 101-1124)

B510. **U.S. CONGRESS. SENATE. COMMITTEE ON FOREIGN RELATIONS.** Subcommittee on European Affairs. Soviet disunion: The American response. Hearing, 102nd Congress, 1st Session. Feb. 28–Mar. 6, 1991. Washington, G.P.O., 1991, 125 pp. (Hearing, Senate, 102nd Congress, 1st Session, S. Hrg. 102-17).

Today, it seems that the forces of disintegration in the Soviet Union are gaining momentum....President Gorbachev appears to have adopted preservation of the union as his own highest priority, even if this goal contradicts, and eventually destroys, his own policies of glasnost and perestroika.

B511. **U.S. CONGRESS. SENATE. COMMITTEE ON FOREIGN RELATIONS.** The future of U.S.–Soviet relations. Hearings, 101st Congress, 1st session,

Washington, G.P.O., 1990, 961 pp. (Hearing, Senate, 101st Congress, 1st session, S. Hrg. 101=365). Hearings held Apr. 4–June 20, 1989.

B512. **U.S. CONGRESS. SENATE. COMMITTEE ON FOREIGN RELATIONS.** Threshold test ban and peaceful nuclear explosions treaties; report to accompany EX N, 94-2 and Treaty Doc. 101-19, Washington, G.P.O., 1990, 196 pp. (Report, Senate, 101st Congress, 2nd session, exec. report 101-31).

B513. **U.S. CONGRESS. SENATE. COMMITTEE ON FOREIGN RELATIONS.** Workshop on U.S.–U.S.S.R. commercial relations, Apr. 17, 1989, Washington, G.P.O., 1990, 224 pp. (Print, Senate, 101st Congress, 2nd session, committee print S. Prt. 101-106).

B515. **U.S. CONGRESS. SENATE. COMMITTEE ON FOREIGN RELATIONS.** The future of U.S.–Soviet relations: hearings before the Committee on Foreign Relations, U.S. Senate, 101st Congress, 1st session, April 4, 12, 19 and May 3, 15, 18, and June 1 and 20, 1989, Washington, DC: U.S. G.P.O. Includes bibliographical references.

B516. **U.S. CONGRESS. SENATE. COMMITTEE ON FOREIGN RELATIONS.** Nuclear testing issues: hearing before the Committee on Foreign Relations, United States Senate, 101st Congress, 1st session, November 9, 1989, Washington, DC: U.S. G.P.O.

B517. **U.S. CONGRESS. SENATE. SELECT COMMITTEE ON INTELLIGENCE.** U.S. capability to monitor Soviet compliance with the Threshold Test Ban Treaty (TTBT) and the Treaty on Peaceful Nuclear Explosions (PNET); report. Washington, G.P.O., 1990, 12 pp. (Report, Senate, 101st Congress, 2nd session, no. 101-462).

B518. **U.S. PRESIDENT (1989– : BUSH).**

Agreement with the Union of Soviet Socialist Republics on the maritime boundary; message from the President of the United States transmitting the agreement between the United States of American and the Union of Soviet Socialist Republics on the maritime boundary, with annex, signed at Washington, June 1, 1990, Washington, G.P.O., 1990, 8 pp. (Document, Senate, 101st Congress, 2nd session, treaty doc. 101-22). Territorial seas and continental shelf jurisdiction in the Arctic Ocean, Bering and Chukchi Seas, and a portion of the North Pacific Ocean.

B519. **U.S. PRESIDENT (1989– : BUSH).**

Protocols to the threshold test ban and peaceful nuclear explosions treaties with the Union of Soviet Socialist Republics; message. Washington, G.P.O., 1990, 356 pp. (Treaty doc., Senate, 101st Congress, 2nd session, no. 101–19).

B520. **U.S.S.R.–U.S.A. SUMMIT** (1990: Washington, DC)

U.S.S.R.–U.S.A. Summit: Washington, May 30–June 3, 1990: documents and materials. Moscow: Novosti, 1990, 110 pp., 20 cm.

B521. **U.S.-SOVIET GOALS IN THE ASIA-PACIFIC REGION: COINCIDENCE OR CONFRONTATION?** Edited by R.A. Brooks. Washington, Heritage Foundation, 1990, 24 pp. (Heritage Lectures No. 266).
At head of title: A Heritage Foundation Conference.

B522. **U.S.-SOVIET RELATIONS.** Alexandria, VA: Close Up Foundation, c1990, 127 pp., ill., maps, 23 cm.
Includes bibliographical references (pp. 125-127). Examines the relationship between the United States and the Soviet Union from World War I to the present day.

B523. **UNDERSTANDING SOVIET FOREIGN POLICY: READINGS AND DOCUMENTS.** Edited by V. Wozniuk, New York, NY: McGraw-Hill, c1990, xxv, 323 pp., map, 24 cm.
Includes bibliographical references

B524. **UNDERSTANDING SOVIET FOREIGN POLICY.** Washington, DC: Institute for National Strategic Studies, Supt. of Docs., U.S. G.P.O. distributor, 1990, 44 pp., 23 cm.

B525. **THE U.S.S.R. AND MARXIST REVOLUTIONS IN THE THIRD WORLD.** Edited by M.N. Katz, Washington, DC: Woodrow Wilson International Center for Scholars, Cambridge, New York, NY: Cambridge University Press, 1990, ix, 153 pp., 23 cm.
Revisions of papers presented at a conference held at the Wilson Center, Sept. 25-26, 1986. Includes bibliographical references and index.

B526. Valenta, J. **"NEW THINKING" AND SOVIET POLICY IN LATIN AMERICA.** *Washington Quarterly*, Vol. 13, Spring 1990, pp. 135-151.
Many aspects of the new Soviet approach to the Third World remain unclear. What do the new concepts really mean and how relevant are they to Soviet foreign policy-making? Are they causing a substantive shift or merely a tactical change in Soviet strategy in Latin America?

B527. Valenta, J. **SOVIET INTERVENTION IN CZECHOSLOVAKIA, 1968: ANATOMY OF A DECISION.** With a new foreword by A. Dubcek. Baltimore, MD: Johns Hopkins University Press, c1991.
Includes index.

B528. Van Voorst, B. **STALKING THE RED INTRUDERS.** *Time*, Vol. 137, May 20, 1991, pp. 24-25.
Describes how the CIA's counterintelligence chief virtually paralyzed the agency at the height of the cold war with his obsessive pursuit of Soviet moles.

B529. Van Atta, D. **BACK TO THE FUTURE IN THE SOVIET COUNTRYSIDE?** *Problems of Communism*, Vol. 40, Jan.-Apr. 1991, pp. 155-164.
Reviews recent works which examine the role of the collective farm in Soviet politics, government, economics, and culture. Considers directions for this institution under Gorbachev.

B530. Van Dyke, C. **RUSSIAN IMPERIAL MILITARY DOCTRINE AND EDUCATION, 1832–1914.** New York, NY: Greenwood Press, 1990, xvi, 193 pp., ill., maps, 25 cm.
Includes bibliographical references (pp. 165–179) and index.

B531. Van Oudenaren, J. **DETENTE IN EUROPE: THE SOVIET UNION AND THE WEST SINCE 1953.** Durham, NC: Duke University Press, 1991.
Includes bibliographical references and index.

B532. Vanneman, P. **SOVIET STRATEGY IN SOUTH AFRICA: GORBACHEV'S PRAGMATIC APPROACH.** Stanford, CA: Hoover Institution Press, c1990, xi, 142 pp., 1 map, 24 cm.
Includes bibliographical references (pp. 133–136) and index.

B533. Vinton, L. **SOVIET UNION BEGINS WITHDRAWING TROOPS - BUT ON ITS OWN TERMS.** *Report on Eastern Europe*, Vol. 2, Apr. 26, 1991, pp. 19–25.
Soviet military officials announced that the formal withdrawal of Soviet troops from Poland would begin on April 9. Despite seven months of negotiations, the Soviet side has not yet reached agreement with Poland on the timetable or the conditions of the withdrawal.

B534. Vivian, P.H. **THE SOVIET ARMY: COMING TO TERMS WITH ITS AFGHAN EXPERIENCE.** *Infantry*, Vol. 80, Jan.–Feb. 1880, pp. 14–17.
Defeat for any army, whether political or military or both, is traumatic. Considers whether the exodus from Afghanistan - was it a military defeat? There are some dangers in comparing the Soviet experience in Afghanistan with the U.S. experience in Vietnam.

B536. Voas, J. **PREVENTING AFGHANISTANS: REFORM IN SOVIET POLICY-MAKING ON MILITARY INTERVENTION ABROAD.** Alexandria, VA, Center for Naval Analyses, 1990, 52 pp. (CNA occasional paper, August 1990).
Partial contents - Who is to blame? What went wrong? What is to be done?

B537. Volkov, Y.E. **PERESTROIKA, EDUCATION, AND THE SOVIET ECONOMY.** *Forum for Applied Research and Public Policy*, Vol. 6., Spring 1991, pp. 89–97.
Argues that in order to tailor the Soviet education system to the needs of the scientific and technological revolution, it is necessary to make radical economic changes, reorganize the education system, and improve education and training methods. Within the next few years, the Soviet Union must increase education's share of the national budget from its present two percent to 10 to 12 percent - the level in most industrialized countries. Without this investment, Soviet education will continue to decline, and the economy and living standards of the Soviet people will continue to fall as well.

B538. Von Hagen, M. 1954–. **SOLDIERS IN THE PROLETARIAN DICTATORSHIP: THE RED ARMY AND THE SOVIET SOCIALIST STATE, 1917–1930.** Ithaca, NY: Cornell University Press, 1990, xviii, 369 pp., ill., 25 cm.
Studies in Soviet history and society. Includes bibliographical references (pp. 344–357) and index.

B539. Wallace, W.V. **THE SOVIET UNION AND EASTERN EUROPE.** *Futures,* Vol. 22, June 1990, pp. 451–461.

Looks at the political and economic situation and its probable evolution in Eastern European countries and the U.S.S.R., and finds some common factors for both favorable and problematic long-term prospects....Argue(s) that the European Community has an important role to play in the economic recovery of these countries.

B540. Walter, N. **BEYOND GERMAN REUNIFICATION.** *International Economy,* Vol. 4, Oct.–Nov. 1990, pp. 58,60–62.

Presents an optimistic view of the process of and prospects for an integrating single German economy. Predicts an increase in growth rates for Europe with Germany taking the lead. Shows less confidence in the prospects for Eastern Europe and argues the West can help best with a hard-nosed policy regarding the conditions under which it grants loans.

B541. Wanner, B. **SUMMIT CONTINUES SLOW THAW IN JAPANESE-SOVIET RELATIONS.** Washington, Japan Economic Institute, 1991, 14 pp. (JEI Report No. 18A)

Argues that while not a breakthrough summit, the Kaifu-Gorbachev meeting, nevertheless, continued the slow thaw in bilateral relations that began about four years ago. Perhaps most important, Moscow for the first time since 1956 formally acknowledged that the jurisdiction of the four northern islands is a topic of negotiation.

B542. Warner, G. and Shuman, M. **CITIZEN DIPLOMATS: PATHFINDERS IN SOVIET–AMERICAN RELATIONS AND HOW YOU CAN JOIN THEM.** Foreword by C. Sagan. New York, NY: Continuum, 1991.

B543. Watts, A.J. **THE IMPERIAL RUSSIAN NAVY.** London: Arms and Armour, New York, NY: Distributed in the U.S.A. by Sterling Pub. Co., 1990, 192 pp., ill., 26 cm.

Includes bibliographical references (pp. 187) and index.

B544. Weber, S., 1961– . **COOPERATION AND SICORD IN U.S.–SOVIET ARMS CONTROL.** Princeton, NJ: Princeton University Press, 1991.

Includes bibliographical references and index.

B545. Weeks, A.L. **THE SOVIET DEFENSE COUNCIL: THE KREMLIN'S TOP ECONOMIC, MILITARY-INDUSTRIAL AND WAR-FIGHTING ORGAN.** *Defense and Diplomacy,* Vol. 8, May 1990, pp. 42–47.

Considers why in the era of glasnost, so little information i available on this supreme ruling body. Sees economic modernization as one of its key roles.

B546. Weinbaum, M.G. **WAR AND PEACE IN AFGHANISTAN: THE PAKISTANI ROLE.** *Middle East Journal,* Vol. 45, Winter 1991, pp. 71–85.

Without Pakistan there could have been no effective Afghan resistance movement and little prospect for its success against the Soviets. The sanctuary of Pakistan allowed the mujahidin (holy warriors) to organize military operations, and the Islamabad government became a conduit for multinational arms deliveries to those fighting in Afghanistan.

B547. Weiss, T.G., Kessler, M.A. **THIRD WORLD SECURITY IN THE POST-COLD WAR ERA.** Boston, World Peace Foundation, 1991, 31 pp.

This report summarizes the results from a collaborative project between Brown University's Thomas J. Watson Jr. Institute for International Studies and the World Peace Foundation. Our purpose was to explore the possibilities of cooperation between the United States and the Soviet Union in mitigating or resolving Third World conflicts.

B548. Weiss, T.G. and Kessler, M.A. **MOSCOW'S U.N. POLICY.** Foreign Policy, No. 79, Summer 1990, pp. 94–112.

Much as did the American experience in Vietnam, Moscow's counterinsurgency in Afghanistan revealed the pitfalls of unilateral superpower intervention....As a result, the Kremlin has become perhaps the most active and vocal advocate for a more dynamic United Nations. This new Soviet attitude departs radically from previous Soviet positions.

B549. Weitz, R. **THE U.S.S.R. AND THE CONFRONTATION IN THE GULF.** *Report on the U.S.S.R.*, Vol. 2, No. 33, 1990, pp 1–7.

Moscow's response to the current conflict provides strong evidence of a new calculation of interests by Soviet officials regarding regional conflicts.

B550. **THE WEST AND THE SOVIET UNION: POLITICS AND POLICY.** Edited by G. Flynn and R.E. Greene; foreword by T.L. Hughes, New York, NY: St. Martin's Press in association with the Carnegie Endowment for International Peace, 1990, xiv, 266 pp., 23 cm.

Includes edited papers from a conference held in Versailles, France in 1987 under the auspices of the Atlantic Institute for International Affairs. Includes bibliographical references and index.

B551. Wettig, G. **WEST EUROPEAN INTEGRATION AND PAN-EUROPEANISM IN SOVIET FOREIGN POLICY.** Koln: Bundesinstitut fur Ostwissenschaftliche und Internationale Studien, c1990, 26 pp., 30 cm. Berichte des Bundesinstituts fur Ostwissenschaftliche und Internationale Studien, 10-1990.

Summary in German. Includes bibliographical references.

B552. Wettig, G. **THE SOVIET CONCEPT OF SECURITY IN A "COMMON EUROPEAN HOUSE."** Cologne, Ger., Bundesinstitut fur Ostwissenschaftliche und Internationale Studien, 1990, 28 pp. (Berichte No. 13).

Contents - The traditional problem of European Security. The first phase of defining Soviet attitude. Differentiation of Soviet attitude. Detailed discussion of U.S. military presence in Europe. Implications of political change in Eastern Europe. Assessment of options for European security.

B553. Wettig, G. **THE GERMAN PROBLEM IN SOVIET POLICY.** *Aussenpolitik*, Vol. 41, first quarter 1990, pp. 38–51.

The gates have been opened to discussion of the German problem - but to discussion only for the present. In the midst of the upheavals now taking place in the Soviet Union and Eastern Europe, Gorbachev would be ill-advised to set further change in motion whose consequences cannot be foreseen.

Germans will have to be content for the time being with the Soviet Union's having acknowledged the existence of their unresolved national problem.

B554. Wettig, G. **THE POLITICAL IMPLICATIONS OF CHANGE IN EASTERN EUROPE.** *Aussenpolitik*, Vol. 41, Apr.–June 1990, pp. 107–117.

Sees resolving the "German question" as the central problem in European East–West countries. Argues that if Germany transcends the nation-state and finds a place in a community of nations, the center of Europe can develop its natural strength without threatening neighboring countries.

B555. Whelan, J.G. **THE MOSCOW SUMMIT, 1988: REAGAN AND GORBACHEV IN NEGOTIATION.** Boulder, CO: Westview Press, 1990, xvi, 141 pp., 23 cm.

Includes bibliographical references (pp. 127–141).

B556. White, G.L. **RETOOLING SOVIET DEFENSE SECTOR PROVES DIFFICULT.** Wall Street Journal, Sept. 6, 1990, A10.

Factories that once made rockets and tanks are now supposed to churn out everything from saucepans to baby carriages.

B557. White, A. 1959–. **DE-STALINIZATION AND THE HOUSE OF CULTURE: DECLINING STATE CONTROL OVER LEISURE IN THE U.S.S.R., POLAND, AND HUNGARY, 1953–1989.** London, New York: Routledge, 1990, p. cm.

Includes bibliographical references.

B558. Whitney, C.R. **GORBACHEV'S SEARCH FOR A NEW RIGHT-HAND MAN; REPLACING SHEVARDNADZE: WITH WHOM AND WHAT?** *New York Times*, Jan. 6, 1991, 3 pp.

Among the considerations in picking a new foreign minister: reassuring the army's officer corps and other hard-liners.

B559. Wirtschafter, E.K. **FROM SERF TO RUSSIAN SOLDER.** Princeton, NJ: Princeton University Press, c1990, xix, 241 pp., 25 cm.

Includes index.

B560. Wishnevsky, J. **THAT "LAW-BASED STATE," SOVIET-STYLE.** *Report on the U.S.S.R.*, Vol. 3, Mar. 8, 1991, pp. 1–4.

Examines the status of constitutional conflict between the central Soviet government and the republics. The central Soviet government accuses the leaders of local and republican governments - in particular, those in the Baltic republics - of unleashing "a war of laws" against the all-Union government and of violating human rights and the U.S.S.R. Constitution. Asserts that his is not the case, but suggests that those most guilty of anticonstitutional activity are not the leaders of local and republican governments but the Soviet president himself and the Communist Party of which he is general secretary.

B561. Wood, A. 1943–. **STALIN AND STALINISM.** London, New York, NY: routledge, 1990, xvii, 68 pp., ill., 22 cm.

Includes bibliographical references (pp. 67–68).

B562. Woodward, J.K. **PERESTROIKA AND GRAND STRATEGY.** *Global Affairs,* Vol. 5, Winter 1990, pp. 19–37.

The author considers the possibility that perestroika and glasnost are deliberate policy, intending consequences somewhat less noble than the regime's accepting its own passing from power. What are the intentions that lie behind these policies?

B563. **WORLD REPORT.** *Advocate,* No. 579, June 18, 1991, pp. 29–46,48–49.

Five articles on developments in the situation for gays in Mexico, by D. Lido; Eastern Europe (D. Tuller); Australia (B. Calder); Argentina (R. Julian); and the U.S.S.R. (M. Gessen). In addition, Rex Wockner interviews the editors of gay magazines in Great Britain, Norway, Germany, Costa Rica, and Australia.

B564. Wren, C.S. (Christopher Sale), 1936–. **THE END OF THE LINE: THE FAILURE OF COMMUNISM IN THE SOVIET UNION AND CHINA.** New York, NY: Simon and Schuster, c1990, 352 pp., 25 cm.

Includes bibliographical references (pp. 317–338) and index.

B565. Yazov, D.T. **SOVIET MILITARY DOCTRINE.** In RUSI and Brassey's Defense Yearbook, 1990, London, Brassey's Defense Publishers, 1990, pp. 27–39.

The military doctrine of the Soviet State reflects in full measure the political, social and economic essence of socialism.

B566. Yergin, D. **SHATTERED PEACE: THE ORIGINS OF THE COLD WAR.** New York, NY.: Penguin Books, c1990, xiii, 544 pp., 23 cm.

Reprint. Originally published: Boston, MA: Houghton Mifflin, 1977. Includes bibliographical references (pp. 509–530) and index.

B567. Yetiv, S.A. **HOW THE SOVIET MILITARY INTERVENTION IN AFGHANISTAN IMPROVED THE U.S. STRATEGIC POSITION IN THE PERSIAN GULF.** *Asian Affairs: an American review,* Vol. 17, summer, 1990, pp. 62–81.

The object of this study is to show how the Afghanistan intervention, a classic case of the failure of the use of force in international relations, improved the U.S. strategic position in a region that remains of major relevance to U.S. national security - the Persian Gulf.

B568. Zaloga, S. **THE MISSILES OF OCTOBER: SOVIET BALLISTIC MISSILE FORCES DURING THE CUBAN CRISIS.** *Journal of Soviet Military Studies,* Vol. 3, June 1990, pp. 307–323.

The aim of this article is to describe, in more detail than the military aspects of the Soviet missile deployment, and to examine some of the unexplored military questions about the missile crisis in 1962.

B569. Zaloga, S.J. **THE SOVIET NUCLEAR BOMB PROGRAMME - THE FIRST DECADE.** *Jane's Soviet Intelligence Review,* Vol. 3, Apr. 1991, pp. 174–181.

Over the past year, new Soviet memoirs and other accounts have been released which permit the first detailed description of the development of the Soviet fission bomb (A-Bomb), and the later fusion bomb (H-Bomb).

B570. Zamascikov, S. **CHANGES IN THE SOVIET MILITARY LEADERSHIP SINCE 1987.** Prepared for Under Secretary of Defense for Policy. Santa Monica, CA (1700 Main St., P.O. Box 2138, Santa Monica 90406-2138), RAND, 1990, xiii, 38 pp., 28 cm.

December 1990. Includes bibliographical references.

B571. Zenova, N. **THE DEADLY CLOUD OVER SVERDLOVSK.** *Wall Street Journal*, Nov. 28, 1990, A22.

Why, if it was "simply" anthrax, did people in military uniforms play first violin in the investigation? Why was the whole story of the illness eliminated along with all records and all documentation?

B572. Zwick, P. 1942–. **SOVIET FOREIGN RELATIONS: PROCESS AND POLICY.** Englewood Cliffs, NJ: Prentice Hall, c1990, xiv, 350 pp., ill, 23 cm.

C. DOMESTIC POLITICS; ELECTIONS

C001. **17 MARCH REFERENDUM.** FBIS Daily Report (Soviet Union), Mar. 20, 1991, suppl., whole issue (73 pp.).

C002. **A TALK WITH YURI SKUBCO: LEADER OF THE DEMOCRATIC UNION.** *New Leader*, Vol. 73, Aug. 6–20, 1990, pp. 14–17.

Interviews political activist, Yuri Skubco, a founding member of the Democratic Union, the first and arguably the most radical of the new political parties.

C003. Afanasyev, Y. **THE COMING DICTATORSHIP.** *New York Review of Books*, Vol. 38, Jan. 31, 1991, pp. 36–39.

Today we have to realize that this transitional stage consists of two processes that are at once interrelated and independent. The first is the transition from empire to a commonwealth of independent states, and the second is the transition from a centralized, planned economy to a market economy and private enterprise.

C004. **AFTER PERESTROIKA: DEMOCRACY IN THE SOVIET UNION.** B. Roberts and N. Belyaeva, eds. With a foreword by W. Laqueur. Moscow (Russia): Interlegal Research Center; Washington, DC: Center for Strategic and International Studies, 1991.

C005. Alexander, E. 1920–. **THE SERPENT AND THE BEES: A KGB CHRONICLE.** Lanham, MD: University Press of America, c1990, p. cm.

Includes bibliographical references and index.

C006. Alexeyeva, L. **UNREST IN THE SOVIET UNION.** *Washington Quarterly*, Vol. 13, Winter 1990, pp. 63–77.

The agony of the Soviet multinational empire is evident. An analysis of the unrest in the Soviet Union in the second half of the 1980s confirms the fact that the principal source of violence is the imperial apparatus of the state.

C007. **ALL-UNION REFERENDUM.** *Report on the U.S.S.R.*, Vol. 3, Mar. 29, 1991, pp. 1–23.

Contents - The all-union referendum in Central Asia, by B. Brown. The all-union referendum in the Transcaucasus, by E. Fuller. The referendum in Ukraine: preliminary results, by R. Solchanyk. The all-union referendum in Belorussia: appeals to the community of Slavs, by K. Mihalisko. Moldavia resists pressure and boycotts union referendum, by V. Socor. The U.S.S.R. referendum: a nonevent in Latvia, by D. Bungs. Referendum in Lithuania, by S. Girnius. Round three in Estonia's referendum season, by R. Kionka.

C008. Andrew, C and Gordievsky, O. **INSIDE THE KGB: A DOUBLE AGENT'S TALE.** *Time*, Vol. 136, Oct. 22, 1990, pp. 72–76,78,80,82.

C009. Andrews, W.G., 1930– . **THE LAND AND PEOPLE OF THE SOVIET UNION.** New York, NY: Harper Collins, c1991, xv, 304 pp., ill., 24 cm.

Includes bibliographical references (pp. 287–291). Discography, 292 pp. Filmography, pp. 292–293.

Introduces the history, geography, people, culture, government, and economy of the Soviet Union.

C010. **THE ANTI-COMMUNIST MANIFESTO: WHOM TO HELP IN RUSSIA.** Edited by L. Timofeyev. Translated from the Russian by V. Kisin and O. Glebov, foreword by R. Pipes. Bellevue, WA: Free Enterprise Press. Distributed by Merril Press, c1990, xvii, 96 pp., 22 cm.

A Project of the Referendum Foundation. Includes index.

C011. **ARBATOV SPILLS THE BEANS.** Washington, Heritage Foundation, 1990. 2 pp. (Backgrounder No. 121).

Presents experts from Soviet foreign policy expert Georgiy Arbatov's statements to the Soviet Congress of People's Deputies on Soviet military spending.

C012. **ARMENIA AT THE CROSSROADS: DEMOCRACY AND NATIONHOOD IN THE POST-SOVIET ERA: ESSAYS, INTERVIEWS, AND SPEECHES BY THE LEADERS OF THE NATIONAL DEMOCRATIC MOVEMENT IN ARMENIA.** Edited by G.J. Libaridian. Watertown, MA: Blue Crane Books, c1991.

Includes bibliographical references.

C013. Arnett, R.L. **PERESTROIKA IN DECISION-MAKING IN SOVIET NATIONAL SECURITY POLICY.** *Journal of Soviet Military Studies*, Vol. 3, Mar. 1990, pp. 32–45.

In the past four-and-a-half years, Gorbachev has made important changes in both Soviet national security policy and in the national security decision-making process. The author reviews the changes and discusses their implications.

C014. Aron, L. **YELTSIN: RUSSIA'S ROUGE POPULIST; IS GORBACHEV'S MAVERICK NEMESIS POISED TO PROFIT FROM BAD TIMES?** *Washington Post*, June 3, 1990, D1,D4.

Yeltsin's triumph will allow us at last to see the real Boris Yeltsin, and to judge him by what he does rather than what he says. For despite his assiduously cultivated image of a simple Siberian parent (guy), he remains a largely enigmatic figure, yet to make public his own detailed blueprint for the future of the enormous republic he now leads.

C015. Bahry, D. and Silver, B.D. **PUBLIC PERCEPTIONS AND THE DILEMMAS OF PARTY REFORM IN THE U.S.S.R..** *Comparative Political Studies*, Vol. 23, July 1990, pp. 171–209.

This study examines the relationship of individual differences in the perceptions of the honesty and competence of local and central party leaders to four background factors: ideological commitment, satisfaction with the material quality of life, the qualities of primary party secretaries, and direct experiences in citizen-initiated contacts with the party. The study also examines the reasons people give the joining or not joining the party.

C016. Bahry, D. and Silver, B.D. **SOVIET CITIZEN PARTICIPATION ON THE EVE OF DEMOCRATIZATION.** *American Political Science Review,* Vol. 84, Sept. 1990, pp. 821–847.

Reassesses the debate over Soviet citizen politics in the U.S.S.R. during the Brezhnev era. Shows that political participation under the "old regime" was not nearly as one-dimensional and devoid of effect as many previous researchers (and current Soviet leaders) have described it. Many forms of political participation in the Soviet Union before Gorbachev did not fit the stereotype of a psychologically disengaged citizenry driven to participate only by coercion, a desire to conform, or a quest for particularized benefits from public officials.

C017. Barnard, F.M. **PLURALISM, SOCIALISM, AND POLITICAL LEGITIMACY: REFLECTIONS ON OPENING-UP COMMUNISM.** Cambridge (England), New York, NY: Cambridge University Press, 1991.

Includes bibliographical references.

C018. Barry, D.D. et al. **PERESTROIKA AT THE CROSSROADS.** Edited by A.J. Rieber and A.Z. Rubinstein. Armonk, NY: M.E. Sharpe, c1991, x, 387 pp., 24 cm.

Includes bibliographical references and index.

C019. Barry, D.D. and Barner-Barry, C. **CONTEMPORARY SOVIET POLITICS: AN INTRODUCTION.** Englewood Cliffs, NJ: Prentice-Hall, c1991, xi, 398 pp., map, 23 cm.

Includes bibliographical references and index.

C020. Belousovitch, I.N. **NEW SOVIET PARLIAMENT: PROCESS, PROCEDURES AND LEGISLATIVE PRIORITY.** *Cornell International Law Journal,* Vol. 23, Symposium 1990, pp. 275–286.

Article examines the Soviet Union's restructured legislative process, which has altered the relationships between the regime, the legislature, and the bureaucracy. Formerly, the bureaucracy served as the regime's instrument for transforming party policy into state legislation. By shifting that responsibility to the legislature, the regime for the first time provided the Soviet public, through their elected deputies, with a voice in the formulation of national policy and legislation - areas the party leadership has always guarded jealously.

C021. Berman, H.J. **THE RULE OF LAW AND THE LAW-BASED STATE (RECHTSSTAAT).** *Harriman Institute Forum,* Vol. 4, May 1991, pp. 1–12.

Explores the theoretical implications of the expressions "rule of law" and "law-based state" in the....ways in which both concepts are reflected in recent Soviet legal thought.

C022. **BETWEEN TSAR AND PEOPLE: EDUCATED SOCIETY AND THE QUEST FOR PUBLIC IDENTITY IN LATE IMPERIAL RUSSIA.** Edited by E.W.

Clowes, S.D. Kassow and J.L. West. Princeton, NJ: Princeton University Press, 1991.

Includes index.

C023. Bialer, S. **THE PASSING OF THE SOVIET ORDER?** *Survival*, Vol. 32, Mar.–Apr. 1990, pp. 107–120.

This article examines three propositions that define the Soviet situation and the probable direction of its development. First, the U.S.S.R. has passed from a guided reform, perestroika, into a revolution. Second, the main political process under way in the U.S.S.R. is that of polarization and radicalization, to the left and right of Gorbachev. And third, the convulsions and conflicts that are shaking the U.S.S.R. are trends that are likely to persist and intensify for a long time to come.

C024. Billington, J.H. **THE CRISIS OF COMMUNISM AND THE FUTURE OF FREEDOM.** *Ethics and International Affairs*, Vol. 5, 1991, pp. 87–97.

The most important of all the searches for cultural identity is that which is currently raging within the dominant Russian nationality within the U.S.S.R.. The key question is: How, if at all, can Russians find a posttotalitarian identity and can enable them to live at peace with themselves and thus with the outside world?....For the Russians must simultaneously deal with a potentially dissolving empire as well as a demonstrably dead ideology.

C025. Billington, J.H. **RUSSIA'S QUEST FOR IDENTITY.** Washington Post, Jan. 21, 1990, B7; Jan. 22, A11.

When Gorbachev turned from economic to political reform, he opened up a crisis of legitimacy that he has not been able to resolve....Gorbachev and any successor in ruling this deeply disillusioned people can probably find only four possible answers to the question of Russian identity.

C026. Blank, S.J. et al. **ECONOMIC PERESTROIKA: THE CONSEQUENCES OF SUCCESS.** Carlisle Barracks, PA: Strategic Studies Institute, U.S. Army War College, 1990, vi, 23 pp., 23 cm.

C027. Blank, S. and Stanley, G. **IS CANADIAN FEDERALISM A MODEL FOR EUROPE AND THE SOVIET UNION?** *International Economy*, Vol. 4, Oct.–Nov. 1990, pp. 73–75.

The EC comprises a looser version of what Canadians have achieved for themselves over the last 123 years. Indeed, Canadian-style federalism is what other big transcontinental empires, like the Soviet Union, may have to embrace.

C028. Boettke, P.J. **SOVIET ADMISSIONS: COMMUNISM DOESN'T WORK.** *Freeman*, Vol. 40, Feb. 1990, pp. 50–56.

Communism, plain and simple, has revealed itself for the whole world to see as an unfortunate and terrible historical mistake.

C029. Bogert, C. **WHY RUSSIA CANNOT FEED ITSELF.** *Newsweek*, Vol. 116, Oct. 15, 1990, pp. 44–46.

Provides a rare look at how a Soviet farm really works. Based on author's experience: a week working on a farm in the U.S.S.R.

C030. Bogomolov, O. **THE CHANGING NATURE OF SOCIALISM.** *Soviet Review*, Vol. 31, May–June 1990, pp. 46–59.

What new qualities can society acquire in these countries as a result of modernization? In what way will such a society differ from the most progressive forms of modern capitalism? These questions are asked by many since the answer to them determines the content of perestroika and the new vision of socialism.

C031. Bohr, A. **TURKMENISTAN UNDER PERESTROIKA: AN OVERVIEW.** *Report on the U.S.S.R.*, Vol. 2, Mar. 23, 1990, pp. 20–30.

While the Turkmen have used perestroika to make significant cultural and religious gains during the first years of Gorbachev's rule, the more recent calls by many Turkmen for a fundamental restructuring of the republic's economic relationship with Moscow promise to have the most far-reaching consequences.

C032. Bond, A.R. and Piepenburg, K. **LAND RECLAMATION AFTER SURFACE MINING IN THE U.S.S.R.: ECONOMIC, POLITICAL, AND LEGAL ISSUES.** *Soviet Geography*, Vol. 31, May 1990, pp. 332–365.

This paper surveys economic, political, and legal factors involved in decisions to reclaim surface-mined land in the U.S.S.R., with particular emphasis on coal and iron ore....An initial section presents estimates of areas disturbed by surface mining and subsequently reclaimed. An analysis of selected economic, political, and legal factors follows. These include changing ratios of surface to underground production; a price system which undervalues mineral raw materials relative to finished products; Gorbachev's economic reforms; fragmentation of jurisdiction over reclamation activities; and extant reclamation law and its interpretation.

C033. Bonner, E. **ON GORBACHEV.** *New York Review of Books*, Vol. 37, May 17, 1990, pp. 14–17.

The following was given as an address at the University of California, Berkeley, on March 22, 1990.

C034. Borovik, A. 1960–. **THE HIDDEN WAR: A RUSSIAN JOURNALIST'S ACCOUNT OF THE SOVIET WAR IN AFGHANISTAN.** New York, NY: Atlantic Monthly Press, c1990, 288 pp. (8) pp. of plates, ill., map, 24 cm.

Translation of: Afghanistan. Originally published: U.S.S.R.: International Relations Publishing House, 1990. A Morgan Entrekin book.

C035. Bozzo, R. **GORBACHEV AND THE NATIONALITIES PROBLEM.** *Global Affairs*, Vol. 5, Summer–Fall 1990, pp. 19–35.

Resolving nationalities issue is not only consistent with the spirit of reform, but failure to do so constitutes a serious impediment to its success.

C036. Brovkin, V. **FIRST PARTY SECRETARIES: AN ENDANGERED SOVIET SPECIES?** *Problems of Communism*, Vol. 39, Jan.–Feb. 1990, pp. 15–27.

Communist Party secretaries in the oblasts and districts of U.S.S.R. constitute the most important source of resistance to Mikhail Gorbachev's program of perestroika. These apparatchiki blame the reform efforts for threatening the authority of the party, bringing about economic chaos, and calling into question the credibility of Marxism–Leninism. To repair the damage, the party secretaries call for safeguarding Marxist–Leninist ideology, and preserving the party's leading role in society. Concurrently, they are seeking to establish a role for themselves in the new political era by identifying with nationalists unlikely to succeed in such efforts; they face certain extinction in the years ahead.

C037. Brovkin, V.N. **THE MAKING OF ELECTIONS TO THE CONGRESS OF PEOPLE'S DEPUTIES (CPD) IN MARCH 1989.** *Russian Review*, Vol. 49, Oct. 1990, pp. 417–442.

In March 1989, for the first time since 1918, contested elections to a Soviet legislative body, specifically to a Congress of People's Deputies (CPD), took place in the Soviet Union. This step represents an important stage in Gorbachev's plan to restructure the Soviet political system. To what extent were these elections really contested? What were the mechanics of the electoral process?....Does the Communist Party have a chance to maintain its "leadership role" or will it be swept away by the new political forces? Nominally a supreme legislative institution, the CPD's role is limited to electing the Supreme Soviet, the actual legislature.

C038. Brown, B. **THE FALL OF MASALIEV: KYRGYZSTAN'S "SILK REVOLUTION" ADVANCES.** *Report on the U.S.S.R.*, Vol. 3, Apr. 19, 1991, pp. 12–15.

Kyrgyzstan's conservative Communist Party leader, Absamat Masaliev, has resigned and left for Moscow after unsuccessfully seeking to derail the liberalization drive of republican President Askar Akaev.

C039. Brown, B. **UNREST IN TAJIKISTAN.** *Report on the U.S.S.R.*, Vol., 1, Feb. 23, 1990, pp. 28–31.

Discusses recent riots in Tajikistan. Considers reasons for the unrest and likely Soviet action.

C040. Brucan, S. 1916–. **PLURALISM AND SOCIAL CONFLICT: A SOCIAL ANALYSIS OF THE COMMUNIST WORLD.** Foreword by I. Wallerstein, New York, NY: Praeger, 1990, xxx, 186 pp., 23 cm

Includes bibliographical references (pp. 179–180) and index.

C041. Brumberg, A. **THE TURNING POINT?** *New York Review of Books*, Vol. 37, June 28, 1990, pp. 52–59.

The Soviet Union is gripped by fear of sharply rising prices and the worst food shortages in decades but more mistrustful of Gorbachev himself....In addition, there is now a popular political rival for Gorbachev to deal with - the newly elected president of the Russian Republic, Boris Yeltsin.

C042. Brzezinski, Z. **BEYOND CHAOS: A POLICY FOR THE WEST.** National Interest, No. 19, Spring 1990, pp. 3–12.

Argues that if Central Europe falters economically and slide politically into violent nationalist passions, the probability is overwhelming that the Soviet Union - itself the volcano of nations - will explode violently before eventually smoldering into some noxious form of Great Russian nationalist dictatorship. Concludes that the West must today respond to the abrupt collapse of Soviet power in Central Europe and to the internal Soviet crisis with the grand concept of a Trans-European Commonwealth, with the

European Community at its core, but embracing Central Europe and being open also to eventual association with what is still today the Soviet Union.

C043. Brzezinski, Z. **BRZEZINSKI ON THE BREAKUP OF THE U.S.S.R..** *World Monitor*, Vol. 3, Nov. 1990, pp. 30–33.

U.S. policy should radically change, says a top former presidential adviser. Washington should help the soviet republics become independent nations, and that will aid democracy, Yeltsin's Russia - and even Gorbachev.

C044. **BUILDING A DEMOCRATIC EASTERN EUROPE; SPECIAL REPORT.** *World and I*, Vol 5, May 1990, pp. 20–59.

The World and I invited international experts to examine the hard tasks facing Eastern Europe on its road to real democracy.

C045. Bukovsky, V. **MALTA IN RETROSPECT.** *Global Affairs*, Vol. 5, Spring 1990, pp. 71–82.

Only the emergence of a strong, democratic opposition can stabilize the Soviet Union by replacing the Communist Party in power, dissolving the empire, and urgently introducing a market economy.

C046. Burg, S.L. **THE EUROPEAN REPUBLICS OF THE SOVIET UNION.** *Current History*, Vol. 89, Oct. 1990, pp. 321–324,340–342.

The dominant political conflict in the Soviet Union today is between forces supporting democratization and forces opposed to it....The emotional power of nationalism....may accelerate the process of change.

C047. Calzini, P. **THE BREZHNEV DOCTRINE TODAY.** *International Spectator*, Vol. 25, Apr.–June 1990, pp. 106–113.

A brief analysis....of the significance for the Soviets today of the principles of the Socialist International and, in connection with it, the so-called "Brezhnev Doctrine" - the management of relations with socialist countries.

C048. Campeanu, P. **EXIT: TOWARD POST-STALINISM.** Translated by M. Vale. Armonk, NY: M.E. Sharpe, c1990, xiii, 169 pp., 24 cm.

Translated from an unpublished French manuscript., "The text of this translation also appeared in Vol. 20, No. 1–2 of International Journal of Sociology" - T.p. verson. Includes bibliographical references (pp. 157–162) and index.

C049. **CAN GORBACHEV'S REFORMS SUCCEED?** Breslauer, G.W. editor. Berkeley, Center for Slavic and East European Studies, University of California, c1990, 135 pp.

Partial contents - Thinking about the Soviet future, by G.W. Breslauer. If the author were advising Gorbachev: thoughts of an economist, by H. Levine. Gorbachev's economic reforms: international constraints and opportunities, by L. D'Andrea Tyson. The Soviet Union's quiet revolution, by B.A. Ruble. Can Gorbachev manage the nationalities crisis? by G.W. Lapidus. New thinking abroad and the military's stake in reform at home, by D. Holloway. Eastern Europe and its impact on the fate of reform, by J.F. Brown.

C050. **CAN HE LAST? GORBACHEV MUST DIG OUT FROM A WINTER OF DISCONTENT.** *World Press Review*, Vol. 37, Mar. 1990, pp. 11–14,16,18,20,22.

Contents - Gorbachev vs. the "Dark Forces," by P. Smark. Russian nationalism draws its battle lines, by M. Huber. The worst of both worlds, by R. Cornwell.

C051. Cappelli, O. **COMPARATIVE COMMUNISM'S FALL; THE FIRST PHASE: THE "INTELLIGENTSIA REVOLUTION" OF 1989–1990.** *Harriman Institute Forum*, Vol. 3, June 1990, pp. 1–8.

"Comparative Communism's Fall" may be subtitled to indicate the crumbling of such pillars of communism as the centrally planned economy, Marxist–Leninist ideology and political culture, and above all, the one-party system....What follows is an attempt to analyze the intelligentsia revolution of 1989–1990 as the first phase in the process of the fall of communism.

C052. Carnagham, E. and Bahry, D. **POLITICAL ATTITUDES AND THE GENDER GAP IN THE U.S.S.R..** *Comparative politics*, Vol. 22, July 1990, pp. 379–399.

Scholars of Soviet politics have shown that men and women in the U.S.S.R. differ substantially in the political roles they assume....Soviet women do appear to have a diminished sense of personal influence and interest in politics, to be less democratic, less tolerant, and more religious, to support spending for social programs, and not to support a higher defense budget or state control over the economy.

C053. Carter, S. **RUSSIAN NATIONALISM: YESTERDAY, TODAY, TOMORROW.** New York, NY: St. Martin's Press, 1990, 175 pp., 24 cm.

Includes bibliographical references (pp. 159–164).

C054. Cartledge, B. **THE SECOND RUSSIAN REVOLUTION?** *International Relations (England)*, Vol. 10, May 1990. pp. 1–11.

We are at present witnessing a transformation of the relationship between the rulers and the ruled in the Soviet Union which amounts, the author believes, to a revolution if not in the conventional sense.

C055. Carynnyk, M. **THE KILLING FIELDS OF KIEV.** *Commentary*, Vol. 90, Oct. 1990, pp. 19–25.

An unprecedented genocide - the carefully planned murder....of a whole generation of intellectuals.

C056. Chaianov, A.V., 1888–1939. **THE THEORY OF PEASANT COOPERATIVES.** Translated by D.W. Benn. Introduction by V. Danilov. Columbus, OH: Ohio State University Press, 1991.

Translation of: Osnovnye Idei i Formy Organizatsii sel Skokhoziaistvennoi Kooperatsii.

C057. Chiesa, G. **THE 28TH CONGRESS OF THE CPSU.** *Problems of Communism*, Vol. 39, July–Aug. 1990, pp. 24–38.

The 28th CPSU Congress initiated a new political era in the Soviet Union. Mikhail Gorbachev, with the help of Boris Yeltsin, defeated the most important and dangerous group hostile to reform - the conservative party apparatus....It is now virtually impossible for party conservatives to turn back the clock. Having scored his most significant political victory since becoming general secretary, Gorbachev can now proceed with dismantling the "monster" party-state built up over the past 70 years of Soviet history.

C058. Clemens, W.C., Jr. **WHY GORBACHEV HAS GEORGIA ON HIS MIND.** *World Monitor*, Vol. 3, Sept. 1990, pp. 52–54,56–58.

From tyrant Stalin to diplomat Shevardnadze, the sunny California of the U.S.S.R. has contributed more than its share to Moscow's corridors of power. But, despite last year's Bloody Sunday, Georgians still defy Moscow's grip.

C059. Clemens, W.C., Jr. **THE BALTIC WAY.** *World Monitor*, Vol. 3, May 1990, pp. 56–60.

Discusses the Soviet response of the recent events in Lithuania, Estonia, and Latvia.

C060. Clemens, W.C. Jr. **BALTIC INDEPENDENCE AND RUSSIAN EMPIRE.** New York, NY: St. Martin's Press, 1991, xxii, 346 pp., maps, 22 cm.

Includes bibliographical references and index.

C061. Cohen, S.F. **RETHINKING THE SOVIET EXPERIENCE: POLITICS AND HISTORY SINCE 1917.** New York, NY: Oxford University Press, 1991.

Includes bibliographical references.

C062. Cole, J.P. **CHANGES IN THE POPULATION OF LARGER CITIES OF THE U.S.S.R., 1979–1989.** *Soviet Geography*, Vol. 31, Mar. 1990, 160–172.

Reviews the dynamics of Soviet cities for the period 1979–1989, based largely on maps and tables depicting five key "subsets" or city groupings: (a) cities increasing by over 100,000 inhabitants; (b) the fastest growing cities, 1959–1979; (d) the slowest growing cities in percentage terms; and (e) their comparison with slowest growing cities, 1959–1979.

C063. Connor, W.D. **THE ACCIDENTAL PROLETARIAT: WORKERS, POLITICS, AND CRISIS IN GORBACHEV'S RUSSIA.** Princeton, NJ: Princeton University Press, 1991.

Includes index.

C064. Conquest, R. **THE GREAT TERROR: A REASSESSMENT.** New York, NY: Oxford University Press, 1990, viii, 570 pp., 24 cm.

Includes bibliographical references.

C065. **THE CONSTITUTION, PROGRESSIVISM AND REFORM.** *Presidential Studies Quarterly*, Vol. 20, Summer 1990, pp. 459–620.

Partial contents - The new freedom in the Soviet Union and Eastern Europe, by J.C. Whitehead. Proposals for constitutional reform: an evaluation of the Committee on the Constitutional System, by M.P. Petracca. Publicity in the interest of the people: Theodore Roosevelt's conservation crusade, by S. Ponder. Management science and the great engineer: governing the White House during the Hoover Administration, by C. Walcott and K.M. Hult. Norman Thomas as presidential conscience, by J.C. Duram. Reappraising the presidency of Lyndon B. Johnson, by V. Davis Bornet. Early returns: assessing Jimmy Carter, by G.W. Reichard.

C066. Cooper, L., 1922– . **SOVIET REFORMS AND BEYOND.** New York, NY: St. Martin's Press, c1991.

Includes bibliographical references and index.

C067. Corn, D. **LIFE WITHOUT THE RED MENACE.** *Nation*, Vol. 250, Apr. 9, 1990, pp. 484–486.

Communism may be dead, but anti-Communism is alive and kicking - at least, within certain conservative circles. But since some on the right are willing to let go of the Red Menace, a split has been growing within the movement, as was demonstrated at the recent three-day Conservative Political Action Conference (CPAC) in Washington.

C068. **THE CRISIS OF LENINISM AND THE DECLINE OF THE LEFT: THE REVOLUTIONS OF 1989.** Edited by D. Chirot. Seattle, WA: University of Washington Press, c1991.

Papers from a conference held at the Henry M. Jackson School of International Studies. Includes index.

C069. Crow, S. **THE RESIGNATION OF SHEVARDNADZE.** *Report on the U.S.S.R.*, Vol. 3, Jan. 11, 1991, pp. 6–8.

Profiles Eduard Shevardnadze and considers his reasons for resigning as Soviet Foreign Minister. Considers implications of his resignation on Soviet foreign and domestic policy.

C070. **THE CULTURE OF THE STALIN PERIOD.** Edited by H. Gunther. New York, NY: St. Martin's Press, 1990, xxi, 291 pp. (20) pp. of plates, ill., 22 cm.

Published in association with the School of Slavonic and East European Studies, University of London. Papers from a conference held Oct. 20–23, 1986 at the Center for Interdisciplinary Research of the University of Bielefeld; sponsored by the Center. Includes bibliographical references and index.

C071. **CURRENT SOVIET STRATEGY: DISSENTING VIEWS.** *Global Affairs*, Vol. 2, Spring 1990, whole issue (pp. 1–172).

Contents - Strategies for the 1990s, by D. Quayle. The changing U.S.–Soviet strategic balance. The Soviet threat in the 1990s, by C.S. Gray. The balance of power conflicts of Eurasia, by A.J. Gregor. Malta in retrospect, by V. Bukovsky. Eastern Europe: the revolution in its future, by M. Djilas. Market communism at the brink, by S. Rosefielde. Red star over Afghanistan, by E.D. Krakowski. Moscow's Third World empire, by M. Leighton. The illusion of strategic stability, by M. Ruhle.

C072. Daniels, R.V. **TROTSKY, STALIN, AND SOCIALISM.** Boulder, CO: Westview Press, 1991.

Includes index.

C073. Daniels, R.V. **GLASNOST REVISED: THE LIMITS OF GORBACHEV'S REFORM.** *New Leader*, Vol. 74, Jan. 28, 1991, pp. 7–9.

Concludes that Gorbachev can stall reform for a time, but it is inconceivable that he can stop the clock indefinitely. Soviet society is now far too modern, sophisticated and complex to be run in the old monolithic way.

C074. Deriabin, P. and Bagley, T.H. 1921–. **KGB: MASTERS OF THE SOVIET UNION.** New York, NY: Hippocrene Books, 1990, xxiv, 466 pp., 24 cm.
Includes bibliographical references (pp. 443–457) and index.

C075. Desai, P. **PERESTROIKA IN PERSPECTIVE: THE DESIGN AND DILEMMAS OF SOVIET REFORM.** Princeton, NJ: Princeton University Press, c1990, viii, 221 pp., ill., 22 cm. Princeton paperbacks.
Includes bibliographical references (pp 209–211) and index.

C076. DeSomma, V.V. **UNION OF SOVIET SOCIALIST REPUBLICS.** New York, NY: Chelsea House Publishers, c1991.
Includes index.
Examines the history, geography and society of the Soviet Union.

C077. **DEVELOPMENTS IN SOVIET POLITICS.** Edited by S. White, A. Pravda and Z. Gitelman. Houndmills, Basingstoke, Hampshire: Macmillan, 1990, xvi, 310 pp., ill., maps, 23 cm.
Includes bibliographical references (pp. 298–304) and index.

C078. Dima, N. **IS SOVIET MOLDAVIA NEXT?** *Conservative Review,* Vol. 1, May 1990, pp. 2–4.
The Moldavians, too, were once a proud province within an independent Romania, but were grabbed by Stalin. Stalin has been denounced by Gorbachev but who in the Soviet empire or in the West have taken steps to give self-determination back to the peoples whose freedom he took away? Forty-five years of forced economic integration, of enforced population movements, and of intense brainwashing have still not deprived these captive peoples of their desire for freedom.

C079. Diuk, N. and Karatnycky, A. **NATIONALISM - PART OF THE SOLUTION.** *Orbis,* Vol. 35, Fall 1990, pp. 531–546.
The national movements deserve Western support. This is so for two reasons. First, they are pro-freedom, democratic, and peaceful. Second, they represent a process of decolonialization.

C080. Dobkin, J.A. and Burt, J.A. **SOVIET JOINT VENTURE LEGISLATION AND REGULATIONS AND RECENT RELATED LEGAL DEVELOPMENTS.** *International Quarterly,* Vol. 2, July 1990, pp. 156–173.
Contents - Restrictions on the use of convertible currencies. Structure of the joint venture. Purchasing, sales and other operational issues. Dissolution of the venture. Approval of the joint venture agreement. Conclusion.

C081. Doder, D. and Branson, L. **GORBACHEV: HERETIC IN THE KREMLIN.** New York, NY: Viking, 1990, x, 450 pp., 24 cm.
Includes bibliographical references and index.

C082. Drachman, E.R., 1940– . **CHALLENGING THE KREMLIN: THE SOVIET JEWRY FREEDOM MOVEMENT, 1967–1990.** New York, NY: Paragon House Publishers, 1991.
Includes bibliographical references and index.

C083. Dukes, P. 1934–. **THE MAKING OF RUSSIAN ABSOLUTISM, 1613–1801.** London, New York, NY: Longman, 1990, x, 240 pp., ill., maps, 24 cm.

Includes bibliographical references (pp. 224–230) and index. Longman history of Russia.

C084. Ehrenfeld, R. **NARCO-TERRORISM: THE SOVIET CONNECTION.** *Defense and Diplomacy*, Vol. 8, Sept. 1990, pp. 11–15.

Is it suggesting too much that Moscow knew perfectly well what was going on inside its empire, and that the Soviets are the responsible architects of the infrastructure for international narco-terrorism?

C085. Evans, A. Jr. **GORBACHEV'S UNFINISHED REVOLUTION.** *Problems of Communism*, Vol. 40, Jan.–Apr. 1991, pp. 133–143.

The Gorbachev phenomenon has called forth a flood of writings on reform in the Soviet Union, even through the rapid pace of change there renders most such reports out-of-date as soon as they appear in print, if not before. As the books under review demonstrate, analyses of the reforms initiated by Gorbachev have offered widely differing interpretations of the purposes and implications of those changes in structures and policies, and have advanced contrasting assessments of the prospects for the success of perestroika.

C086. Fink, L. **MUTINY IN THE U.S.S.R.** *Defense and Diplomacy*, Vol. 9, Mar.–Apr. 1991, pp. 59–62.

Mikhail Gorbachev these days must also deal with 15 mutinous republics that continue to chip steadily away at Moscow's authority. The Soviet Union is a huge multi-ethnic empire consisting of well over 100 separate national or ethnic groups.

C087. **FIVE YEARS THAT SHOOK THE WORLD: GORBACHEV'S UNFINISHED REVOLUTION.** Edited by H.D. Balzer, Boulder, CO. Westview Press, 1990, xi, 267 pp., map, 23 cm.

Includes index.

C088. **FIVE YEARS OF GORBACHEV.** With contributions by Y.N. Afanasyev et al., editors, N. Adler et al., Amsterdam: Second World Center, 1990, 133 pp., 22 cm.

Includes bibliographical references.

C089. Foteyev, V.K. **EFFECTIVENESS OF RECENT PARLIAMENTARY LEGISLATION VIEWED.** JPRS Report (Soviet Union: Political Affairs). Oct. 16, 1990, pp. 5–8.

Translation of an interview with the chairman of the U.S.S.R. Supreme Soviet Committee for Questions of Glasnost and Citizens' Rights and Appeals, originally appearing in Pravda, Sept. 7, 1990 (second ed.), 3. Foteyev focuses on the "second function" of the legislature, oversight and monitoring of enacted legislation.

C090. Freidin, G. **THE GORBACHEV TEAM: COMMUNIST REFORMERS CONSPIRE.** *New Republic*, Vol. 203, July 30–Aug. 6, 1990, pp. 10–12.

A secret question-and-answer session offers a glimpse of what the Communist Party's reformist faction really thinks.

C091. Frye, T. **A PORTRAIT OF ANATOLII SOBCHAK.** *Report on the U.S.S.R.*, Vol. 2, Aug. 17, 1990, pp. 8–11.

Profiles the recently elected reformist chairman of the Leningrad City Soviet, Anatolii Sobchak. Argues that Sobchak merits special attention as a potential leader because he is fairly young (aged fifty-two) and enjoys a broad national following and strong support in reformist circles. Most important, Sobchak's skills and background seem ideally suited to the new Soviet political environment.

C092. Fuller, E., Foye, S. **SPECIAL STATUS, STATE OF EMERGENCY, AND PRESIDENTIAL RULE.** *Report on the U.S.S.R.*, Vol. 3, Feb. 1, 1991, pp. 33–35.

The Soviet authorities have a number of means at their disposal to counter violence and reimpose some semblance of order in cases of severe interethnic unrest. They may introduce a curfew (kommendantsky chaos): "special status" (osoboe polozhenie): and, as of March, 1990, a "state of emergency" (chrezvychainoe polozhenie) and presidential rule (prezidentskoe pravlenie).

C093. Fuller, G.E. **SOVIET NATIONALITIES AND DEMOCRATIC REFORM.** *Global Affairs*, Vol. 6, Winter 1991, pp. 23–39.

At this point in Soviet history the nationalities issue eclipses virtually every other internal issue in its threat to the very integrity of the Soviet Union itself.

C094. Fuller, E. **GAMSAKHURDIA'S FIRST 100 DAYS.** *Report on the U.S.S.R.*, Vol. 3, Mar. 8, 1991, pp. 10–13.

Analyzes recent political events in Georgia, including the election of Zviad Gamsakhurdia as chairman of the parliament.

C095. Galichenko, N. **GLASNOST - SOVIET CINEMA RESPONDS.** Edited by R. Allington. Austin, TX: University of Texas Press, 1991.

Includes bibliographical references and index.

C096. Gill, G.J. **STALINISM.** Atlantic Highlands, NJ: Humanities Press International, 1990, p. cm.

Includes bibliographical references.

C097. Gitelman, Z. **GLASNOST, PERESTROIKA AND ANTISEMITISM.** *Foreign Affairs*, Vol. 70, Spring 1991, pp. 141–159.

There are 1.45 million Jews in the Soviet Union. They enjoy more cultural and religious freedom than at anytime since 1948, but they also perceive themselves as more vulnerable than at any time since.

C098. **THE GLASNOST PAPERS: VOICES ON REFORM FROM MOSCOW.** Edited by A.Melville and G.W. Lapidus, compiled and with a commentary by O. Aliakrinskii et al., Boulder, CO: Westview Press, 1990, vii, 359 pp., 24 cm.

Includes bibliographical references (pp. 341–342) and index.

C099. **THE GLASNOST READER.** Compiled and edited by J. Eisen, with an introduction by W.C. McWilliams. New York, NY: New American Library, Markham, Ont.: Penguin Books Canada, c1990, xvii, 445 pp., ill. 22 cm.

NAL books. Includes bibliographical references.

C100. Gleason, G. **FEDERALISM AND NATIONALISM: THE STRUGGLE FOR REPUBLICAN RIGHTS IN THE U.S.S.R.** With a foreword by J.N. Hazard. Boulder, CO: Westview Press, 1990, xiii, 170 pp., map; 23 cm.

C101. Goble, P.A. **FEDERALISM AND HUMAN RIGHTS IN THE SOVIET UNION.** *Cornell International Law Journal*, Vol. 23, No. 2, 1990, pp. 399–404.

This essay examines how ethnicity was an essential element in the U.S.S.R.'s formation, contributing to its coercive character, ethnic inequality, and pattern of human rights abuses....Explores how Gorbachev's revitalization campaign has changed the nature of human rights abuses in the Soviet Union by transforming ethnic and power relationships.

C102. Goble, P. **NATIONAL-STATE RELATIONS: GORBACHEV'S NEW FEDERALISM WON'T WORK.** *Report on the U.S.S.R.*, Vol. 2, July 6, 1990, pp. 13–14.

Mikhail Gorbachev's much-praised call for a new Union treaty has only one major drawback: it won't work as he intends. His suggestion that each republic set its own relationship with Moscow will only radicalize ever more nationalities, thus diminishing the treaty's utility as a brake on disintegration. Furthermore, his failure to discuss what will happen if republics that initially agree to federal relations later want looser ties virtually guarantees chaos or repression in the not-too-distant future.

C103. Goldhagen, E. **THE IDEOLOGICAL BELIEFS OF MIKHAIL GORBACHEV.** *Midstream*, Vol. 36, Feb.–Mar. 1990, pp. 3–9.

Discusses the ongoing evolution of Gorbachev's views. concludes that he has broken loose from the moorings of Marxism–Leninism and appears to have concluded that the only practicable course for him to follow is that of a pragmatic, piecemeal social engineer broadly guided by socialist values whose nature is still to be determined in the crucible of praxis.

C104. Goldman, M.I. **THE CATASTROPHE OF THE SOVIET ECONOMY.** *International Economy*, Vol. 4, Aug.–Sept. 1990, pp. 54–57.

The very nature of the Soviet economic system may make it impossible for it to recover from the debacle it has created.

C105. Goldman, S.D. **DECENTRALIZATION AND THE COHESION OF THE SOVIET UNION.** *Congressional Research Service Review*, Vol. 11, Mar.–Apr. 1990, pp. 23–24.

Decentralization is one of the guiding principles of the Gorbachev reforms and is the basis of many of the changes considered most praiseworthy in the West. But decentralization has had some unanticipated results and may be escaping Gorbachev's control, threatening to fragment the U.S.S.R.

C106. Goldman, M.I. **WHAT WENT WRONG WITH PERESTROIKA.** New York, NY: Norton, 1991.

Includes index.

C107. Goldman, K. **POGROMS AND PERESTROIKA.** *World Monitor*, Vol. 3, May 1990, pp. 16,18–19.

A young American in the Soviet Union finds fear - and defiance - among Jews who choose to stay.

C108. Goldman, S.D. **THE NEW SOVIET LEGISLATIVE BRANCH.** *Congressional Research Service Review*, Vol. 11, Mar.–Apr. 1990, pp. 20–22.

The new legislative system is in the forefront of democratization in the Soviet Union and may be the strongest protection against the reversal of Gorbachev's reforms in the future.

C109. Gooding, J. **THE XXVIII CONGRESS OF THE CPSU IN PERSPECTIVE.** *Soviet Studies*, Vol. 43, No. 2, 1991, pp. 237–253.

Describes the 18th congress of the Communist Party of the Soviet Union (CPSU) concentrating on the activities of party traditionalists. Finds that by the end of the XXVIII Congress the attempt at counter-revolution, which had never been very serious, had fizzled out. Most party traditionalists had already accepted, with however bad grace, the loss of the party's oligarchic absolutism as irreversible....Ligachev, who had instead chosen a course of outright confrontation, had been decisively defeated.

C110. **GORBACHEV AND PERESTROIKA.** Edited by M. McCauley, New York, NY: St. Martin's Press, 1990, xii, 222 pp., 23 cm.

Includes bibliographical references (pp. 208–214) and index.

C111. **GORBACHEV'S U.S.S.R.: A SYSTEM IN CRISIS.** Edited by U. Ra'anan and I. Lukes, foreword by G.R. Urban, New York, NY: St. Martin's Press, 1990, xxi, 154 pp., 23 cm.

Includes bibliographical references and index.

C112. Gryazin, I. **CONSTITUTIONAL DEVELOPMENT OF ESTONIA IN 1988.** *Notre Dame Law Review*, Vol. 65, No. 2, 1990, pp. 141–164.

Article concludes that at the first stage, the constitutional reform in the Estonian SSR was aimed at dismantling federal dictatorship in the Republic and at preserving Estonia's membership in the Union on the basis of democratic federalism.

C113. Gusev, S.I. **THE INTERNATIONAL INSTRUMENTS ON THE PROTECTION OF HUMAN RIGHTS IN THE U.S.S.R. AND THEIR INTERPRETATION IN U.S.S.R. JUDICIAL PRACTICE**. Bulletin of Human Rights, No. 1, Mar. 1990, pp. 48–59.

In this period of reconstruction and improvement of the political system, the individual and his rights, needs and interests are increasingly at the center of the Soviet State's attention.

C114. Hahn, J.W. **BOSS GORBACHEV CONFRONTS HIS NEW CONGRESS.** *Orbis*, Vol. 34, Spring 1990, pp. 163–178.

On March 26, 1989, the Soviet Union held its first competitive national election since 1917. Despite structural arrangements favoring the Communist Party of the Soviet Union (CPSU), several leading party candidates were defeated and a substantial number of party critics were elected. Is the Congress of People's Deputies the first manifestation of a proto-parliament? Is it the beginning of the democratic representation?

C115. Hammer, D.P. **THE U.S.S.R.: THE POLITICS OF OLIGARCHY.** Boulder, CO: Westview Press, 1990, xvi, 319 pp., 24 cm.

Includes bibliographical references and index.

C116. Hart, G., 1936– . **RUSSIA SHAKES THE WORLD: THE SECOND RUSSIAN REVOLUTION AND ITS IMPACT ON THE WEST.** New York, NY: Cornelia and Michael Bessie Books, c1991.
Includes index.

C117. Hawkes, N. 1952– **GLASNOST AND PERESTROIKA.** Vero Beach, FL: Rourke Enterprises, 1990, 48 pp., ill. (some col.), maps, 26 cm. World issues.
Includes index. Examines the meaning of Glasnost and Perestroika in the context of current Soviet history and describes the social and economic changes that have taken place within the Soviet Union and in the newly-independent countries of Eastern Europe.

C118. Heitman, S. **THE RIGHT TO LEAVE: THE NEW SOVIET DRAFT LAW ON EMIGRATION.** Koln: Bundesinstitut fur Ostwissenschaftliche und Internationale Studien, c1990, iii, 53 pp., 30 cm. Berichte des Bundesinstituts fur Ostwissenschaftliche und Internationale Studien, 26-1990.
Summary in German. Includes bibliographical references.

C119. Hemans, S. **WHITHER THE SOVIET UNION?** *RUSI Journal*, Vol. 135, autumn 1990, pp. 21–25.
What Mr. Gorbachev has unleashed is indeed a revolution....A review of the key areas affecting, or rather determining, the future of the Soviet Union.

C120. Henderson, M.B. 1951–. **THE PALACE GUARD: A CALL TO INTERCESSION AND ACTION FOR RELEASE OF THE SOVIET JEWS.** Florence, SC: Rt. 8, Box 13-A, Florence 29501): Sh ma Pub., c1990, xiv, 231 pp., ill., 22 cm.

C121. Heresch, E. **BLOOD ON THE SNOW: EYEWITNESS ACCOUNTS OF THE RUSSIAN REVOLUTION.** New York, NY: Paragon House, 1990, xiii, 250 pp. (85) pp. of plates: ill., 24 cm.
Translation of: Blutiger Schnee. Includes bibliographical references and index.

C122. Herlin, H., 1925– . **SIBERIAN TRANSFER.** New York, NY: St. Martin's Press, 1991.

C123. Herspring, D.R. (Dale Roy) **THE SOVIET HIGH COMMAND, 1967–1989: PERSONALITIES AND POLITICS.** princeton, NJ: Princeton University Press, c1990, xv, 322 pp. (1) p. of plates, ill., 25 cm.
Includes bibliographical references and index.

C124. Hiden, J. and Salmon, P. **THE BALTIC NATIONS AND EUROPE: ESTONIA, LATVIA, AND LITHUANIA IN THE TWENTIETH CENTURY.** London (England), New York, NY: Longman, 1991.
Includes bibliographical references and index.

C125. Hill, R.J. **THE CPSU: FROM MONOLITH TO PLURALIST?** *Soviet Studies*, Vol. 43, No. 2, 1991, pp. 217–235.
Examines the factionalism within the Communist Party of the Soviet Union. Notes that the ban on factionalism has never been rescinded, and

democratic centralism remains the organizing principle of intra-party life. Concludes that the willingness of the CPSU to function within the conventions of pluralist democracy remains unproven, and the suspicions of alternative organizations may seal the party's fate over the next few years.

C126. Hofheinz, P. **THE NEW RUSSIAN REVOLUTION.** *Fortune*, Vol. 122, Nov. 19, 1990, pp. 127–128,130,134.

In the vacuum created by Gorbachev's foot dragging, control of economic reform is rapidly shifting to a group of men who have been more decisive - the leaders of Russia, the mightiest of the 15 republics that make up the Soviet Union. Led by the charismatic Boris Yeltsin, they are pushing ahead with their own version of a 500-day forced march to a market economy that Gorbachev considered and then greatly watered down.

C127. Hofheinz, P. **THE SOVIET WINTER OF DISCONTENT.** *Fortune*, Vol. 123, Jan. 28, 1991, pp. 78–79,82,84–85.

After six years of zigzagging between left and right, Gorbachev is fast running out of wiggle room. The liberals, whose rise he encouraged, no longer trust him. His new friends on the right, whose views of the Soviet Union seem in so many ways fundamentally different from his own, undoubtedly feel the same way. As winter deepens, the liberator of Eastern Europe desperately needs to find some way to offer his own people the hope of a better life. If he fails, few of his countrymen....will shed a tear should he fall.

C128. **HOLDING A BAD HAND.** *Newsweek*, Vol. 115, June 4, 1990, pp. 16,18–27.

Contents - Why he's failing. Too little and too late? On reform: prime time for crime. The leaders next time. Neither ally nor enemy. The death of Democracy.

C129. Holman, P. et al. **THE SOVIET UNION AFTER PERESTROIKA: CHANGE AND CONTINUITY.** Washington, DC: Brassey's (US), 1991. Special Report.

A publication of the Institute for Foreign Policy Analysis, Inc., Cambridge, MA, and Washington, DC.

Includes bibliographical references.

C130. Horyn, M. **BUILDING AN INDEPENDENT AND DEMOCRATIC UKRAINE.** Washington, Heritage Foundation, 1990, 4 pp. (Heritage Lectures 282).

Ukraine has taken great strides on the road toward a rebirth of national consciousness....National rebirth goes hand in hand with the construction of a Ukrainian national state, writes the author, chairman of the Secretariat of Rukh, the Popular Movement of Ukraine.

C131. Hosking, G.A. **THE PARADOX OF PERESTROIKA.** *Atlantic Monthly*, Vol. 265, Feb. 1990, pp. 20,22,24.

Argues that Gorbachev faces two unenviable alternatives, either the reforms will fail, in which case perestroika as a whole is doomed, and the Soviet Union will probably fall apart and certainly cease to be a great power. Or they will succeed, engendering working-class unrest and ethnic tension to a degree that may well strain the resources of the state. Moreover, the combination of relative political freedom and access to information with disappointing economic performance - more or less the current juncture in the

Soviet Union - has in the past been thought to create a classic revolutionary situation.

C132. Hosking, G.A. **THE AWAKENING OF THE SOVIET UNION.** London: Heinemann, 1990, viii, 182 pp., 24 cm.
Includes bibliographical references (pp. 163–176) and index.

C133. Hosking, G.A. **THE AWAKENING OF THE SOVIET UNION.** Cambridge, MA: Harvard University Press, 1990, viii, 182 pp., 25 cm.
Includes bibliographical references (pp. 163–176).

C134. Hough, J.F. **GORBACHEV'S ENDGAME.** *World Policy Journal*, Vol. 7, Fall 1990, pp. 639–672.
If Gorbachev is going to remain in power until at least 1995, it is incumbent upon the United States to deal with him until and unless the next election produces a new national leader....Under the circumstances, to speak of supporting Yeltsin against Gorbachev is not just a mistake but madness.

C135. Hunter, S.T. **NATIONALIST MOVEMENTS IN SOVIET ASIA.** *Current History*, Vol. 89, Oct. 1990, pp. 325–328,337–339.
Soviet Asian republics have developed assertive popular movements and are emerging as budding independent actors. These popular movements are essentially anticolonial, reformist and nationalist.

C136. Hutchinson, J.F. **POLITICS AND PUBLIC HEALTH IN REVOLUTIONARY RUSSIA, 1890–1918.** Baltimore, MD: Johns Hopkins University Press, c1990, xx, 253, pp., ill., 24 cm.
Includes bibliographical references (pp. 231–238) and index.

C137. Hyman, A. **SOVIET CENTRAL ASIA: MUSLIM UNREST THREATENS SOVIETS.** Middle East, No. 188, June 1990, 20 pp.
Reports on how the appeal of full independence for Muslims of Central Asia is rapidly overtaking any doubts about its economic viability.

C138. **THE IMPACT OF GORBACHEV, 1985–1990.** Edited by D.W. Spring. London (England), New York, NY: Pinter Publishers, 1991.
Includes bibliographical references and index.

C139. **THE IMPACT OF PERESTROIKA ON SOVIET LAW.** Edited by A.J. Schmidt. Dordrecht, Boston, MA: M. Nijhoff, Norwell, MA: Sold and distributed in the U.S.A. and Canada by Kluwer Academic, c1990, xxvii, 558 pp., ill., 25 cm.
Includes bibliographical references and index.

C140. **THE IMPOVERISHED SUPERPOWER: PERESTROIKA AND THE SOVIET MILITARY BURDEN.** Edited by H.S. Rowen and C. Wolf, Jr. San Francisco, CA.: ICS Press, Lanhan, MD: Distributed to the trade by National Book Network, c1990, xiv, 372 pp., ill., 24 cm.
Includes bibliographical references (pp. 287–353) and index.

C141. **IN SEARCH OF CIVIL SOCIETY: INDEPENDENT PEACE MOVEMENTS IN THE SOVIET BLOC.** Edited by V. Tismaneanu, New York, NY: routledge, 1990, x, 193 pp., 24 cm.

A Foreign Policy Research Institute book - P. (ii). Includes bibliographical references and index.

C142. Josephson, P.R. **PHYSICS AND POLITICS IN REVOLUTIONARY RUSSIA.** Berkeley, CA: University of California Press, 1991.
Includes bibliographical references and index.

C143. Kagarlitsky, B. **"AND THUS, THE MOSSOVIET...."** *Harriman Institute Forum*, Vol. 4, Jan. 1991, pp. 1–6.
Last spring, when Muscovites elected a majority from the "Democratic Russia" bloc to the city council, thereby opting decisively for the transfer of power from party institutions to the people's choice, no one expected the transition period to be easy....Clearly, the democratic experiment in the capital has failed....Its gravediggers turned out to be....the new oligarchy arising under the banner of the struggle for democracy and renewal.

C144. Kagarlitsky, B. 1958–. **FAREWELL PERESTROIKA: A SOVIET CHRONICLE.** Translated by R. Simon, London, New York, NY: Verso, 1990, vii, 217 pp. (2) pp. of plates, 1 map, 24 cm.
Includes bibliographical references and index.

C145. Kaiser, R.G. **GORBACHEV: TRIUMPH AND FAILURE.** *Foreign Affairs*, Vol. 70, Spring 1991, pp. 160–174.
In just over five years, Mikhail Gorbachev transformed the world....Then he discovered that he had started a revolution he could not control....Gorbachev was often working with the forces of history, not against them....Mikhail Gorbachev's historical reputation will depend largely now on how far the violence goes - on how willing he proves to be to reverse his own civilizing reforms....Moreover he has assured himself a large place in history, and a large part of his reputation will be positive, despite his ultimate failures. Yet the future doesn't belong to Gorbachev, but to others.

C146. Kaiser, R.G., 1943– . **WHY GORBACHEV HAPPENED: THE MAN AND HIS REVOLUTION.** New York, NY: Simon and Schuster, 1991.
Includes bibliographical references and index.

C147. Kalmykov, Y. **PROCEDURES, STRATEGY OF LEGISLATIVE PROCESS EXAMINED.** JPRS Report (Soviet Union: Political Affairs), July 20, 1990, pp. 9–11.
Translation of an article by the chairman of the Supreme Soviet Committee on Legislation, originally appearing in the newspaper Pravda, May 15, 1990, 2 pp.

C148. Kaplan, M.A. **THE TRAGEDY OF MIKHAIL GORBACHEV.** *World and I*, Vol. 6, Apr. 1991, pp. 58–63.
Western pressure must be brought to bear upon Gorbachev to reverse course, give up the party, and lead the Soviet republics into a democratic future.

C149. Kassow, S.D. **SHOULD SOVIET JEWS LEAVE?** *Tikkun*, Vol. 5, Sept.–Oct. 1990, pp. 27–30,99–101.

For many Jews, fear or the desire for economic security will be enough reason to emigrate. We should respect that choice. It may be morally sublime to tell Soviet Jews to fight for nascent democracy at home, but that is up to those who may have to live with the physical consequences of that decision....The safety and security of Israel should still be the number-one Jewish concern. In this regard, heavy Soviet Jewish immigration will not only bolster the Jewish population but may also increase the chances for peace.

C150. Katsenelinboigen. A. **THE SOVIET UNION: EMPIRE, NATION, AND SYSTEM.** New Brunswick, NJ: Transaction Publishers, c1990, xx, 471 pp., 24 cm.
Includes bibliographical references and index.

C151. Kaw. M. **CHOOSING SIDES: TESTING A POLITICAL PROXIMITY MODEL.** *American Journal of Political Science*, Vol. 34, May 1990, pp. 441–470.
To explain and predict how great powers choose sides in others' conflicts by examining Soviet support behavior in 403 diverse conflicts during 1950–87.

C152. Keller, B. **BORIS YELTSIN TAKING POWER.** New York Times Magazine, Sept. 23, 1990, pp. 32,34,80–81,84.
Once dismissed as a yokel, he is now setting the pace on domestic issues and pushing Gorbachev to the wall.

C153. Keller, B. **YEARNING FOR AN IRON HAND.** New York Times Magazine, Jan. 28, 1990, pp. 18–21,46,48,50.
Ethnic Russians may be next to challenge Gorbachev.

C154. Khrushchev, N.S, 1894–1971. **KHRUSHCHEV REMEMBERS: THE GLASNOST TAPES.** Foreword by S. Talbott. Translated and edited by J.L. Schecter with V.V. Luchkov, Boston, MA: Little, Brown, 1990, xvi, 219 pp. (8) pp. of plates, ill., 24 cm.
Includes index.

C155. Kirichenko, V.N. **THE STATISTICS CORNER: RETURN CREDIBILITY TO STATISTICS.** *Business Economics*, Vol. 25, Oct. 1990, pp. 52–57.
The Soviet Union's chief statistician reflects on the state of official statistics in that country and the traditional ideological function played by statistics In shaping illusions of well-being and infallibility in the activities of the command-bureaucratic system.

C156. Kirkpatrick, J.J. **THE WITHERING AWAY OF THE TOTALITARIAN STATE.** Washington, DC: AEI Press; Lanham, MD: Distributed by National Book Network, c1991.
Includes index.

C157. Kirkwood, M. **GLASNOST', "THE NATIONAL QUESTION" AND SOVIET LANGUAGE POLICY.** *Soviet Studies*, Vol. 43, No. 1, 1991, pp. 61–81.
The causes of the present ethnic unrest are at once historical, economic, political, cultural and linguistic....I intend to concentrate on the question of Soviet language policy and to evaluate the extent to which it can be said to have contributed to the stimulation of national awareness among the multitudinous ethnic groups which comprise the Soviet population.

C158. Klein, J. **THE REAL SUMMIT.** *New York*, Vol. 23, June 18, 1990, pp. 12–15.

The Gorbachev–Yeltsin negotiations of the next few weeks, in anticipation of the July Communist Party Congress, are the real summit of 1990. It's a wonderfully symbolic confrontation: the president of the Soviet Union vs. the President of Russia, the new Soviet man vs. the unreconstructed peasant, the intellectual vs. the populist, the internationalist vs. the nationalist....It is no secret that more than a few members of Gorbachev's inner circle now believe that a deal with Yeltsin is mandatory: He's the only public figure with the credibility to sell the economic pain necessary to move the Soviet Union toward a functioning economy.

C159. Knight, A.W. 1946–. **THE KGB: POLICE AND POLITICS IN THE SOVIET UNION.** Boston, MA: Unwin Hyman, 1990, xx, 357, pp., ill., 24 cm.

Includes bibliographical references (pp. 343–349) and index.

C160. Koerner, W. **THE SOVIET UNION: PROSPECTS FOR REFORM.** Ottawa, Research Branch, Library of Parliament, 1991, 5 pp. (Mini-Review MR-84E (Feb. 20, 1991))

This paper provides an analysis of the problematic character of the present reform movement in the Soviet Union. The discussion is placed in historical perspective and argues that the motives for reform are to be found in the concrete circumstances with which Gorbachev is confronted rather than in any "democratic sentiment" on his part.

C161. Kory, W. **GLASNOST AND SOVIET ANTI-SEMITISM.** New York, American Jewish Committee, 1991, 44 pp. (Working Papers on Contemporary Anti-semitism).

Indicates how anti-Semitism has taken on new forms to fit changing political, economic, and social conditions.

C162. Kotkin, S. **PERESTROIKA IN THE SOVIET RUSTBELT.** *Harriman Institute Forum*, Vol. 4, Feb. 1991, pp. 1–16.

The profound economic and social ills that were to have been remedied by perestroika loom larger than ever....The focus here is Magnitogorsk, a medium-sized industrial city in the heartland of Russia.

C163. Kovalev, E.V. **U.S.S.R. SUPREME SOVIET PRESS CENTER FUNCTIONS DETAILED.** JPRS Report (Soviet Union: Political Affairs), Sept. 13, 1990, pp. 31–32.

Translation of an interview with the consultant to the newly established press center of the Soviet legislative body, originally appearing in the publication Sovetskaya Latvia of May 5, 1990, 2 pp.

C164. Krupnik, I.I. **MULTINATIONAL SOCIETY.** *Soviet Review*, Vol. 31, Mar.–Apr. 1990, pp. 3–15.

The issue now raised is whether our society is able to find a harmonious....combination of the interests of the peoples composing it, or whether we should expect a further buildup in tension of interethnic relations.

C165. Kull, S. **DATELINE MOSCOW: BURYING LENIN.** Foreign Policy, No. 78, Spring 1990, pp. 172–191.

What does the decline of Leninism portend for future Soviet behavior? Will policies traditionally rationalized in ideological terms gradually fade? Will a more pragmatic Soviet Union withdraw into itself and simply attend to its burgeoning domestic problems.

C166. Kux, S. **SOVIET FEDERALISM.** *Problems of Communism*, Vol. 38, Mar.–Apr. 1990, pp. 1–20.

It is difficult to isolate specific deficiencies in the Soviet federal system or to suggest optimal solutions for center-periphery relations....So far, the Soviet leadership has taken an administrative approach. It continues to deal with minority questions on a case-by-case basis.

C167. Kux, S. 1956–. **SOVIET FEDERALISM: A COMPARATIVE PERSPECTIVE.** New York, NY: Institute for East–West Security Studies, Boulder, CO: Distributed by Westview Press, c1990, vi, 117, pp., 23 cm. Occasional paper series, 18.

Includes bibliographical references.

C168. Laber, J. **STALIN'S DUMPING GROUND.** *New York Review of Books*, Vol. 37, Oct. 11, 1990, pp. 50–53.

As ethnic conflicts erupt through the U.S.S.R. and demands for independence, autonomy, and secession become increasingly insistent, it is important to investigate events to understand how Moscow is seen from other parts of the Soviet Union.

C169. Lane, D.S. **SOVIET SOCIETY UNDER PERESTROIKA.** Boston, MA: Unwin Hyman, 1990, xv, 401 pp., ill., 24 cm.

Includes bibliographical references and index.

C170. Laqueur, W. 1921–. **THE LONG ROAD TO FREEDOM: RUSSIAN AND GLASNOST.** New York, NY: Collier Books, 1990, c1989, xviii, 325 pp., 23 cm.

Includes bibliographical references and index.

C171. Laqueur, W., 1921– . **SOVIET UNION 2000: REFORM OR REVOLUTION?** New York, NY: St. Martin's Press, 1991.

C172. Laqueur, W. 1921–. **STALIN: THE GLASNOST REVELATIONS.** New York, NY: Scribner's, c1990, xi, 382 pp., 25 cm.

A Robert Steward book. Includes bibliographical references (pp. 333–367) and index.

C173. Laqueur, W., Erickson, J., et al. 1921–. **SOVIET UNION 2000: REFORM OR REVOLUTION.** New York, NY: St. Martin's Press, c1990, xx, 201 pp., 23 cm.

Includes bibliographical references and index.

C174. Laqueur, W. 1921–. **SOVIET REALITIES: CULTURE AND POLITICS FROM STALIN TO GORBACHEV.** New Brunswick, NJ: Transaction Publishers, c1990, xix, 231 p., 24 cm.

Includes bibliographical references.

C175. LeBlanc, P. **LENIN AND THE REVOLUTIONARY PARTY.** Atlantic Highlands, N.J., Humanities Press International, 1990, 399 pp.

Partial contents - Introduction: authentic Leninism. The context of Lenin's early organizational perspectives. Revolutionary program, cohesive organization. The birth of Leninism. Questions and problems. The test of revolution. The meaning of democratic centralism. Preparing for revolution. The almost revolution. Party and war. party and revolution. After taking power. Conclusion.

C176. **LEGAL REFORM IN THE SOVIET UNION.** *Columbia Journal of Transnational Law*, Vol. 28, No. 1, 1990, whole issue (pp. 1–328).

Partial contents. Soviet legal reform in historical context, by R. Sharlet. The party and the rule of law, by M.R. Bessinger. Law reform and the Soviet courts, by J. Quigley. Gorbachev's attack on Stalin's etatization of ownership, by J.H. Hazard. Economic reform and contract law in the U.S.S.R., by A. Klishin. International law in an interdependent world, by P.B. Maggs, V.S. Vereshchetin, and R.A. Mullerson.

C177. Levin, A.E. **NEW DRAFT LEGISLATION ON SCIENCE POLICY IN THE U.S.S.R.** *Report on the U.S.S.R.*, Vol. 3, May 31, 1991, pp. 6–9.

Legislation to govern science policy in the U.S.S.R. was prepared at the end of 1990. Since then it has been submitted for review by interested parties before being debated by the U.S.S.R. Supreme Soviet. The legislation is intended to establish a sound basis for formulation and execution of national science policy in the future.

C178. Lewin, M., 1921– . **STALINISM AND THE SEEDS OF SOVIET REFORM: THE DEBATES OF THE 1960's.** Armonk, NY: M.E. Sharpe, c1991.

Includes bibliographical references and index.

C179. Lewin, M., 1921– . **THE GORBACHEV PHENOMENON: A HISTORICAL INTERPRETATION.** Berkeley, CA: University of California Press, 1991, xii, 209 pp., 24 cm.

Includes bibliographical references (pp. 187–194) and index.

C180. Lewis, J. and Whitehead, P. **STALIN: A TIME FOR JUDGMENT.** New York, NY: Pantheon Books, c1990, xvi, 254 pp., ill., maps, 25 cm.

Originally published: London: Methuen, 1990. Includes bibliographical references (pp. 237–243) and index.

C181. Library of Congress. **NEW SOVIET AND BALTIC INDEPENDENT SERIALS AT THE LIBRARY OF CONGRESS: A HOLDINGS LIST.** Compiled by E.A. Johnson and M.E. Neubert, with the assistance of B. Yasinsky. Edited and with an introduction by H.M. Leich. Washington, DC: The Library, 1991.

May 1991. Includes indexes.

C182. Lih, L.T. **SOVIET POLITICS: BREAKDOWN OR RENEWAL?** *Current History*, Vol. 89, Oct. 1990, pp. 309–312,339–340.

To the tensions inherited from the past are added the frustrations engendered by today's economic and political crisis. The most obvious response is mutually destructive measures of self-protection....It is the race between breakdown and renewal that will decide the fate of Soviet society.

C183. Linden, C.A. **KHRUSHCHEV AND THE SOVIET LEADERSHIP: WITH AN EPILOGUE ON GORBACHEV.** Baltimore, MD: Johns Hopkins University Press, 1990, xi, 287 pp., 21 cm.

Originally published in cooperation with the Institute for Sino-Soviet Studies, George Washington University. Includes bibliographical references (pp. 259–271) and index.

C184. Lipset, M. **PARLIAMENTARY DEMOCRACY IN THE LAND OF LENIN.** Washington, Progressive Policy Institute, 1990, 12 pp. (Lecture Series No. 1).

What is evolving in Moscow is a Presidential-Congressional system, a government which can be institutionalized and constitutionalized along the lines it is developing.

C185. **LITHUANIAN INDEPENDENCE: THE REESTABLISHMENT OF THE RULE OF LAW.** Edited by S.P. Zumbakis. Chicago, IL: Ethnic Community Services, 1990, xi, 164 pp., ill. 28 cm.

Documents pertaining to relations between the Republic of Lithuania and the Union of Soviet Socialist Republics. Translated and compiled by the Information Bureau of the Supreme Council of the Republic of Lithuania, pp. 53–163.

C186. Loginov, V. **IS THERE A WAY OUT OF THE CRISIS?** *Soviet Review*, Vol. 32, Mar.–Apr. 1991, pp. 3–20.

Claims that the economic program adopted at the Twenty-seventh CPSU Congress was unrealistic, politically nearsighted, and that precious time was lost in the course of its implementation. Negative processes in the economy intensified, the working people began losing faith in perestroika, and the living standard declined significantly, which led to the most terrible evil of our time - social and labor apathy, indifference, the growth of individualism, selfishness, and nationalistic feelings and tendencies.

C187. **THE LOST EMPIRE: PERCEPTIONS OF SOVIET POLICY SHIFTS IN THE 1990s.** Edited by J. Hemsley. London (England), Washington, DC: Brassey's, 1991.

Includes index.

C188. Lowry, M.J. 1930–. **GLASNOST: DECEPTION, DESPERATION, DIALECTICS.** New York, NY: P. Lang, 1990, p. cm.

Includes bibliographical references and index.

C189. Ludlam, J. **REFORM AND THE REDEFINITION OF THE SOCIAL CONTRACT UNDER GORBACHEV.** *World Politics*, Vol. 43, Jan. 1991, pp. 284–312.

The concept of "social contract" is useful in understanding the process of reform currently under way in the Soviet Union. The social contract "concluded" by Khrushchev and Brezhnev provided the population with economic guarantees but deprived it of any political power. Reviews recent books on this topic.

C190. Madigan, C.M. **SOVIET NATIONALISM.** Chicago Tribune, May 20, 1990, pp. 1,15 May 21, pp. 1,6.

Contents - Nationalism endangering U.S.S.R.: Gorbachev's reforms set loose passion for independence. Soviet nationalism: repressed threat.

C191. Malcolm, N. and Jenkins, T. **SOCIALIST REFORM.** South, No. 111, Jan. 1990, pp. 22–25.

Two scenarios stretch out before an embattled Mikhail Gorbachev. The first envisages limited success in changing the Soviet economy. The second sees chaos and the end to communist dominance. Meanwhile Third World socialist countries are facing up the implications of perestroika.

C192. Maley, W. 1957–. **THE POLITICS OF BALTIC NATIONALISM.** Canberra: Research School of Pacific Studies, Australian National University, 1990, 22 pp., 30 cm. Working paper, 1990/6.

Includes bibliographical references (pp. 16–22).

C193. Malia, M. **A MANIFESTO FOR SOVIET DEMOCRACY.** *New York Review of Books*, Vol. 37, Mar. 29, 1990, pp. 26–27.

During the past two years innumerable "informal" organizations, voluntary associations, and even proto-political parties have sprung up across the Soviet Union's eleven time zones.

C194. Mally, L **CULTURE OF THE FUTURE: THE PROLETKULT MOVEMENT IN REVOLUTIONARY RUSSIA.** Berkeley, CA: University of California Press, c1990, xxix, 306 pp., (8) pp. of plates, ill., 24 cm.

Includes index.

C195. **MANAGING THE SOVIET REVOLUTION.** *World and I*, Vol. 5, Apr. 1990, pp. 56–77.

Contents - The world's most power president? by R.W. Judy. Nationalism shakes the U.S.S.R., by H. R. Huttenbach. The financial crisis - from their view, by A. Anikin.

C196. Mandel, E. **BEYOND PERESTROIKA: THE FUTURE OF GORBACHEV'S RUSSIA.** Translated by G. Fagan. London (England), New York, NY: Verso, 1991.

Includes bibliographical references.

C197. Mann, D. **BETWEEN TWO STOOLS: THE CPSU PONDERS ITS FUTURE ROLE.** *Report on the U.S.S.R.*, Vol. 2, July 6, 1990, pp. 6–9.

The principal goal of the radical-reformist wing of the CPSU: the Democratic Platform, at the Twenty-eighth Party Congress is the transformation of the CPSU from a vanguard party into a parliamentary party. The majority of congress delegates, however, would like to see the CPSU become a parliamentary party while retaining its customary role as a vanguard party - a hybridization that cannot work. Both sides correctly view the difference between a vanguard and a parliamentary party as profound, and they recognize that the choice of one option over the other will have serious implications both for the future of the Party and for the shape of the Soviet political system.

C198. Mann, D. **BRINGING THE CONGRESS OF PEOPLE'S DEPUTIES TO ORDER.** *Report on the U.S.S.R.*, Vol. 2, Jan. 19, 1990, pp. 1–5.

Outlines the basic provisions of the new Soviet Congress's legislative orders, adopted during its second session in Dec. 1989.

C199. Marcy, S. 1911–1. **PERESTROIKA: A MARXIST CRITIQUE.** New York, NY: WW Publishers. Distributed by World View Forum, c1990, xxiv, 409 pp., 22 cm.

Includes bibliographical references (pp. 391–395) and index.

C200. Marples, D., Skrypnyk, O. **PATRIARCH MYSTYSLAV AND THE REVIVAL OF THE UKRAINIAN AUTOCEPHALOUS ORTHODOX CHURCH.** *Report on the U.S.S.R.*, Vol. 3, Jan. 11, 1991, pp. 10–12.

On October 20, 1990, Patriarch Mystyslav arrived in Kiev, some five months after he had been elected patriarch by the Sobor of the Ukrainian Autocephalous Orthodox Church. The visit to Ukraine of the ninety-two-year-old Church leader, a resident of the United States, culminated in his formal installation as patriarch on November 17–18. Ukraine is now in the confusing position of having two Orthodox Churches: the Autocephalous Church and the Ukrainian Autonomous Orthodox Church, which was previously subordinate to the Russian Orthodox Church.

C201. McGwire, M. **PERESTROIKA AND SOVIET NATIONAL SECURITY.** Washington, DC: Brookings Institution, c1991, xi, 481 pp., 24 cm.

Includes bibliographical references and index.

C202. McClellan, W. **RUSSIA: A HISTORY OF THE SOVIET PERIOD.** Woodford McClellan. Englewood Cliffs, NJ: Prentice Hall, c1990, x, 371 pp., ill., 24 cm.

Includes bibliographical references and index.

C203. McFaul, M. **RSFSR: THE SOCIAL DEMOCRATS AND REPUBLICANS ATTEMPT TO MERGE.** *Report on the U.S.S.R.*, Vol. 3, Jan. 18, 1991, pp. 10–13.

The multitude of new parties, the splits within old coalitions, and the appearance of several Communist Party front organizations have flooded the market. Within the Soviets, the proliferation of parties, blocs, and factions has served to paralyze action, as the latest session of the Moscow City Soviet demonstrated. Outside the government structures, intellectuals gather at weekly meetings to argue among themselves, while the rest of the population is fast losing interest in all politics, whether they are democratic or not.

C204. McGuire, S.O. **THE SOVIET–JAPANESE ECONOMIC RELATIONS.** Santa Monica, CA: Rand Corp., 1990, xv, 106 pp., ill., 23 cm.

May 1990, R-3817. Includes bibliographical references.

C205. McNair, B., 1959– . **GLASNOST, PERESTROIKA, AND THE SOVIET MEDIA.** London (England), New York, NY: Routledge, 1991. Communication and society.

Includes bibliographical references and index.

C206. **MEDIA ANALYSIS IN THE ERA OF GLASNOST.** Washington, Foreign Broadcast Information Service, 1991, 61 pp.

FB AR 91-10005, April 5, 1991. Contents - Soviet media today and tomorrow. Glasnost and media analysis methods. Conclusion.

C207. Medish, V. 1924–. **THE SOVIET UNION.** Englewood Cliffs, NJ: Prentice Hall, c1990, xvi, 411 pp., ill., 23 cm.

Includes bibliographical references.

C208. Meerovich, A. **THE EMERGENCE OF RUSSIAN MULTIPARTY POLITICS.** *Report on the U.S.S.R.*, Vol. 2, Aug. 24, 1990, pp. 8–16.

Inspired and unfettered by the historic CPSU Central Committee plenum in February that announced the end of the Party's monopoly on power, more than a hundred parties and other political organization have appeared in the U.S.S.R., with most to be found in the RSFSR itself.

C209. Meissner, B. **GORBACHEV IN A DILEMMA: PRESSURE FOR REFORM AND THE CONSTELLATION OF POWER.** Aussenpolitik, No. 2, Apr.–June 1990, pp. 118–134.

Argues that without comprehensive social reform, with the reform of the political system as its central element, economic reform in the Soviet Union is doomed to failure. Concludes that a system of dual rule, based on the power of the Communist Party and the power of the "central organs of the state," has evolved during the course of reform so far. Asserts that constitutional limitations of the Party and further consolidation of Gorbachev's personal power position would "make it easier for him to take on the risks associated with future fundamental decisions."

C210. Mendras, M. **THE SOVIET UNION AND ITS RIVAL SELF.** *Journal of Communist Studies*, Vol. 6, Mar. 1990, pp. 1–23.

Like the Russia of the tsars, the U.S.S.R. locates its identity in opposition to the West. The dynamic of Soviet foreign policy lies in a competition, even if peaceful, against a Western rival that is at one and the same time enemy and model....The Gorbachev experience certainly affects the traditional approach to Russia's relations with the outside world....nevertheless (it) continues to be carried out in the sustained face a face with Russia's rival self, the East.

C211. Mihalisko, K. **THE ALL-UNION REFERENDUM IN BELORUSSIA: APPEALS TO THE COMMUNITY OF SLAVS.** *Report on the U.S.S.R.*, Vol. 3, Mar. 29, 1991, pp. 7–9.

Belorussians voted overwhelmingly in favor of preservation of the Union, but in the conduct of the campaign by the Communist Party prior to the referendum, glasnost' and pluralism were the losers. The authorities effectively silenced opponents of the Union. A constant refrain in the Communist-controlled press was that Belorussians, Russians, and Ukrainians are a community whose interests, it was argued, lie in the maintenance of the present Soviet state.

C212. Mihalisko, K. **THE WORKERS' REBELLION IN BELORUSSIA.** *Report on the U.S.S.R.*, Vol. 3, Apr. 26, 1991, pp. 21–25.

Thousands of Belorussian workers have downed tools this month in a series of strikes. The protest action was sparked by economic problems, but it quickly took on a political purpose: its organizers want nothing less than the introduction of political democracy in Belorussia. This is the most serious challenge ever to the republic's Communist regime and adds a Belorussian dimension to mounting labor unrest in the U.S.S.R.

C213. Mitchell, R.J. **GETTING TO THE TOP IN THE U.S.S.R.: CYCLICAL PATTERNS IN THE LEADERSHIP SUCCESSION PROCESS.** Stanford, CA: Hoover Institution Press, c1990, xiv, 237 pp., 24 cm.
Includes bibliographical references (pp. 225 –230) and index.

C214. Mitchell, J. **MANAGERIAL DISCIPLINE, PRODUCTIVITY, AND BANKRUPTCY IN CAPITALIST AND SOCIALIST ECONOMIES.** *Comparative Economic Studies*, Vol. 32, Fall 1990, pp. 93–137.
In this paper the author analyzes the potential functions of bankruptcy laws in reforming socialist economies in relation to its functions in capitalist economies. The author considers how the focus of socialist bankruptcy laws might be expected to change as an economy becomes progressively market-dominated and how problems of enforcement may vary at differing stages of reform. Finally, the author discusses the implications of these issues for enterprise behavior.

C215. **MOSCOW'S BIG STICK: KGB.** *U.S. News and World Report*, Vol. 110, mar. 25, 1991, pp. 33–41.
Amid the chaos of a disintegrating society, the KGB is amassing new powers and wielding ever greater political and economic influence. Contents - Too little and too late, by J. Trimble. Moscow's big stick, by J. Trimble. The KGB decided to stop Gorbachev, by O. Gordievsky.

C216. Motyle, A.J. **SOVIETOLOGY, RATIONALITY, NATIONALITY: COMING TO GRIPS WITH NATIONALISM IN THE U.S.S.R.** New York, NY: Columbia University Press, c1990, xii, 263 pp., 25 cm.
Includes bibliographical references (pp. 227–253) and index.

C217. Mukhametshin, B., 1942– . **GORBYSHOW: ANTI-POSTERS FOR OUR TIME.** Preface and notes by G. Kern. Riverside, CA: Xenos Books; San Bernardino, CA: Distributed by the Borgo Press, c1991, xx, 156 pp., ill., 28 cm.

C218. Muravchik, J. **GORBACHEV'S INTELLECTUAL ODYSSEY.** *New Republic*, Vol. 202, Mar. 5, 1990, pp. 20–25.
Traces changes in Gorbachev's ideology since his coming to power. Concludes that Gorbachev's evolution seems so far to have brought him to some form of "democratic socialism." Given this the U.S. should do everything, not reckless, to support and deepen glasnost and perestroika.

C219. Muravchik, J. **GORBACHEV, THE TRUE COMMUNIST.** *American Enterprise*, Vol. 1, Mar.–Apr. 1990, pp. 38–45.
Gorbachev's intellectual odyssey may lead him to reject Marx and Lenin.

C220. Myles, B. 1942–. **NIGHT WITCHES: THE UNTOLD STORY OF SOVIET WOMEN IN COMBAT.** Chicago, IL: Academy Chicago, 1990, 272 pp., (8) pp. of plates: ill., ; 18 cm.

C221. Nahaylo, B. and Swoboda, V. **SOVIET DISUNION: A HISTORY OF THE NATIONALITIES PROBLEM IN THE U.S.S.R.** London: Hamish Hamilton, 1990, xvi, 432 pp. (8) pp. of plates, ill., maps, 24, cm.
Includes bibliographical references (pp. 412–417) and index.

C222. Nahaylo, B. and Swoboda, V. **SOVIET DISUNION: A HISTORY OF THE NATIONALITIES PROBLEM IN THE U.S.S.R..** New York, NY: Free Press, 1990, xvi, 432 pp. (8) pp. of plates, ill., maps, 24 cm.
Includes bibliographical references (pp. 412–417) and index.

C223. **THE NATIONALITIES FACTOR IN SOVIET POLITICS AND SOCIETY.** Edited by L. Hajda, M. Beissinger, Boulder, CO: Westview Press, 1990, vii, 332 pp., 24 cm.
Includes bibliographical references and index.

C224. Nelan, B.W. **LASHED BY THE FLAGS OF FREEDOM.** *Time,* Vol. 135, Mar. 12, 1990, pp. 26,29–36,38–40,44–48,50–52.
Once a gray monolith, the Soviet Union is collapsing into a clamor of independent-minded republics and ethnic groups. What Gorbachev does to save the empire will affect not only his country but the world.

C225. Nepomnyashchy, C.T. **FAMINE IN TIME OF FEAST: SOVIET LITERARY PUBLISHING UNDER GLASNOST.** *Harriman Institute Forum,* Vol. 3, Mar. 1990, pp. 1–8.
Soviet readers these days frequently voice the lament....that it is virtually impossible to keep up with the pace of publishing under glasnost....Yet....in the midst of the current publishing boom, books - at least those books most people want to read - remain a deficit commodity.

C226. Nincic, M. **U.S. SOVIET POLICY AND THE ELECTORAL CONNECTION.** *World Politics,* Vol. 42, Apr. 1990, pp. 370–396.
Examine(s) the possibility that United States attitudes toward the Soviet Union are not only....determined by that country's capacities and behavior, but that they are substantially shaped by domestic political rhythms within the United States and, in particular, by the electoral cycle.

C227. Norden, E. **THE INGATHERING.** *Commentary,* Vol. 91, Apr. 1991, pp. 35–41.
Aliyah....the effort to integrate the newcomers is going to have to be as much an individual as a collective one.

C228. Nove, A. **GLASNOST' IN ACTION: CULTURAL RENAISSANCE IN RUSSIA.** Boston, MA: Unwin Hyman, 1990, xi, 259 pp., 23 cm.
Includes bibliographical references (pp. 245–246) and index.

C229. Olcott, M.B. **THE LITHUANIAN CRISIS.** *Foreign Affairs,* Vol. 69, Summer 1990, pp. 30–46.
Gorbachev clearly recognizes the threat he faces in the Baltics. Since Lithuania's declaration his position has been constant: any republic can leave as long as it abides by the provisions of the new Soviet law on secession....A basic tension still remains, however, between Moscow's will to enforce most of the provisions of its secession law and Lithuania's desire to protect its declaration of independence.

C230. Olcott, M.B. **PERESTROIKA IN KAZAKHSTAN.** *Problems of Communism,* Vol. 39, July–Aug. 1990, pp. 65–77.
Under the direction of Kazakhstan's communist party and its leader, Nursultan Nazarabayev, perestroika has taken root in that republic. Party

and government leaders have supported such popular causes as making Kazakh the official state language of the republic, filing in the "blank pages" of Kazakh history, endorsing a more open official attitude toward Islam, protecting the environment, and gaining economic sovereignty for the republic. So far, this regime flexibility has made it difficult for radical informal groups to gain popular support, but continued party dominance will depend on whether Nazarbayev and the party elite can reduce rising inter-ethnic tensions and resolve questions concerning the republic's economic autonomy.

C231. Olcott, M.B. **THE SOVIET (DIS)UNION.** *Foreign Policy*, No. 82, Spring 1991, pp. 118–136.

Gorbachev's inexperience with nationality relations has cost him dearly. It has undermined his authority, cost him the support of close political allies, crippled his reform programs, resulted in the deaths of what some estimate to be more than a thousand citizens, and could well lead to the bloody dissolution of the country that he is seeking to preserve.

C232. Parker, J.W., 1945–. **KREMLIN IN TRANSITION.** Boston, MA: Unwin Hyman, 1991–, v. 2, 24 cm.

Includes bibliographical references and index.

C233. Parks, M.L. **INTELLECTUAL PROPERTY LAWS - SOVIET STYLE.** *Export Today*, Vol. 7, June 1991, pp. 39–40.

To understand current developments in Soviet intellectual property protection laws, you must understand the history of these laws. You must also know something about the Soviet economy - past and present - and Soviet laws regarding the creation of joint ventures and of the cooperatives that comprise its corporate structures.

C234. Parks, M. **GORBACHEV'S GATHERING STORM.** *Los Angeles Magazine*, Apr. 7, 1991, pp. 28–30,32,68,70,72.

The Soviet leader may have only months to pull his country out of its deepening crises - or see his reforms consumed by them.

C235. **THE PARTY AND PERESTROIKA.** Editorial council, V.N. Kudryavtsev, V.V. Sogrin, editor-in-chief. Moscow: Social Sciences Today. Editorial Board, Nauka Publishers, 1990, 159 pp., 21 cm.

Title in colophon: Partiia i perestroika. At head of title: U.S.S.R. Academy of Sciences. Includes bibliographical references.

C236. **PERESTROIKA FROM BELOW: SOCIAL MOVEMENTS IN THE SOVIET UNION.** Edited by J.B. Sedaitis and J. Butterfield. Boulder, CO: Westview, 1991.

Includes bibliographical references and index.

C237. **PERESTROIKA IN THE COUNTRYSIDE: AGRICULTURAL REFORM IN THE GORBACHEV ERA.** Edited by W. Moskoff. Armonk, NY: M.E. Sharpe, c1990, xiii, 135 pp., 24 cm.

Includes bibliographical references and index.

C238. **PERESTROIKA, SOVIET DOMESTIC AND FOREIGN POLICIES.** Edited by T. Hasegawa and A. Pravda. London: Royal Institute of International Affairs, Lond, Newbury Park: Sage Publications, 1990, xii, 276 pp., 23 cm.

Includes bibliographical references and index.

C239. **PERESTROIKA-ERA POLITICS: THE NEW SOVIET LEGISLATURE AND GORBACHEV'S POLITICAL REFORMS.** Edited by R.T. Huber and D.R. Kelley. Armonk, NY: M.E. Sharpe, c1991.

Includes bibliographical references.

C240. **PERSPECTIVES ON THE LEGAL PERESTROIKA: SOVIET CONSTITUTIONAL AND LEGISLATIVE CHANGES.** *Cornell International Law Journal*, Vol. 23, No. 2, 1990, whole issue (pp. 187–398).

Contents - The Soviet Union as a state under the rule of law: an overview, by J. Quigley. The restructuring of Perestroika: pragmatism and ideology (the Preamble to the Soviet Constitution of 1977 revisited), by S.L. Levitsky. The new Soviet parliament: process, procedures, and legislative priority, by I.N. Belousovitch. The Committee of Constitutional Supervision of the U.S.S.R., by H. Hausmaninger. The politics of constitutional reform: the new power structure and the role of the party, by V.N. Brovkin.

C241. Pethybridge, R.W. 1934–. **ONE STEP BACKWARDS, TWO STEPS FORWARD: SOVIET SOCIETY AND POLITICS IN THE NEW ECONOMIC POLICY.** Oxford: Clarendon Press, New York, NY: Oxford University Press, 1990, p. cm.

Includes bibliographical references.

C242. Petro, N.N. **REDISCOVERING RUSSIA: NATIONALISM IN THE SOVIET BLOC.** *Orbis*, Vol. 23, Winter 1990, pp. 33–49.

Rising nationalism among the Soviet Union's ethnic minorities is much in the news, especially the nationalism of the Caucasus and Baltic regions. But what about the ethnic majority? Nationalism among Russians is emerging as an increasingly important factor in the Soviet domestic debate.

C243. Pilon, R. **WILL THE WORLDWIDE LIBERAL REVOLUTION BYPASS AMERICA THROUGH JUDICIAL RESTRAINT?** *Cato Policy Report*, Vol, 12, Mar. -Apr. 1990, pp. 1,10–14.

Analyzes the recent developments in the U.S.S.R. and Eastern Europe changing their governments from decentralization to democratization to liberalization. The author argues that unlike these countries, through judicial restraint, the United States is abandoning its liberal stance of protecting individual rights in support of special interests. He contends that it is the special interest that the peoples of the socialist world are attempting to overturn.

C244. Pipes, R. **THE RUSSIAN REVOLUTION.** New York, NY: Knopf, 1990, xxiv, 944 pp., ill., map, 25 cm.

Includes bibliographical references (pp. 915–919) and index.

C245. Pipes, R. **GORBACHEV'S RUSSIA: BREAKDOWN OR CRACKDOWN?** *Commentary*, Vol. 89, Mar. 1990, pp. 13–25.

Argues that one cannot insist too strongly that perestroika and glasnost are neither the result of a change of heart on the part of the Soviet leadership, nor the fulfillment of one man's vision, but the desperate effort by an apparatus composed of millions of parasitic Communist functionaries to stave off revolution.

C246. Pittman, R.H. **PERESTROIKA AND SOVIET CULTURAL POLITICS: THE CASE OF THE MAJOR LITERARY JOURNALS.** *Soviet Studies*, Vol. 42, Jan. 1990, pp. 111–132.

The scope of this essay is limited and it can hope simply, with the help of a few examples, to give a flavor of the way in which many Soviet literary journals have been transformed since Gorbachev's accession to power. To this end, a number of journals are discussed here with some reference to the key editorial personnel changes which have taken place in them, as well as to issues which the journals have taken up.

C247. **POGROMS: ANTI-JEWISH VIOLENCE IN MODERN RUSSIAN HISTORY.** Edited by J.D. Klier and S. Lambroza. Cambridge (England), New York, NY: Cambridge University Press, 1991.

Includes bibliographical references and index.

C248. Pope, R. **PUBLIC OPINION RESEARCH IN THE SOVIET UNION: A FIRSTHAND ACCOUNT.** *Report on the U.S.S.R.*, Vol. 2, Oct. 1990, pp. 8–12.

American political scientist describes the results of his polling in the city of Vladimir and discusses the state of Soviet survey research. An encouraging development in the U.S.S.R. today is the growing availability of the findings of the public opinion studies being conducted by an increasing number of Soviet survey research institutes.

C249. Popov, G. **PERESTROIKA AND THE PRIMACY OF POLITICS.** *Dissent*, Vol. 37, Winter 1990, pp. 91–96.

Argues that the first efforts at reform, introduced in 1985–1986, support three conclusions: First, that what our country needs is not reform but fundamental economic restructuring - that is to say, a new economic system. Second, that the new economic system requires a political system that is congruous with it. And third, that further economic reorganization is impossible without radical changes in our political institutions.

C250. Pospielovsky, D. **RUSSIAN NATIONALISM: AN UPDATE.** *Report on the U.S.S.R.*, Vol. 2, Feb. 9, 1990, pp. 8–17.

After several visits to the Soviet Union as a tourist, observer and participant in an international conference the author, a university professor claims that Russian "neonationalism" is very widespread and that it is predominantly defensive, rather than offensive, in character, and then draws some conclusions.

C251. Pozner, V. **PARTING WITH ILLUSIONS.** Introduction by B. Kahn. New York, NY: Atlantic Monthly Press, c1990, 324 pp., 24 cm.

Includes index.

C252. Putintsev, A.D. **U.S.S.R., PERESTROIKA.** Written and compiled by A. Putintsev. Moscow: Novosti Press Agency Pub. House, 1990, 1 v. (unpaged), ill. (some col.), 22 cm.

Title on p. (2) of cover: SSSR perestroika.

C253. Ra'anan, U. 1926–. **INSIDE THE APPARAT: PERSPECTIVES ON THE SOVIET SYSTEM FROM FORMER FUNCTIONARIES.** Edited by U. Ra'anan, I. Lukes. Lexington, MA: Lexington Books, c1990, xxviii, 281 pp., 24 cm.

Includes bibliographical references and index.

C254. Rahr, A. **STATE SECURITY: NEW EVIDENCE OF THE KGB'S POLITICAL COMPLEXION PUBLISHED.** *Report on the U.S.S.R.*, Vol. 3, Jan. 18, 1991, pp. 1–5.

The dramatic changes that have affected Soviet society since the inception of perestroika have put increasing pressure on all Soviet institutions to adapt. Not even the most conservative among them - such as the KGB and the armed forces - have been able to circumvent this imperative, which has forced them to adjust their traditional roles and attitudes to the present political realities. Discusses information which the KGB released about its work and mission.

C255. Rahr. A. **THE RUSSIAN TRIANGLE: GORBACHEV—YELTSIN—POLOZKOV.** *Report on the U.S.S.R.*, Vol. 2, July 5, 1990, pp. 4–6.

Contends that the birth of the Russian Communist Party is a further step towards the fragmentation of the Soviet Union and a personal defeat for President Mikhail Gorbachev. The election of hardliner Ivan Polozkov as first secretary of the Russian Party also dramatically reduces Gorbachev's control over....Party organizations in the republic. At the same time, the election of Gorbachev's political rival Boris Yeltsin as chairman of the RSFSR Supreme Soviet deprives the Soviet president of the power to directly supervise the Russian legislature.

C256. Reddaway, P. **EMPIRE ON THE BRINK.** New York Review of Books, Jan. 31, 1991, pp. 7–9.

The world's last major empire is no longer just fraying at the edges....Looks like the early stages of a prolonged and probably far from peaceful death....Since 1988 the Soviet Union's fifteen republics have....won steadily more freedom from the control of the central government. But now the conservative forces of the center....are urgently rallying to attack it.

C257. Reddaway, P. **REFORM OF SOVIET PSYCHIATRY: IS THE ESTABLISHMENT BEGINNING TO PANIC?** *Report on Eastern Europe*, Vol. 1, Nov. 2, 1990, pp. 1–14.

The struggle over the political abuse and reform of Soviet psychiatry. Sustained reform has not yet begun, and the long-discredited psychiatric leadership continues to hang to grimly, resisting real change.

C258. Remnick, D. **PERESTROIKA NURTURED AT SIBERIAN THINK TANK: GENERATION OF LIBERALS AWAITED GORBACHEV.** Washington Post, Feb. 10, 1990, A1,A18.

The dreams of Agenbegyan and the small core of progressives within the Communist Party are taking shape.

C259. Remnick, D. **COMRADE PERSONALITY.** *Esquire*, Vol. 113, Feb. 1990, pp. 74–76,78–81.

Gorbachev's personality will play an essential role in the immediate future of the Soviet Union....More and more, Gorbachev will be forced to look inside himself and make choices that depend on the conflicts within his own career and personality.

C260. **RENEWAL AND CHALLENGE: THE BALTIC STATES, 1988–1989.** prepared by the staff of the U.S. Commission on Security and Cooperation in Europe. Washington, DC: U.S. G.P.O.

C261. **REVOLUTION IN LAW: CONTRIBUTIONS TO THE DEVELOPMENT OF SOVIET LEGAL THEORY, 1917–1938.** Edited by P. Beirne, Armonk, NY: M.E. Sharpe, c1990, xiii, 202 pp., 24 cm.

Includes bibliographical references and index.

C262. Reznik, S.E. **SOVIET JEWS IN THE GLASNOST ERA.** *Society*, Vol. 28, May–June 1991, pp. 73–83.

The situation for the Jews in the Soviet Union in the post-glasnost era has become extremely volatile. The struggle for power between democratic forces and the communist party bureaucracy is becoming more acute.

C263. Rich, V. **SOVIET ENERGY....POWER AND THE PEOPLE.** *New Scientist*, Vol. 125, Mar. 3, 1990, pp. 44–47.

Discusses the opposition to the Soviet Union's centrally planned energy program. For the foreseeable future, the Soviet Union's main energy problem will not be a lack of resources, but the cost of exploiting the reserves in increasingly remote areas of the country, and public hostility to environmentally polluting forms of fuel.

C264. Rigby, T.H. (Thomas Henry), 1925–. **POLITICAL ELITES IN THE U.S.S.R.: CENTRAL LEADERS AND LOCAL CADRES FROM LENIN TO GORBACHEV.** Aldershot, Hants, England: E. Elgar, Brookfield, VT.: Gower Pub. Co., c1990, vii, 301 pp., 23 cm.

Includes bibliographical references and index.

C265. Rigby, T.H. (Thomas Henry), 1925–. **THE CHANGING SOVIET SYSTEM: MONO-ORGANIZATIONAL SOCIALISM FROM ITS ORIGINS TO GORBACHEV'S RESTRUCTURING.** Aldershot, Hants, England, Brookfield, VT: E. Elgar Pub., c1990, vii, 256 pp., 24 cm.

Includes bibliographical references and index.

C266. **THE RISE OF NATIONS IN THE SOVIET UNION: AMERICAN FOREIGN POLICY AND THE DISINTEGRATION OF THE USSR.** Edited by M. Mandelbaum. New York, NY: Council on Foreign Relations Press, c1991, viii, 120 pp., 1 map, 23 cm.

Includes bibliographical references and index.

C267. Rittersporn, G.T., 1948– . **STALINIST SIMPLIFICATIONS AND SOVIET COMPLICATIONS: SOCIAL TENSIONS AND POLITICAL CONFLICTS IN THE USSR, 1933–1953.** Chur, New York, NY: Harwood Academic Publishers, c1991.

Translation of: Simplifications Staliniennes et complications sovietiques. Includes bibliographical references and index.

C268. Ro'i, Y. **THE STRUGGLE FOR SOVIET JEWISH EMIGRATION, 1948–1967.** Cambridge (England), New York, NY: Cambridge University Press, 1991, xvii, 458 pp., 24 cm.

Includes bibliographical references (pp. 429–435) and index.

C269. Roeder, P.G. **SOVIET FEDERALISM AND ETHNIC MOBILIZATION.** *World Politics*, Vol. 43, Jan. 1991, pp. 196–232.

Over the past three decades three changes have transformed Soviet developmental strategy into a source of ethnofederalism....With the trimming of the terror apparatus under Krushchev....the cadres had greater leeway in pressing their particularistic agendas....As the cadres built institutional and even popular support within their ethnic communities, their dependence upon the center declined. These new power bases enabled the cadres to take more assertive policy stands against Moscow.

C270. Roi, Y. **THE ISLAMIC INFLUENCE ON NATIONALISM IN SOVIET CENTRAL ASIA.** *Problems of Communism*, vol. 39, July–Aug. 1990, pp. 49–64.

Both Islam and nationalism are becoming increasingly assertive in Soviet Central Asia, and the two currents have merged in some cases, particularly among the young. It remains to be seen whether Islam will ultimately serve as a cement uniting diverse Central Asian peoples against Moscow, or whether nationalism will set the nations of the region against one another.

C271. Romerstein, H. **IN CRISIS: THE RULERS OF THE SOVIET UNION.** *International Freedom Review*, Vol. 3, Winter 1990, pp. 65–80.

The present Soviet crisis requires drastic solutions. It is possible that they will proceed along a democratic path and dismantle the repressive, Communist one party system....On the other hand, Soviet rulers may decide that the solution to the crisis is a return to Stalinism, with its internal repression and international aggression. Either path could be taken under the leadership of Gorbachev, or as a result of Gorbachev's ouster.

C272. Rosefielde,S. **GORBACHEV'S TRANSITION PLAN: STRATEGY FOR DISASTER.** *Global Affairs*, Vol. 6, Spring 1991, pp. 1–21.

Examines Gorbachev's transition plan adopted on Oct. 19, 1990. Concludes that the program will fail because shock therapy cannot revive a market that does not exist, and will only serve to undermine Gorbachev's legitimacy by further destabilizing an economy already in an acute state of crisis.

C273. Rummel, R.J. (Rudolph J.). 1932–. **LETHAL POLITICS: SOVIET GENOCIDE AND MASS MURDER SINCE 1917.** New Brunswick, NJ: Transaction Publishers, c1990, xvii, 268 pp., ill., 24 cm.

Includes bibliographical references (pp. 245–257) and indexes.

C274. Sakwa, R. **GORBACHEV AND HIS REFORMS, 1985–1990.** New York, NY: Prentice-Hall, 1991, xiv, 459 pp., 24 cm.

Includes bibliographical references (pp. 421–439) and index.

C275. Salitan, L.P. **POLITICS AND NATIONALITY IN CONTEMPORARY SOVIET JEWISH EMIGRATION, 1968–1989.** New York, NY: St. Martin's Press, 1991.

Includes bibliographical references and index.

C276. Satter, D. **MOSCOW BELIEVES IN TEARS.** *National Review*, Vol. 43, Apr. 29, 1991, pp. 30–34.

The Soviet Union was permeated by an ideology which, although absurd, created its own peculiar form of social consensus. Soviet citizens were provided with a minimum level of security and, in return, denied certain basic rights....If they are now given rights and deprived of security, how will they react?

C277. Schoenfeld, G. **THE SOVIET UNION: A STORM RISING.** *Atlantic Monthly*, Vol. 266, Dec. 1990, pp. 44,46,50–52,54.

Reports on the problems the Soviet Union has in handling radioactive material, lack of safety procedures at nuclear power plants, and the level of radioactive contamination throughout country.

C278. Schultz, S.S. and Rafferty, M.P. **SOVIET HEALTH CARE AND PERESTROIKA.** *American Journal for Public Health*, Vol. 80, Feb. 1990, pp. 193–197.

This report briefly describes the current state of Soviet health and medical care, Gorbachev's plans for reform, and the prospects for success. In recent years the Soviet Union has experienced a rising infant mortality rate and declining life expectancy. The health care system has been increasingly criticized for its uncaring providers, low quality of care, and unequal access. The proposed measures will increase by 50 percent the state's contribution to health care financing, encourage private medicine on a small scale, and begin experimentation with capitation financing.

C279. Senn, A.E. **TOWARD LITHUANIAN INDEPENDENCE: ALGIRDAS BRAZAUSKAS AND THE CPL.** *Problems of Communism*, Vol. 39, Mar.–Apr. 1990, pp. 21–28.

December 1989, the decision of the Communist Party of Lithuania (CPL) to declare its independence from the Communist Party of the Soviet Union (CPSU) caught the attention of the world and gave Algirdas Brazauskas, the first secretary of the CPL, considerable international publicity....The Communist Party of Lithuania in fact took a giant step along the road that led eventually to its declaration of independence.

C280. Sheehy, A. **REVISED DRAFT ON THE UNION TREATY.** *Report on the U.S.S.R.*, Vol. 3, Mar. 22, 1991, pp. 1–4.

The revised draft of the Union treaty published on March 9 makes significant concessions to the republics but retains essential elements of a federal state, such as the primacy of federal laws in matters of federal competence. The representatives of only eight of the present fifteen Union republics have signaled their approval of the draft, and point of dispute between the republics remain. There are, moreover, grave doubts about the viability of the system being proposed. The draft must now be approved by the republican Supreme Soviets.

C281. Sheehy, A. **NATIONAL-STATE RELATIONS: MOVES TO DRAW UP NEW UNION TREATY.** *Report on the U.S.S.R.*, Vol. 2, July 6, 1990, pp. 14–17.

There can be no doubt that Gorbachev's failure to respond to the demand for a new Union treaty when it was first made has rendered the task of holding the Soviet Union together much more difficult today. Many, if not all, of the republics would probably have settled for less autonomy two years ago than they will demand now.

C282. Sheehy, A. **FACT SHEET ON QUESTIONS IN THE REFERENDUM OF MARCH 17 AND LATER REFERENDUMS.** *Report on the U.S.S.R.*, Vol. 3, Mar. 22, 1991, pp. 4–6.

Several republics, and also some oblasts and cities, are taking advantage of the all-Union referendum of March 17 on the preservation of the Soviet Union to hold their own polls on a variety of issues on the same day. Presents republic by republic information on these referendums.

C283. Sheehy, A. **THE ALL-UNION AND RSFSR REFERENDUMS OF MARCH 17.** *Report on the U.S.S.R.*, Vol. 3, Mar. 29, 1991, pp. 19–23.

The preliminary results of the all-Union referendum on the preservation of the Soviet Union and the RSFSR referendum on the institution of the Post of a popularly elected president show that both Mikhail Gorbachev and his political archrival Boris Yeltsin secured the mandate they sought from the electorate. Gorbachev has already said that this should speed up the signing of a new Union treaty, while Yeltsin has stated that he will stand for the RSFSR presidency.

C284. Sheehy, A. **THE STATE OF THE MULTINATIONAL UNION.** *Report on the U.S.S.R.*, Vol. 3, Jan. 1991, pp. 16–19.

In the past year, the Soviet Union has moved appreciably closer to breaking up. In the course of 1990, the three Baltic republics, Armenia, and Georgia either declared their independence or their intention of regaining independence after a transitional period, and all the other Union republics adopted declarations of sovereignty that challenged the authority of the center. President Mikhail Gorbachev has not wavered in his determination to hold the country together, but his indecisiveness and reluctance to revolve power to the republics except under pressure has only made his task more difficult.

C285. Sherr, J., 1951– . **SOVIET POWER, THE CONTINUING CHALLENGE.** New York, NY: St. Martin's Press, 1991, xxxiii, 283 pp., 23 cm.

Includes bibliographical references (pp. 272–278) and index.

C286. Shipler, D.K. **BETWEEN DICTATORSHIP AND ANARCHY.** *New Yorker*, Vol. 66, June 25, 1990, pp. 42–45,48–51,54–60,62–64,66–70.

Like Russia under the czars, the Soviet Union under the Communist Party had never codified the allocation of political powers....Now Gorbachev is trying to transfer political authority from the Party to the government - a delicate exercise.

C287. Simon, G. **NATIONALISM AND POLICY TOWARD THE NATIONALITIES IN THE SOVIET UNION: FROM TOTALITARIAN DICTATORSHIP TO POST-STALINIST SOCIETY.** Translated by K. Forster and O. Forster. Boulder, CO: Westview Press, 1991, xvii, 483 pp., 23 cm.

Rev. and updated translation of: Nationalismus und Nationalitatenpolitik in der Sowjetunion.

Includes bibliographical references (pp. 423–456) and index.

C288. Smart, C. **GORBACHEV'S LENIN: THE MYTH IN SERVICE TO PERESTROIKA.** *Studies in Comparative Communism*, Vol. 23, Spring 1990, pp. 5–21.

Argues that Gorbachev calls up two visions of Lenin in support of perestroika, the first is the revolutionary Lenin just off the train from Finland and ready to remold - almost single-handedly - Russia's government, people and culture....The other is the kinder, gentler Lenin of the later years, the pragmatic Lenin who called for calm, rational problem-solving. Concludes that, although Gorbachev uses the Lenin myth, as did his predecessors, to reinforce his authority and support his programs, the kind of Lenin he calls differs markedly from previous Soviet leaders.

C289. Smith, H. **THE NEW RUSSIANS.** New York, NY: Random House, 1990, xxxi, 621 pp., 24 cm.

Includes bibliographical references (pp. 575–580) and index.

C290. Smolowe, J. **AND NOW, DIVORCE?** *Times*, Vol. 135, Jan. 22, 1990, pp. 30–34.

As Lithuanians demand independence, Mikhail Gorbachev contemplates an empire endangered by the flames of secession. Briefly outlines the background of the unrest in the Soviet Union's non-Russian republics.

C291. Sobhani, S.C. **AZERBAIJAN: A PEOPLE IN SEARCH OF INDEPENDENCE.** *Global Affairs*, Vol. 6, Winter 1991, pp. 40–53.

Like the other republics within the Soviet Union, Azerbaijan's independence is not likely to be easy to achieve nor is its triumph inevitable, concludes the author after a visit to Azerbaijan.

C292. Socor, V. **MOLDAVIANS REJECT UNION TREATY.** *Report on the U.S.S.R.*, Vol. 3, Jan. 11, 1991, pp. 12–14.

The Moldavian Grand National Assembly and its resolutions not only underscore the political and ethnic polarization in the republic but also appear to presage a realignment of political forces - affecting, in particular, the position of the Moldavian Communist Party. Under its new, reformist, and pro-Gorbachev leadership, the Party has sought to attune itself to the basic interests and values of the Moldavian majority, alienating in the process much of the Party's disproportionately high Russian membership. Moldavian demands have, however, seemed recently to outrun the Party's capacity to adapt.

C293. Socor, V. **THE MOLDAVIAN COMMUNISTS: FROM RULING TO OPPOSITION PARTY.** *Report on the U.S.S.R.*, Vol. 3, Apr. 5, 1991, pp. 15–21.

The moldavian Communist Party's attempt to introduce perestroika in Moldavia has not prevented it from losing power to the national democratic forces. Split along ideological and ethnic lines, the Party has also experienced substantial losses of membership.

C294. Socor, V. **MOLDAVIA RESISTS PRESSURE AND BOYCOTTS UNION REFERENDUM.** *Report on the U.S.S.R.*, Vol. 3, Mar. 29, 1991, pp. 9–14.

The Moldavian parliament voted on February 19 to boycott the all-Union referendum. The growing conservative trend in Moscow added to Moldavia's reasons for seeking what the republican leaders now call "independence" from the center....Moscow exerted heavy pressure on Moldavia by means of hostile media coverage, the dispatch of additional military units, and the threat of legal proceedings against the republic, but these tactics appear to have backfired, stiffening Kishinev's resolve to pursue its chosen course.

C295. Solchanyk, R. **UKRAINIAN-JEWISH RELATIONS: AN INTERVIEW WITH OLEKSANDR BURAKOVS'KYI.** *Report on the U.S.S.R.* Vol. 3, Jan. 18, 1991, pp. 13–17.

Oleksandr Burakovs'kyi, a writer and scientist, is cochairman of the Shalom Aleichem Jewish Cultural and Educational Society in Kiev, which was established at the Ukrainian Writers' Union and publishes the bulletin Einikait. Burakovs'kyi discusses problems with Ukraine-Jewish relations, anti-semitism, and other issues.

C296. Solchanyk, R. **UKRAINIAN COMMUNIST PARTY ON THE OFFENSIVE.** *Report on the U.S.S.R.*, Vol. 3, Mar. 8, 1991, pp. 13–14.

Profiles the leadership of the Communist party of the Ukraine and discusses the role of the party with regard to recent reforms.

C297. **SOLDIERS AND THE SOVIET STATE: CIVIL-MILITARY RELATIONS FROM BREZHNEV TO GORBACHEV.** Edited by T.J. Colton and T. Gustafson. Princeton, NJ: Princeton University Press, c1990, xiii, 370 pp., 25 cm.

A research study of the Center for Strategic and International Studies. Includes bibliographical references and index.

C298. Solomon, P.H., Jr. **THE U.S.S.R. SUPREME COURT: HISTORY, ROLE, AND FUTURE PROSPECTS.** *American Journal of Comparitive Law*, Vol. 38, Winter 1990, pp. 127–142.

Since its founding in 1924 the U.S.S.R. Supreme Court has experienced radical changes in its character....With the launching in the late 1980s of M.S. Gorbachev's program of reform, leading Soviet jurists called for the revival of the Court's constitutional role.

C299. Solomon, B. **BUSH SUCCEEDS IN HUSHING LITHUANIA....AN ISSUE THAT CAN DO HIM NO GOOD.** *National Journal*, Vol. 22, May 12, 1990, pp. 1176–1177.

Lithuania's sinuous quest for liberty carries implications for Gorbachev's effort to refashion the Soviet Union and thus has meaning for the rest of the world. For Bush, it creates a dangerous dilemma: how to pursue his pragmatic judgment that what happens to Gorbachev mattes more than what happens to Lithuania while sidestepping the political danger of alienating wary conservatives or giving Democrats a political opening.

C300. Soros, G. **UNDERWRITING DEMOCRACY.** New York, NY: Free Press, c1991.

C301. Sovetnikov, S. **DEPUTY ASSESSES WORK OF ESTONIAN SUPREME SOVIET.** JPRS Report (Soviet Union: Political Affairs), Sept. 26, 1990, pp. 19–22.

Translation of an article by the chairman of the Estonian Republic Supreme Soviet's International Relations Commission, originally appearing in the Tallinn newspaper Sovetskaya Estonia of July 27, 1990, p. 2.

C302. **THE SOVIET DISUNION.** *Reason*, Vol. 23, July 1991, pp. 20–43.

Contents - Searching the Soviet soul, by C. Young. Privileged privatization, P.C. Roberts. An island of capitalism?, by P. Walker. Coping with collapse, by A. Garfinkle. Yeltsin's chess game, by L. Aron. The new opposition, by W.D. Eggers.

C303. **THE SOVIET EMPIRE: THE CHALLENGE OF NATIONAL AND DEMOCRATIC MOVEMENTS.** Edited by U. Ra'anan. Lexington, MA: Lexington Books, c1990, xvi, 254 pp., 24 cm.

Includes bibliographical references and index.

C304. **THE SOVIET MULTINATIONAL STATE: READINGS AND DOCUMENTS.** Edited by Martha B. Olcott with Lubomyr Hajda and Anthony Olcott, Armonk, NY.: M.E. Sharpe, c1990, xii, 605 pp., map, 24 cm.

C305. **SOVIET NATIONAL SECURITY POLICY UNDER PERESTROIKA.** Edited by G.E. Hudson, Boston, MA: Unwin Hyman, 1990, xv, 343 pp., 24 cm.

Book began as a Mershon Center faculty seminar at Ohio State University between Dec. 1986 and Oct. 1987. Includes bibliographical and index. Mershon Center series on international security and foreign policy, v. 4.

C306. **SOVIET NATIONALITIES PROBLEMS.** Edited by I.A. Bremmer and N.M. Naimark, Stanford, CA: Stanford University, 1990, p. cm.

Includes bibliographical references.

C307. **SOVIET NATIONALITY POLICIES: RULING ETHNIC GROUPS IN THE U.S.S.R.** Edited by H.R. Huttenbach. London, New York, NY: Mansell, 1990, p. cm.

Nationalities papers. Monograph series "Studies in issues", No. 6.

C308. **THE SOVIET NATIONALITY QUESTION: THE CRISIS IN CONTEXT.** Edited by R. Denber. Boulder, CO: Westview Press, 1990.

Includes index.

C309. **SOVIET PRESS COVERAGE OF THE GULF WAR.** JPRS Report (Soviet Union), Mar. 18, 1991, whole issue (31 pp.)

Translations of 33 articles originally appearing in various Soviet publications from late January through February 1991.

C310. **THE SOVIET SOBRANIE OF LAWS: PROBLEMS OF CODIFICATION AND NON-PUBLICATION.** R.M. Buxbaum and K. Hendley, eds. Berkeley, CA: International and Area Studies, University of California at Berkeley, c1991. Research Series, No. 78.

Papers presented at the Conference on the Codification of Soviet Law, held on Aug. 3–5 at Berkeley, CA, sponsored by the International and Area Studies, University of California at Berkeley.

Includes bibliographical references.

C311. **SOVIET UNION.**
Treaty between the United States of America and the Union of Soviet Socialist Republics on the Limitation of Underground Nuclear Tests and the Treaty between the United States and the Union of Soviet Socialist Republics on Underground Nuclear Explosions for Peaceful Purposes: texts of treaties and protocols. Washington, DC: U.S. Arms Control and Disarmament Agency, 1990, 99 pp., 23 cm.

C312. **THE SOVIET UNION, 1990.** *Current History*, Vol. 89, Oct. 1990, whole issue (pp. 305–352).

Contents - Soviet–Americans relations: the Cold War ends, by L.T. Caldwell. Soviet politics: breakdown or renewal?, by L.T. Lih. Soviet energy runs out of gas, by M.I. Goldman. Confusion in Soviet economic reform, by J.R. McKinney. The European republics of the Soviet Union, by S.L. Burg. Nationalist movements in Soviet Asia, by S.T. Hunger. Soviet agriculture under Perestroika, by K.M. Brooks.

C313. **SOVIET UNION, A COUNTRY STUDY.** Federal Research Division, Library of Congress. Edited by R.E. Zickel. Washington, DC: The Division. For sale by the Supt. of Docs., U.S. G.P.O., 1991.

Research completed May 1989. Supersedes the 1971 edition of Area Handbook for the Soviet Union written by E.K. Keefe, et al.

Includes bibliographical references and index.

C314. **SOVIET UNION: FIVE YEARS OF PERESTROIKA.** *World Focus*, Vol. 11, Apr. 1990, pp. 3–28.

Contents - Political, economic upheaval, by D. Kaushik. New thinking in international affairs, by R. Khan. Disturbing economic trend, by Jayashekar. Baltic republics in revolt, by S. Chakravartty. Relations with East Europe, by A. Gupta.

C315. **SOVIET UNION (MICROFORM): SPECIAL STUDIES, 1985–1988.** Supplement. Frederick, MD: University Publications of America, c1989. Microfilm reels. The Special Studies series.

Accompanied by printed reel guide compiled by N. Dobrosky.

C316. **THE SOVIET UNION, 1988–1989. PERESTROIKA IN CRISIS?** Edited by the Federal Institute for Soviet and International Studies, Boulder, CO: Westview Press, 1990, xv, 410 pp., 23 cm.

Translation of: Sowjetunion, 1988–1989. Includes bibliographical references and index.

C317. Sproule, A. **MIKHAIL GORBACHEV: REVOLUTIONARY FOR DEMOCRACY.** Milwaukee, WI: Gareth Stevens Children's Books, 1991, 68 pp., ill. (some col.), 22 cm.

Includes bibliographical references and index.

An account of Mr. Gorbachev's role in the Soviet Union at the present time, as events unfold which portend a much freer way of life for the Russian people.

C318. **THE STALIN REVOLUTION: FOUNDATIONS OF THE TOTALITARIAN ERA.** Lexington, MA: D.C. Heath, c1990, x, 269 pp., ill., 21 cm.
Includes bibliographical references (pp. 264–269).

C319. Starua, G. **IN THE U.S.S.R. SUPREME SOVIET: DEFENSE, STATE SECURITY COMMITTEE VIEWED.** JPRS Report (Soviet Union: World Economy and International Relations), June 19, 1990, pp. 52–58.
Translation of an article by the sector chief of the Soviet Academy of Sciences World Economics and International Relations Institute, originally appearing in the magazine Mirovaya Ekonomika i Mezhdunarodnyee Otnosheniya, Jan. 1990, pp. 79–85.

C320. Stebelsky, I. **RESTRUCTURING SOVIET AGRICULTURE: TOWARDS A SPATIAL DIMENSION.** *Soviet Geography*, Vol. 31, Sept. 1990, pp. 500–508.
Examines recent legislation to reform Soviet agriculture. Collective, family, and individual contracting (and in some areas family farming on isolated farmsteads, or khutors) are altering the way collective and state farms are organized. Since provisions of the new legislation grant local soviets considerable authority in decisions on land tenure issues, the paper investigates how regional preferences and traditions in agriculture may reshape the rural landscape into one of greater diversity and increased spatial differentiation.

C321. Steffen, L. **CASTING THE FIRST STONE.** *Christianity and Crisis*, Vol. 50, Feb. 5, 1990, pp. 11–18.
Argues that capital punishment is still a moral problem. Includes articles, Churches and capital punishment, by J. Gittings and Death penalty debates: U.S./U.S.S.R. by A. Henze.

C322. Stein, G. **A PORTRAIT OF ALEKSANDR NEVZOROV.** *Report on the U.S.S.R.*, Vol. 3, Mar. 8, 1991, pp. 8–9.
Profiles investigative reporter Nevzorov and discusses his relationship with the Soviet authorities.

C323. Sternthal, S. and Bernstein, J. **TAKING THEIR OWN PLACE ON THE MAP.** *Insight (Washington Times)*, Vol. 6, Feb. 26, 1990, pp. 8–19.
The nations and peoples forcibly incorporated into the Soviet are finding their voice, thanks to glasnost, and heralding the breakup of the monolithic communist state.

C324. Stewart, G. 1949–. **THE SOVIET UNION.** New York, NY: Crestwood House, Toronto: Collier Macmillan Canada, c1990, 48 pp., ill. (chiefly col.), 23 cm. Places in the news.
Includes index. Examines the Soviet Union's changing political scene, status as a superpower, and relationship with the United States.

C325. Surovell, J. **LIGACHEV AND SOVIET POLITICS.** *Soviet Studies*, Vol. 43, No. 2, 1991, pp. 355–374.

Examines Ligachev's positions as culled from speeches, interviews, etc. on a number of issues, including new thinking in foreign policy; market mechanisms; political reform; agricultural reform; the nationalities question; and culture, history, and the media.

C326. Taylor, S.J. (Sally J.) **STALIN'S APOLOGIST: WALTER DURANTY, THE NEW YORK TIME'S MAN IN MOSCOW.** New York, NY: Oxford University Press, 1990, 404 pp. (14) pp of plates, ill., 25 cm.

Includes bibliographical references (pp. 391–397).

C327. Teague, E. **BORIS YELTSIN INTRODUCES HIS BRAIN TRUST.** *Report on the U.S.S.R.*, Vol. 3, Apr. 12, 1991, pp. 14–19.

Boris Yeltsin has appointed a twenty-two member brain trust, composed almost exclusively of prominent intellectuals. The creation of the new body seems to be partly an exercise in image-building on Yeltsin's part, but the high proportion of well-known reformers in it underlines the fact that there has, in recent months, been a significant shift in the support of the liberal intelligentsia away from Mikhail Gorbachev and towards Yeltsin.

C328. Teague, E. **AIRBRUSHING IN THESE DAYS OF GLASNOST.** *Report on the U.S.S.R.*, Vol. 2, Nov. 9, 1990, pp. 11–14.

Since the advent of glasnost, the Soviet Party press has been unearthing archive materials that demonstrate how Stalin had Trotsky and other rivals were airbrushed out of group photographs in which they appeared with Lenin. Even today, however, it seems that there is still work for the airbrushers to do.

C329. Teague, E. and Mann, D. **GORBACHEV'S DUAL ROLE.** *Problems of Communism*, Vol. 39, Jan.–Feb. 1990, pp. 1–14.

Faced by an intractable Communist Party apparatus, General Secretary Mikhail Gorbachev decided to breathe life into the Soviets as an alternative institution of government. The U.S.S.R. Supreme Soviet, of which Gorbachev was elected chairman, has begun to act like a genuine parliament instead of a rubber stamp for decisions of the CPSU Central Committee. However, Gorbachev has apparently felt constrained by the newly assertive legislature. At the February 1990 Central Committee plenum, he proposed the creation of a presidency with strong executive powers independent of the Supreme Court.

C330 Thaler, J. **CONFRONTING CRISES: THE NATURE OF CHANGE IN THE SOVIET UNION.** *Harvard International Review*, Vol. 12, Spring 1990, pp. 38–42.

Contends that the simplest explanation of the current reversal in the U.S.S.R., is that the Soviet Union is in the midst of an internal crisis, largely economic in nature. Struggling to stave off economic disaster, the government has focused all its attention on domestic policy. As never before, foreign policy considerations have taken a back seat to internal affairs. Further the lessons of Eastern Europe have not been lost on the Communist leadership.

C331. Theen, R.H.W. **ON THE PROSPECTS FOR DEMOCRACY IN THE U.S.S.R.** *World and I*, Vol. 6, Apr. 1991, pp. 545–561.

Perestroika may end in failure simply because it came too late, because too many problems were allowed to accumulate and fester under the apparently solid surface of the old Stalinist order.

C332. Thompson, L.M. **SOVIET STRAITJACKET PSYCHIATRY: NEW LEGISLATION TO END THE PSYCHIATRIC REIGN OF TERROR IN THE U.S.S.R.** *Syracuse Journal of International Law and Commerce*, Vol. 16, Spring 1990, pp. 271–291.

Briefly develop(s) the history of psychiatric abuse in the Soviet Union....Provide(s) a thorough analysis of the two legal procedures for psychiatric confinement, along with an analysis of legal reforms implemented under Gorbachev.

C333. Thornburgh, D. **THE RULE OF LAW IN THE SOVIET UNION: A NECESSARY FRAMEWORK FOR DEMOCRATIC REFORM.** Washington, Heritage Foundation, 1990, 6 pp. (Heritage Lectures, 271).

President Gorbachev's stated desire to create a "law-based state" - a Soviet Union founded on the rule of law....It is my view that the rule of law provides the only basis upon which such a government can eventuate from the upheaval under way in the Soviet Union and in Eastern Europe, argues the author.

C334. Thornburgh, R. **THE SOVIET UNION AND THE RULE OF LAW.** *Foreign Affairs*, Vol. 69, Spring 1990, pp. 13–26.

Attorney General of the United States examines the changes in the Soviet legal system.

C335. **THREE SOVIET SCENARIOS: YOU PICK.** *International Economy*, Vol. 5, Jan.–Feb. 1991, pp. 52–55.

The authors asked several Soviet experts to rate the scenario considered most likely over the next one to three years. Experts were allowed to briefly modify, or to outline another scenario. In addition, participants were asked to characterize Western policies appropriate to the scenario considered most likely. The participants include: Helmut Sonnenfeldt, Senator Bill Bradley, Paul H. Nitze, Peter Reddaway, Carl A. Linden, Heinrich Vogel, Horst Teltschik, Harald Malmgren.

C336. Timmermann, H. **THE DECLINE OF COMMUNISM AND ITS CONSEQUENCES FOR EAST-WEST RELATIONS: AN OVERVIEW.** *Issues and Studies*, Vol. 27, Jan. 1991, pp. 70–83.

Examines the main reasons for the decline and loss of authority of communism in the Soviet Union and Eastern Europe, including: the uncompetitiveness of the command economies; the crisis of political legitimacy; and the weakening of the Soviet communist party. Discusses the repercussions of these changes on the international scene and outlines the tasks now faced by western policy-makers.

C337. Tishkov, V.A. **AN ASSEMBLY OF NATIONS OR AN ALL-UNION PARLIAMENT?** *Journal of Soviet Nationalities*, Vol. 1, Spring 1990, pp. 101–127.

Soviet director of the U.S.S.R. Institute of Ethnography examines the ethnic group makeup of the new Soviet legislative institutions. He finds that the new bodies reflect both the full complexity of the ethnic situation that exists in the country and the insufficiently-thought-out and halfway political reform in the way that the higher legislative organ of the country was formed....Even if the most ideal organizational "recipes" are used, the multinational character of the Soviet citizens and the federal nature of the state structure, should and will define the contradictory nature of the federal parliament.

C338. Tolz, V. **THE U.S.S.R. IN 1989: A RECORD OF EVENTS.** Compiled by V. Tolz. Edited by M. Newton, foreword by V.G. Treml, Boulder, CO: Westview Press, 1990, x, 740 pp., 24 cm.

Published in cooperation Radio Free Europe/Radio Liberty - P. facing t.p., Includes indexes.

C339. Tolz, V. **RECENT DEVELOPMENTS IN THE SOVIET AND BALTIC MEDIA.** *Report on the U.S.S.R.*, Vol. 3, Apr. 5, 1991, pp. 10–14.

The central Soviet leadership is continuing the efforts it launched at the beginning of the year to reimpose political censorship on the Soviet media.

C340. Tolz, V. **SOVIET CENTRAL MEDIA COVERAGE OF EVENTS IN THE BALTIC REPUBLICS.** *Report on the U.S.S.R.*, Vol. 3, Feb. 1, 1991, pp. 6–9.

The massive campaign of disinformation about the situation in the Baltic republics, which the official Soviet media launched immediately after Lithuania declared its independence in early 1990, reached a new intensity following the recent violence in Vilnius. Reporting on Lithuania, Latvia, and Estonia, Central Television and TASS currently provide only the viewpoint of the forces in the region opposed to independence and ignore the opinions of the freely elected republican parliaments - this is particularly so in the case of Lithuania.

C341. Tolz, V. **THE U.S.S.R.'S EMERGING MULTIPARTY SYSTEM.** New York, Praeger, 1990, 123 pp. (Washington Papers No. 148).

Contents - Introduction. Chronology of development of unofficial movements. Activities of unofficial movements. Attitude of the authorities: constant changes. Challenges to the policy for the CPSU. Case studies: political groups in Moscow and Leningrad. Conclusion.

C342. Tolz, V. **ADOPTION OF THE PRESS LAW: A NEW SITUATION FOR THE SOVIET MEDIA?** *Report on the U.S.S.R.*, Vol. 2, July 6, 1990, pp. 9–11.

Contends that until such time as the existing publishing houses and electronic media are freed from CPSU and government control, private publishing houses are permitted, and paper is sold on the free market, only marginal changes in the situation of the media are likely.

C343. Tolz, V. **JOURNALIST REVEALS MATERIAL FROM KGB ARCHIVES.** *Report on the U.S.S.R.*, Vol. 3, Jan. 18, 1991, pp. 5–7.

Discusses information about Stalin published by Soviet legal journalist, Arkadii Vaksberg. Articles by investigative journalists and historians such as Vaksberg are making a major contribution to the elimination of "blank spots" in Soviet historiography. It can only be hoped that the number of such articles will increase with the adoption of an All-Union law on archives.

C344. **TOWARD INDEPENDENCE: THE BALTIC POPULAR MOVEMENTS.** Edited by J.A. Trapans. Boulder, CO: Westview Press, 1991, vii, 166 pp., 23 cm.

Published in cooperation with Radio Free Europe/Radio Liberty, Inc. This publication arises from a conference convoked by Radio Free Europe/Radio Liberty, Inc., in September 1989 - P. vii.

Includes bibliographical references.

C345. Trimble, J. **IS BORIS GOOD ENOUGH? YELTSIN'S TRUCE WITH GORBACHEV CANNOT HALT THE GREAT SOVIET SLIDE.** *U.S. News and World Report*, Vol. 110, May 20, 1991, pp. 32–34.

Contends that Yeltsin's fortunes are likely to take a turn for the worse, too. His assurance that sovereignty is coming for Russia does not impress a populace more concerned about where to find food than about distant prospects of greater independence. Moreover, as Yeltsin gains power, he is losing the enviable political position of being free to criticize the Kremlin without having to solve the nation's problems himself.

C346. Trimble, J. **RUNNING OUT OF TIME.** *U.S. News and World Report*, Vol. 108, Feb. 19, 1990, pp. 30–34.

Mikhail Gorbachev is stronger than ever politically, following a historic Communist Party meeting. But he is beset by enemies from left and right, and the people are more fed up than ever.

C347. Tsipko A. **UKRAINE, RUSSIA, AND THE NATIONAL QUESTION: AN INTERVIEW WITH ALEKSANDR TSIPKO.** *Report on the U.S.S.R.*, Vol. 2, Aug. 17, 1990, pp. 19–24.

Interviews the author of "The Sources of Stalinism," concerning the national question in the Soviet Union.

C348. Tsipko., A.S. **IS STALINISM REALLY DEAD?** Translated from the Russian By E.A. Tichina and S.V. Nikheev. San Francisco, CA: Harper, c1990, x, 278 pp., 25 cm.

Includes bibliographical references and index.

C349. Tucker, R.C. **STALIN IN POWER: THE REVOLUTION FROM ABOVE, 1928–1941.** New York, NY: Norton, c1990, xix, 707 pp., ill., 25 cm.

Includes bibliographical references (pp. 671–683) and index.

C350. Tutland, P. **FROM PERESTROIKA TO PARALYSIS: THE STALEMATE IN LENINGRAD.** *Report on the U.S.S.R.*, Vol. 3, Mar. 22, 1991, pp. 12–17.

During a recent trip to Leningrad, the author interviewed a number of the city's leading politicians and attended sittings of its Soviet. He concluded that the city is in the grip of a political and economic deadlock, with the Communist Party continuing to wield considerable influence in local enterprises.

C351. Unger, A.L. **THE TRAVAILS OF INTRA-PARTY DEMOCRACY IN THE SOVIET UNION: THE ELECTIONS TO THE 19TH CONFERENCE OF THE CPSU.** *Soviet Studies*, Vol. 43, No. 2, 1991, pp. 329–354.

Concludes that two features of the process of intra-party democratization are illuminated with particular clarity by the elections to the 19th

Conference. The first is the will and the capacity for authentic participation of the party rank and file. No one familiar with the rituals of pseudo-participation which have characterized party life for so long can fail to be impressed by the speed with which party members found their "voice."

C352. Urban, M.E. 1947–. **MORE POWER TO THE SOVIETS: THE DEMOCRATIC REVOLUTION IN THE U.S.S.R.** Aldershot, Hants, England: E. Elgar Pub., Brookfield, VT: Gower Pub. Co., c1990, x, 167, p. 23 cm.

Includes bibliographical references and index. The International library of studied in communism.

C353. **THE U.S.S.R. FIRST CONGRESS OF PEOPLE'S DEPUTIES: COMPLETE DOCUMENTS AND RECORDS.** Compiled and with an introduction by R.H.W. Theen. New York, NY: Paragon House, 1991.

First published or broadcast in Russian by Izvestiya, TASS, Pravda, or other Soviet media and was translated into English by the Foreign Broadcast Information Service. Translations were first published by the Foreign Broadcast Information Service as supplements to or political and social sections of the Soviet Union daily report. Includes indexes.

C354. Vaksberg, A. **STALIN'S PROSECUTOR: THE LIFE OF ANDREI VYSHINSKY.** Translated by J. Butler. New York, NY: Grove Weidenfeld, 1991.

Translated from the Russian. Includes index.

C355. Vaksberg, A. **THE SOVIET MAFIA.** Translated from the Russian by J. Roberts and E. Roberts. New York, NY: St. Martin's Press, 1991.

Includes index.

C356. Valentey, A. **1989–1990 DRUG USE STATISTICS COMPARED: TRAFFICKING INCREASE NOTED.** JPRS Report (Narcotics), Feb. 5, 1991, pp. 26–29.

Translation of an article originally appearing in the Soviet magazine Ekonomika I Zhizn, Dec. 1990, 17 pp.

C357. Vanden Heuvel, K. **PERESTROIKA IS RETURNING WOMEN TO "TRADITIONAL ROLES."** Washington Post, May 20, 1990, B5.

Contends that perhaps the only significant benefit Gorbachev's reforms have brought women is the freedom to organize, to address inequalities, "to let steam off."

C358. Vizulis, I.J. 1918–. **THE MOLOTOV-RIBBENTROP PACT OF 1939: THE BALTIC CASE.** New York: Praeger, 1990, vi, 176 pp., maps, 24 cm.

Includes bibliographical references.

C359. Walker, M. 1947–. **SOVIET UNION.** New York, NY: Perennial Library, 1990, c1989, 352 pp., ill., maps, 21 cm.

Includes bibliographical references (pp. 346–348) and index.

C360. Warner, G. **THE INVISIBLE THREADS: INDEPENDENT SOVIETS WORKING FOR GLOBAL AWARENESS AND SOCIAL**

TRANSFORMATION. Washington, DC: Seven Locks Press, c1991, xi, 249 pp., 23 cm.

Includes index.

C361. Watt. D.C. **WHO PLOTTED AGAINST WHOM? STALIN'S PURGE OF THE SOVIET HIGH COMMAND REVISITED.** *Journal of Soviet Military Studies*, Vol. 3, Mar. 1990, pp. 46–65.

The savagery and speed of the operation surprised even the most hardened diplomatic and other observers of the Soviet scheme. Almost immediately there was speculation; had the generals been "framed," and if so, by whom? Or were they perhaps actually plotting Stalin's overthrow?

C362. Wcislo, F.W. 1951–. **REFORMING RURAL RUSSIA: STATE, LOCAL SOCIETY, AND NATIONAL POLITICS, 1855–1914.** Princeton, NJ: Princeton University Press, c1990, xviii, 347, pp. 24 cm.

Includes bibliographical references (pp. 317–339) and index.

C363. Weeks, A.L. **GORBACHEV AND THE KGB.** *Global Affairs*, Vol. 5, Winter 1990, pp. 58–77.

Of the three pillars supporting the Soviet regime - the Communist Party, the army, and the police - the Gorbachev period has seen the upward movement of the third, the police, replacing the military in second-place importance. This article assesses the significance of the KGB's increased authority for Soviet domestic and foreign affairs.

C364. Weeks, A.L. **THE GORBACHEV PROFILE.** *Global Affairs*, Vol. 5, Summer–Fall 1990, pp. 47–59.

When and at what point does Mikhail Gorbachev's ambivalence, capriciousness, and resultant political weakness become a liability, possibly a dangerous one, for his country and the rest of the world? Now that he has accumulated augmented executive powers, the lurking danger exists that a fumbling, errant quasi-dictator is in a position to do much more harm than a leader such as the superannuated Leonid Brezhnev or Konstantin Chernenko.

C365. White, S. **DEMOCRATIZATION IN THE U.S.S.R.** *Soviet Studies*, Vol. 42, Jan. 1990, pp. 3–25.

Finds that the prospects for Soviet democratization are therefore open, changing and ambiguous. There is popular support for political reform - but not necessarily if it appears to lead to economic hardship. Leading reformers acknowledge that, even under the most favorable circumstances, there can be no short-term transformation of the society or even of the operation of its political system.

C366. White, S. 1945–. **GORBACHEV IN POWER.** Cambridge (England), New York, NY: Cambridge University Press, 1990, viii, 268 pp., 23 cm.

Includes bibliographical references (pp. 220–260) and index.

C367. Wilhelm, D. 1915–. **GLOBAL COMMUNICATIONS AND POLITICAL POWER.** New Brunswick, NJ: Transaction Publishers, c1990, xiv, 172 pp., 24 cm.

Includes bibliographical references (pp. 155–166) and index.

C368. Wishnevsky, J. **UNLIKELY SOURCES DEPICT LIFE AT THE TOP.** *Report on the U.S.S.R.*, Vol. 3, Feb. 1, 1991, pp. 30–33.

In the short period of relative press freedom that Mikhail Gorbachev's policy of glasnost' brought to the Soviet media, light was shed on what had until then been a closely guarded secret - the personal lives and activities of the Soviet leaders. The process began with the publication of historical materials - recollections of leaders of the Stalin, Khrushchev and Brezhnev eras, but it was not long before glasnost' reached the lives and careers of the current rulers, Gorbachev himself included.

C369 Wishnevsky, J. **THE PURGE OF "TSN": A BAN ON INFORMATION.** *Report on the U.S.S.R.*, Vol. 3, Apr. 5, 1991, pp. 4–9.

The chairman of the All-Union State Television and Radio Company, Leonid Kravchenko, has suspended four people responsible for production of the non-conformist news service "TSN." Modeled on the American pattern of new presentation, "TSN" has latterly been the only source of objective information on Central Television, a fact that made it markedly different from other Soviet television newscases.

C370. Wishnevsky, J. **TWO RSFSR CONGRESSES: A DIARCHY?** *Report on the U.S.S.R.*, Vol. 2, July 6, 1990, pp. 1–3.

Considers Gorbachev's position regarding the Communist party and his likely support from a Russian Communist party.

C371. Wolf, C., Jr. et al. **GORBACHEV'S ALLOCATIVE CHOICES: CONSTRAINTS, DILEMMAS, AND POLICY DIRECTIONS.** Santa Monica, CA: Rand Corporation, 1990, xiii, 36 pp., ill., 23 cm.

Prepared for the Under Secretary of Defense for Policy, September 1990, R-3891-USDP, Rand library collection - Cover. Includes bibliographical references.

C372. **WORK OF U.S.S.R. DEPUTIES, U.S. CONGRESSMEN COMPARED.** JPRS Report (Soviet Union: Political Affairs), Mar. 22, 1990, pp. 1–6.

Translation of two related articles from the Soviet magazine Soyuz of Jan. 29–Feb. 4, 1990, pp. 12–13. The first, by M. Abullayev, describes the problems and privileges of members of the new Congress of People's Deputies; the second, by New York-based Izvestia correspondent A. Shalnev, explains the duties and activities of Members of the United States Congress.

C373. **WORLD AGRICULTURE SITUATION AND OUTLOOK REPORT, SPECIAL ISSUE: FORCES FOR CHANGE IN THE 1990'S.** Washington, U.S. Dept. of Agriculture, Economic Research, 1990, 76 pp. WAS-59, June 1990.

Partial contents - Dynamics of trade negotiations, by S.L. Magiera and M. Johnson. EC 1992: economic integration and world trade effects, by W. Gardiner, S. Neff, and D. Kelch. The safe food issue: new nontariff barriers? by T. Raney and D. Kelch. Economic restructuring in the U.S.S.R. and its potential impact on agricultural trade, by E.C. Cook. China's agriculture and trade: development and prospects, by F.C. Tuan. The changing structure of Japanese agricultural trade, by W. Coyle. Developing countries: changing closed systems to open ones, by D.W. Skully and T.L. Vollrath. Currency convertibility in Eastern Europe and the U.S.S.R.: issues, effects, and prospects, by F. Urban.

C374. Worrall, N. **REPUBLIC OF MOLDAVIA MOVES AWAY FROM MOSCOW.** Christian Science Monitor, May 29, 1990, 4 pp.

Discusses recent political events in Moldavia. Moldavia's official language is now Romanian in its Latin script; its flags and symbols have been changed; and plans are afoot to take over the Communist Party's numerous lavish buildings for more social uses, such as schools and hospitals.

C375. Yasmann, V. **MASTERING AN IDENTITY CRISIS.** *Report on the U.S.S.R.*, Vol. 3, Jan. 4, 1991, pp. 7–10.

Rather than fading into the background, however, as the CPSU was forced to do, the state security service assumed more and more of the functions of the disintegrating Party and government bodies. Among the tasks entrusted to the KGB were the rehabilitation of the victims of Stalinism and, at the end of the year, overseeing the distribution of food donated by Western countries.

C376. Yasmann, V. **CAN GLASNOST' BE REVERSED?** *Report on the U.S.S.R.*, Vol. 3, Feb, 1, 1991, pp. 26–29.

Did the Soviet president seriously think he could take away the population's newly gained freedom of self-expression? The answer is "No," but Gorbachev would certainly like to restrict that freedom, since its present level is preventing him from manipulating the mass media as he has in the past. Glasnost' has always been cut back at times of crisis.

C377. Yeltsin, Boris. **THE KREMLIN'S CREATURE COMFORTS.** *Washington Monthly*, Vol. 22, May 1990, pp. 24–29.

Member of the Soviet Union's People's Parliament, Boris Yeltsin, examines the force of Communist Party officials' privileges in Soviet politics. Asserts that I do believe that perestroika would not have ground to a halt, despite the tactical mistakes that have been made, if only Gorbachev had been able to get rid of his reluctance to deal with the question of the leadership's privileges - if he himself had renounced all those completely useless, though pleasant, customary prerequisites; if he had not built a new house for himself on the Lenin Hills and a new dacha outside Moscow.

C378. Yevtushenko, Y.A., 1933– . **FATAL HALF MEASURES: THE CULTURE OF DEMOCRACY IN THE SOVIET UNION.** Edited and translated by A.W. Bouis. Boston, MA: Little, Brown and Co., c1991, xiii, 357 pp., 25 cm.

Translated from the Russian. Includes index.

C379. Z, pseud. **TO THE STALIN MAUSOLEUM.** *Daedalus*, Vol. 119, Winter 1990, pp. 295–344.

Z reports on what the expectations of glasnost and perestroika have been, why the accomplishments fall so far short of the much-heralded intentions. With respect to democratization, economic restructuring, and growth, and the complex and diverse nationality issues, the historical record of seventy years of Sovietism permits only great skepticism about the possible outcomes of perestroika; the internal contradictions of the system are simply too overwhelming.

C380. Zaslavskaia, T.I. **THE SECOND SOCIALIST REVOLUTION: AN ALTERNATIVE SOVIET STRATEGY.** Foreword by T. Shanin, translated by

S.M. Davies with J. Warren. Bloomington, IN: Indiana University Press, c1990, xx, 241 pp., 25 cm.

Translated from Russian. Includes bibliographical references (pp. 228–231) and index.

C381. Zubritskaya, N. **DIFFICULTIES OF ANTINARCOTICS POLICE IN NOVOSIBIRSK REPORTED.** JPRS Report (Narcotics), Feb. 12, 1991, pp. 32–34.

Translation of an article originally appearing in the Siberian newspaper Sovetskaya Sibir, published in Novosibirsk, Sept. 29, 1990, 12 pp. This is where the most expensive drugs are found, which are brought here from Central Asia and Kazakhstan. Novosibirsk ranks among the top 10 cities in the Soviet Union in the sale of drugs.

D. CULTURE; HISTORY; EDUCATION

D001. Ambrose, E. **LANGUAGE AND CHURCH IN BELORUSSIA.** *Report on the U.S.S.R.*, Vol. 2, Feb. 9, 1990, pp. 18–24.

The Belorussians....have no single religious tradition that could be taken as a touchstone of national identity. Belorussia....lies where the Greek and Roman Christian traditions meet and, partially, overlap....Activists of "Adradzhen'ne" see this diversity as a virtue, but they are not without a certain apprehension about the danger to national identity.

D002. Andrews, W.G., 1930– . **THE LAND AND PEOPLE OF THE SOVIET UNION.** New York, NY: Harper Collins, c1991, xv, 304 pp., ill., 24 cm.

Includes bibliographical references (pp. 287–291). Discography, 292 pp. Filmography, pp. 292–293.

Introduces the history, geography, people, culture, government, and economy of the Soviet Union.

D003. Antic, O. **DEVELOPMENTS IN CHURCH LIFE.** *Report on the U.S.S.R.*, Vol. 3, Jan. 4, 1991, pp. 15–16.

The positive trends in the development of church life in the Soviet Union that began under perestroika with the government's new policies on state-church relations have gained momentum in 1990. The U.S.S.R. Supreme Soviet has shown a positive attitude towards the Churches by passing a new law on religion that, despite certain limitations, undoubtedly represents an important step towards new freedoms for the Churches in the Soviet Union.

D004. Antic, O. **STATISTICS ON RELIGION SPEAK A LANGUAGE OF THEIR OWN.** *Report on the U.S.S.R.*, Vol. 3, Jan. 11, 1991, pp. 8–9.

Since the introduction of Gorbachev's policy of glasnost, the form in which statistics on religion are presented has changed but not, however, as much as might have been expected. There are still significant discrepancies between data advanced by the representatives of the Church and those provided by the state authorities.

D005. Antic, O. **THE RUSSIAN ORTHODOX CHURCH MOVES TOWARDS COMING TO TERMS WITH ITS PAST.** *Report on the U.S.S.R.*, Vol. 3, Mar. 8, 1991, pp. 4–6.

The leadership of the Russian Orthodox Church has been repeatedly and severely criticized by certain well-known religious publicists for its apparent inability to adjust to the changes taking place in the moral climate of the Soviet Union and for its failure to assume a leading role in the current revival of interest in moral issues.

D006. Barber, J. 1944– and Harrison, M. **THE SOVIET HOME FRONT, 1941–1945: A SOCIAL AND ECONOMIC HISTORY OF THE U.S.S.R. IN WORLD WAR II.** London (England), New York, NY: Longman, 1991.
Includes bibliographical references and index.

D007. Beschloss, M.R. **THE CRISIS YEARS: KENNEDY AND KHRUSHCHEV, 1960–1963.** New York, NY: Edward Burlingame Books, c1991, xii, 816 pp., (32) pp. of plates, ill., 25 cm.
Includes bibliographical references (pp. 709–788) and index.

D008. Bleckmann, K. **MILITARY-PATRIOTIC EDUCATION IN THE SOVIET SCHOOL SYSTEM.** *World Outlook*, No. 11, Summer 1990, pp. 133–172.
This paper will explore the aims of military-patriotic education and their correlation with those of political-ideological indoctrination in Soviet schools; the implementation of these aims; the attitudes toward military-patriotic education among the youth, the party, and the military.

D009. Bodrick, B. 1947–. **FEARFUL MAJESTY: THE LIFE AND REIGN OF IVAN THE TERRIBLE.** New York, NY: Paragon House Publishers, 1990, c1987, p. cm.

D010. **BOLSHEVIK VISIONS: FIRST PHASE OF THE CULTURAL REVOLUTION IN SOVIET RUSSIA.** Edited by W.G. Rosenberg, Ann Arbor, MI: University of Michigan Press, c1990, 2 v., ill., 23 cm. An Arbor paperbacks, AA201-AA202.
Translations from the Russian. Reprint. Originally published: Ann Arbor, MI: Ardis, 1984. Includes bibliographical references.

D011. Bonner, E. **HEALTH CARE IN THE SOVIET UNION.** Freedom at issue, No. 117, Nov.–Dec. 1990, pp. 10–14.
Dr. Elena Bonner, wife of the late Andrei Sakharov, presents her observations of the health care system in the Soviet Union. She contents that the general state of poor health is tied directly to the lack of adequate housing which promotes the rapid spread of disease.

D012. Brands, H.W. **INSIDE THE COLD WAR: LOY HENDERSON AND THE RISE OF THE AMERICAN EMPIRE, 1918–1961.** New York, NY: Oxford University Press, 1991, xiv, 337 pp., 25 cm.
Includes bibliographical references (pp. 315–331) and index.

D013. Carnagham, E. and Bahry, D. **POLITICAL ATTITUDES AND THE GENDER GAP IN THE U.S.S.R..** *Comparative politics*, Vol. 22, July 1990, pp. 379–399.
Scholars of Soviet politics have shown that men and women in the U.S.S.R. differ substantially in the political roles they assume....Soviet women do appear to have a diminished sense of personal influence and interest in politics, to be less democratic, less tolerant, and more religious, to support spending for social programs, and not to support a higher defense budget or state control over the economy.

D014. Carrere d'Encausse, H. **THE RUSSIAN SYNDROME: ONE THOUSAND YEARS OF POLITICAL MURDER (POLITICAL MURDER IN RUSSIAN HISTORY).** Translated by C. Higgit. New York, NY: Holmes and Meier, 1991.
Translation of: Le Malheur Russe.

Includes bibliographical references and index.

D015. Carter, S.K. **THE POLITICAL AND SOCIAL THOUGH OF F.M. DOSTOEVSKY.** New York, NY: Garland, 1991.
Originally presented as the author's thesis.
Includes bibliographical references.

D016. Chernykh, E.N. **ANCIENT METALLURGY IN THE USSR: THE EARLY METAL AGE.** Translated by S. Wright. Cambridge (England), New York, NY: Cambridge University Press, 1991.
Translated from Russian.

D017. Chlenov, M.A. **THE LAST JOURNEY OF SOVIET JEWRY.** *Midstream,* Vol. 36, Jan. 1990, pp. 3–6.
Soviet Jewry is entering the final phase of its history. The Jewish population in the U.S.S.R. - estimated to be about 2 million - is diminishing steadily because of various demographic factors, such as low birth rate, a vestige of the Holocaust; a high urbanization index; assimilation - and emigration. The number of Jews who want to leave the country is growing. If the current situation continues,....close to half a million people, a quarter of all the Soviet Jews, will emigrate in the next five years, leaving about 1.8 million Jews in the Soviet Union.

D018. Clarke, J.C. III. **RUSSIA AND ITALY AGAINST HITLER: THE BOLSHEVIK-FASCIST RAPPROCHEMENT OF THE 1930s.** Foreword by C. Foust. New York, NY: Greenwood Press, 1991, xvii, 218 pp., ill., 25 cm.
Includes bibliographical references (pp. 201–207) and index.

D019. **CLASSIC ISSUES IN SOVIET FOREIGN POLICY: FROM LENIN TO BREZHNEV.** Edited by F.J. Fleron, Jr., E.P. Hoffman and R.F. Laird. New York, NY: Aldine de Gruyter, c1991.
Includes bibliographical references and index.

D020. Cohen, S.F. **RETHINKING THE SOVIET EXPERIENCE: POLITICS AND HISTORY SINCE 1917.** New York, NY: Oxford University Press, 1991.
Includes bibliographical references.

D021. Conroy, M.S. **ABUSE OF DRUGS OTHER THAN ALCOHOL AND TOBACCO IN THE SOVIET UNION.** *Soviet Studies,* Vol. 42, July 1990, pp. 447–480.
Reviews Soviet medical literature on substance abuse from 1917 to the present. Few realize that wide-scale abuse of drugs other than alcohol and tobacco initially appeared during World War I and the Civil War or 1918–1920 and remained a severe problem during the 1920s and early 1930s....Whereas Soviet medical literature candidly discussed narcotic abuse in the 1920s and early 1930s, from the late-1930s to the 1950s hard data on the number of abusers were scanty, as in fact they are today.

D022. Daborn, J. **RUSSIA: REVOLUTION AND COUNTER-REVOLUTION, 1917–1924.** Cambridge (England), New York, NY: Cambridge University Press, 1991, 134 pp., ill., map, 24 cm.
Includes index.

D023. **DEAR COMRADES: MENSHEVIK REPORTS ON THE BOLSHEVIK REVOLUTION AND THE CIVIL WAR.** Edited and translated by V.N. Brovkin. Stanford, CA: Hoover Institution Press, Stanford University, c1991, xxii, 275 pp., 24 cm. Hoover Press publication, 398.

Includes bibliographical references (pp. 247–252) and index.

D024. Desind, P. **JEWISH AND RUSSIAN REVOLUTIONARIES EXILED TO SIBERIA, 1901–1917.** Lewiston: Edwin Mellen Press, 1991. Jewish Studies, vol. 6.

"Part I. From the shtetl to Siberia" is a partial translation of Der durkhgegangener beg by I. Pressman. "Part II. From the general's house to Siberia", "part III. Notes", and "part IV. Historical background" are by P. Desind.

Includes bibliographical references.

D025. DeSomma, V.V. **UNION OF SOVIET SOCIALIST REPUBLICS.** New York, NY: Chelsea House Publishers, c1991.

Includes index.

Examines the history, geography and society of the Soviet Union.

D026. Duffy, C., 1936– . **RED STORM ON THE REICH: THE RUSSIANS MARCH ON GERMANY, 1945.** London (England), New York, NY: Routledge, 1991.

Includes bibliographical references and index.

D027. Duffy, C., 1936– . **RED STORM ON THE REICH: THE SOVIET MARCH ON GERMANY, 1945.** New York, NY: Atheneum: Maxwell Macmillan International, 1991, xi, 403 pp., maps, 24 cm.

Previously published, London (England), New York, NY: Routledge, 1991.

Includes bibliographical references (pp. 385–390) and index.

D028. Dukes, P. 1934–. **A HISTORY OF RUSSIA: MEDIEVAL, MODERN, CONTEMPORARY.** Durham, NC: Duke University Press, 1990, xii, 425 pp., maps, 22 cm.

Includes bibliographical references (pp. 396–415) and index.

D029. Eliason, L.R., 1936– . **PERESTROIKA OF THE RUSSIAN SOUL: RELIGIOUS RENAISSANCE IN THE SOVIET UNION.** Jefferson, NC: McFarland and Co., c1991, x, 150 pp., 23 cm.

Includes bibliographical references (pp. 141–145) and index.

D030. Farber, S. 1939–. **BEFORE STALINISM: THE RISE AND FALL OF SOVIET DEMOCRACY.** London, New York, NY: Verso, 1990, xiii, 288 pp., 24 cm.

Includes bibliographical references (pp. 259–276) and index.

D031. Fenin, A.I. 1866–1943. **COAL AND POLITICS IN LATE IMPERIAL RUSSIA: MEMOIRS OF A RUSSIAN MINING ENGINEER.** Translated by A. Fediaevsky. Edited by S.P. McCaffray. DeKalb, IL: Northern Illinois University Press, 1990, xxii, 228 pp., ill., 24 cm.

Translation of: Vospominaniia inzhenera. Includes bibliographical references and index.

D032. Figner, V., 1852–1925. **MEMOIRS OF A REVOLUTIONIST.** Authorized translation from the Russian. Introduction by R. Stites. DeKalb, IL: Northern Illinois University Press, 1991, xxii, 314 pp., ill., 23 cm.
Translation of: Zapechatlennyi trud.

D033. Gabiani, A.A. **DRUGS AMONG THE STUDENT YOUTH.** JPRS Report (Soviet Union: Sociological Studies), Jan. 10, 1991, pp. 22–27.
Translation of an article originally appearing in the Soviet magazine Sotsiologicheskiye Issledovaniya, Sept. 1990, pp. 84–91. Dr. Gabiani's research is based on a survey of over 5800 senior-grade students.

D034. **GENOA, RAPALLO, AND EUROPEAN RECONSTRUCTION IN 1922.** Edited by C. Fink, A. Frohn and J. Heideking. Washington, DC: German Historical Institute; Cambridge (England), New York, NY: Cambridge University Press, 1991.
Includes bibliographical references.

D035. Gifford, H. **INDOMITABLE PASTERNAK.** *New York Review of Books*, Vol. 37, May 31, 1990, pp. 26–31.
Reviews four works on Pasternak. Discusses his role as a Soviet writer.

D036. Gill, G.J. **THE ORIGINS OF THE STALINIST POLITICAL SYSTEM.** Cambridge, MA, New York, NY: Cambridge University Press, 1990, xv, 454 pp., 24 cm.
Includes bibliographical references (pp. 427–441) and index.

D037. Gitelamn, Z. **GLASNOST, PERESTROIKA AND ANTISEMITISM.** *Foreign Affairs*, Vol. 70, Spring 1991, pp. 141–159.
There are 1.45 million Jews in the Soviet Union. They enjoy more cultural and religious freedom than at anytime since 1948, but they also perceive themselves as more vulnerable than at any time since.

D038. Glantz, D.M. **THE ROLE OF INTELLIGENCE IN SOVIET MILITARY STRATEGY IN WORLD WAR II.** Novato, CA: Presidio, c1990, x, 262 pp., ill., maps, 24 cm.
Includes bibliographical references (pp. 227–245) and index.

D039. Gray, Francine du Plessix. **SOVIET WOMEN.** *New Yorker*, Vol. 66, Feb. 19, 1990, pp. 48–50,52,55,58,60–81.
Examines the status and role of women in Soviet society and reviews the impact of glasnost on their contemporary situation.

D040. Gurevich, D. **FROM LENIN TO LENNON.** San Diego, CA: Harcourt Brace Jovanovich, c1991.

D041. Gurov, A. **MVD OFFICIAL ON ORGANIZED CRIME IN THE U.S.S.R., U.S.** JPRS report (Soviet Union: Political Affairs), June 8, 1990, pp. 41–43.
Translation of an interview with the head of the MVD department for combatting organized crime, originally appearing in the Soviet magazine Pravitelstvennyy Vestnick of Apr. 1990, 9 pp.

D042. Headland, R., 1946– . **MESSAGES OF MURDER: A STUDY OF THE REPORTS OF THE EINSATZGRUPPEN OF THE SECURITY POLICE AND THE SECURITY SERVICE, 1941–1943.** Rutherford, NJ: Fairleigh Dickinson University Press; London (England): Associated University Presses, c1991.
Includes bibliographical references and index.

D043. Hilton, S.E., 1940– . **BRAZIL AND THE SOVIET CHALLENGE, 1917–1947.** Austin, TX: University of Texas Press, c1991, xvi, 287 pp., map, 27 cm.
Includes bibliographical references (pp. 261–271) and index.

D044. Hosking, G.A. **THE FIRST SOCIALIST SOCIETY: A HISTORY OF THE SOVIET UNION FROM WITHIN.** Cambridge, MA: Harvard University Press, 1990, 556 pp. (2) pp. of plates, ill., maps, 24 cm.
Includes bibliographical references (pp. 514–536) and index.

D045. **IMPERIAL RUSSIA: A SOURCE BOOK, 1700–1917.** Edited by B. Dmytryshyn. Fort Worth, TX: Holt, Rinerhart and Winston, c1990, xvii, 558 pp., ill., 24 cm.
Includes bibliographical references (pp. 546–558).

D046. James, W.M. III. **A POLITICAL HISTORY OF THE CIVIL WAR IN ANGOLA 1974–1990: THE UNITA FACTOR.** New Brunswick, NJ: Transaction Publishers, c1991.
Includes bibliographical references and index.

D047. Johnston, R.H., 1937– . **SOVIET FOREIGN POLICY, 1918–1945: A GUIDE TO RESEARCH AND RESEARCH MATERIALS.** Wilmington, DE: Scholarly Resources, 1991, xi, 236 pp., 23 cm.
Includes index.

D048. Karyagin, V. **VIEW FROM THE ELEVENTH FLOOR.** International Affairs (Moscow), No. 7, July 1990, pp. 81–94.
Soviet publication discusses protocol and diplomacy in the U.S.S.R. during the Khruschev period.

D049. Kavass, I.I. **GORBACHEV'S LAW: A BIBLIOGRAPHIC SURVEY OF ENGLISH WRITINGS ON SOVIET LEGAL DEVELOPMENTS, 1987–1990.** Buffalo, NY: W.S. Hein, 1991, xxv, 379 pp., 24 cm.

D050. Kennan, G.F. **COMMUNISM IN RUSSIAN HISTORY.** *Foreign Affairs*, Vol. 69, Winter 1990, pp. 168–186.
What is now emerging ont he territory traditionally known as Russia will not be - cannot be - the Russia of the tsars. Nor can it be the Russia of the communists. It can only be something essentially new, the contours of which are still, for us and for the Russians themselves, obscure. The tasks to be encompassed are immense.

D051. Keres, P., 1916– . **POWER CHESS: GREAT GRANDMASTER BATTLES FROM RUSSIA.** Edited by B. Hochberg. New York, NY: Times Books/Random House, c1991.
Collection of forty columns written by P. Keres for Chess Life Magazine from 1968–1975. Includes index.

D052. Khrushchev, N.S, 1894–1971. **KHRUSHCHEV REMEMBERS: THE GLASNOT TAPES.** Foreword by S. Talbott. Translated and edited by J.L. Schecter with V.V. Luchkov, Boston, MA: Little, Brown, 1990, xvi, 219 pp. (8) pp. of plates, ill., 24 cm.
Includes index.

D053. Kirchner, W. **RUSSIAN HISTORY.** New York, NY: Harper Perennial/Harper Collins Publishers, 1991.
7th ed. of: A History of Russia.
Includes bibliographical references and index.

D054. Koehler, H.W., 1886–1941. **OUR MAN IN THE CRIMEA: COMMANDER HUGO KOEHLER AND THE RUSSIAN CIVIL WAR.** Edited by P.J. Capelotti. Columbia, SC: University of South Carolina Press, c1991, xiv, 218 pp., ill., 25 cm.
Includes bibliographical references (pp. 213–216) and index.

D055. Kory, W. **GLASNOST AND SOVIET ANTI-SEMITISM.** New York, American Jewish Committee, 1991, 44 pp. (Working Papers on Contemporary Anti-semitism).
Indicates how anti-semitism has taken on new forms to fit changing political, economic, and social conditions.

D056. Kotkin, S. **STEELTOWN, USSR: SOVIET SOCIETY IN THE GORBACHEV ERA.** Berkeley, CA: University of California Press, c1991, xxx, 269 pp., ill., map, 24 cm.
A Centennial book. Includes index.

D057. Kowalski, R.I. **THE BOLSHEVIK PARTY IN CONFLICT: THE LEFT COMMUNIST OPPOSITION OF 1918.** Pittsburgh, PA: University of Pittsburgh Press, c1991, x, 244 pp., 23 cm. Pitt. series in Russian and East European Studies, No. 14.
Includes bibliographical references (pp. 228–236) and index.

D058. Krasnov, V. **RUSSIA BEYOND COMMUNISM: A CHRONICLE OF NATIONAL REBIRTH.** Boulder, CO: Westview press, 1991.

D059. Kuroda, H., 1927– . **DESTRUCTION OF THE REVOLUTION.** Translated by the Anti-Stalinism Study Group. Tokyo (Japan): Kaiho-sha. Sales Agent, Kobushi-Shobo, 1991. 129 pp., 21 cm.
Translation of: Kakumei no hakai.

D060. Laqueur, W. 1921–. **STALIN: THE GLASNOST REVELATIONS.** London: Unwin Hyman, 1990, ix, 382 pp., 25 cm.
Includes bibliographical references (pp. 333–367) and index.

D061. LeDonne, J.P., 1935– . **ABSOLUTISM AND RULING CLASS: THE FORMATION OF THE RUSSIAN POLITICAL ORDER, 1700–1825.** New York, NY: Oxford University Press, 1991.
Includes bibliographical references and index.

D062. Lee, T.V., Searle-White, J. **PRISONERS DILEMMA MEETS GLASNOST: A COMPARATIVE ADVANTAGE SOLUTION TO THE UNITED STATES PRISON CRISIS.** *Cornell International Law Journal,* Vol. 24, Winter 1991, pp. 25–56.

Where can we find a place with substantial space, expertise in running prisons, and a desperate need for U.S. dollars, a combination that would make it the perfect place to expand American prison capacity? The answer is obvious: the Soviet Union. A joint project, in which the U.S. Bureau of Prisons built and maintained new prison facilities in the U.S.S.R.: with the assistance of Soviet personnel, would alleviate domestic problems of both countries. Such an undertaking would also build on the emerging spirit of open-mindedness and superpower cooperation.

D063. Lewin, M., 1921– . **STALINISM AND THE SEEDS OF SOVIET REFORM: THE DEBATES OF THE 1960s.** London (England), Concord, MA: Pluto Press, 1991.

Reprint. Originally published: Political Undercurrents in Soviet Economic Debates. Princeton, NJ: Princeton University Press, 1974.

Includes bibliographical references and index.

D064. Lincoln, W.B. **THE GREAT REFORMS: AUTOCRACY, BUREAUCRACY, AND THE POLITICS OF CHANGE IN IMPERIAL RUSSIA.** DeKalb, IL: Northern Illinois University Press, 1990, xxi, 281 pp., 23 cm.

Includes bibliographical references (pp. 249–269) and index.

D065. Lourie, R., 1940– . **RUSSIA SPEAKS: AN ORAL HISTORY FROM THE REVOLUTION TO THE PRESENT.** New York, NY: E. Burlingame Books, c1991, 396 pp., 25 cm.

Includes index.

D066. Lucas, J.S. **WAR ON THE EASTERN FRONT 1941–1945: THE GERMAN SOLDIER IN RUSSIA.** London (England): Greenhill Books; California: Presidio Press, 1991.

Reprint. Originally published, New York, NY: Bonanza Books, c1979.

Includes bibliographical references and index.

D067. Lyons, E., 1898– . **ASSIGNMENT IN UTOPIA.** With a new introduction by E.F. Paul. New Brunswick, NJ: Transaction Publishers, 1991, xxilii, 632 pp., 24 cm.

Reprint. Originally published, New York, NY: Harcourt, Brace, c1937.

D068. Margvelashvili, J. **THE CLASSIC CUISINE OF SOVIET GEORGIA: HISTORY, TRADITIONS, AND RECIPES.** New York, NY: Prentice-Hall, 1991.

Includes index.

D069. Marks, S.G., 1958– . **ROAD TO POWER: THE TRANS-SIBERIAN RAILROAD AND THE COLONIZATION OF ASIAN RUSSIA, 1850–1917.** Ithaca, NY: Cornell University Press, 1991, xxi, 240 pp., ill., maps, 24 cm.

Includes bibliographical references (pp. 227–235) and index.

D070. Marples, D., Skrypnyk, O. **PATRIARCH MYSTYSLAV AND THE REVIVAL OF THE UKRAINIAN AUTOCEPHALOUS ORTHODOX CHURCH.** *Report on the U.S.S.R.*, Vol. 3, Jan. 11, 1991, pp. 10–12.

On October 20, 1990, Patriarch Mystyslav arrived in Kiev, some five months after he had been elected patriarch by the Sobor of the Ukrainian Autocephalous Orthodox Church. The visit to Ukraine of the ninety-two-year-old Church leader, a resident of the United States, culminated in his formal installation as patriarch on November 17–18. Ukraine is now in the confusing position of having two Orthodox Churches: the Autocephalous Church and the Ukrainian Autonomous Orthodox Church, which was previously subordinate to the Russian Orthodox Church.

D071. Maslov, N.N. **SHORT COURSE OF THE HISTORY OF THE ALL-RUSSIAN COMMUNIST PARTY (BOLSHEVIK) - AN ENCYCLOPEDIA OF STALIN'S PERSONALITY CULT.** *Soviet Review*, Vol. 31, Mar.–Apr. 1990, pp. 50–79.

The present article seeks to learn lessons from the history of the writing of the Short Course (Kratkii kurs istorii VKP(b)).

D072. **MASS CULTURE AND PERESTROIKA IN THE SOVIET UNION.** Edited by M. Siefert. New York, NY: Oxford University Press, 1991.

Includes bibliographical references.

D073. Mauer, M. **AMERICANS BEHIND BARS: A COMPARISON OF INTERNATIONAL RATES OF INCARCERATION.** Washington, Sentencing Project, 1991, 20 pp.

Compares and contrasts the rate of incarceration in the U.S. with those of South Africa and the Soviet Union. The United States now has the world's highest known rate of incarceration, with 426 prisoners per 100,000 population. South Africa is second in the world with a rate of 333 per 100,000, and the Soviet Union third with 268 per 100,000 population. Black males in the United States are incarcerated at a rate four times that of Black males in South Africa, 3,109 per 100,000 compared to 729 per 100,000.

D074. McClellan, W. **RUSSIA: A HISTORY OF THE SOVIET PERIOD.** Woodford McClellan. Englewood Cliffs, NJ: Prentice Hall, c1990, x, 371 pp., ill., 24 cm.

Includes bibliographical references and index.

D075. McDermott, K. **PETER THE GREAT.** New York, NY: Chelsea House, c1991, 109 pp., ill., 24 cm.

Includes bibliographical references (p. 108) and index.

A biography of the tsar who began the transformation of Russia into a modern state in the late seventeenth–early eighteenth centuries.

D076. McTernan, O. **RELIGION AND PERESTROIKA.** *Studies (An Irish Quarterly Review)*, Vol. 79, Spring 1990, pp. 18–26.

A significant shift in the Soviet leadership's attitude towards religion: Both Catholics and Communists are looking these days for something which will unite and not separate people....It is no secret that for the past seventy years the Soviet communist party actively pursued an anti-religious policy.

D077. Melancon, M. 1940–. **THE SOCIALIST REVOLUTIONARIES AND THE RUSSIAN ANTI-WAR MOVEMENT, 1914–1917.** Columbus, OH: Ohio State University Press, c1990, xii, 368 pp., ports, 24 cm.
Includes bibliographical references (pp. 337–356) and index.

D078. Merridale, C. 1959–. **MOSCOW POLITICS AND THE RISE OF STALIN: THE COMMUNIST PARTY IN THE CAPITAL, 1925–32.** New York, NY: St. Martin's Press, 1990, xv, 328 pp. (8) pp. of plates, ill., 23 cm.
Includes bibliographical references (pp. 306–315) and index.

D079. **MILITARY HISTORY SYMPOSIUM (U.S.) (12TH: 1986: UNITED STATES AIR FORCE ACADEMY).** Transformation in Russian and Soviet military history: proceedings of the Twelfth Military History Symposium, United States Air Force Academy, 1–3 October 1986. Edited by C.W. Reddel. Washington, DC: United States Air Force Academy, Office of Air Force History, United States Air force, 1990, xxii, 405 pp., ill., 23 cm.

D080. Moskoff, W. **THE BREAD OF AFFLICTION: THE FOOD SUPPLY IN THE U.S.S.R. DURING WORLD WAR II.** Cambridge (England), New York, NY: Cambridge University Press, 1990, xvi, 256 pp., ill., 24 cm.
Includes bibliographical references (pp. 240–247) and index.

D081. Munro, N. **THE QUICK AND THE DEAD: ELECTRONIC COMBAT AND MODERN WARFARE.** New York, NY: St. Martin's Press, 1991, xi, 324 pp., ill., 22 cm.

D082. Nahaylo, B. and Swoboda, V. **SOVIET DISUNION: A HISTORY OF THE NATIONALITIES PROBLEM IN THE U.S.S.R.** London: Hamish Hamilton, 1990, xvi, 432 pp. (8) pp. of plates, ill., maps, 24, cm.
Includes bibliographical references (pp. 412–417) and index.

D083. **THE NEW SOVIET JOURNALISM: THE BEST OF THE SOVIET WEEKLY OGONYOK.** Edited by V. Korotich. Edited and translated by C. Porter. Boston, MA: Beacon Press, c1990.
Translation from the Russian.

D084. Owen, T.C. **THE CORPORATION UNDER RUSSIAN LAW, 1800–1917: A STUDY IN TSARIST ECONOMIC POLICY.** Cambridge (England), New York, NY: Cambridge University Press, 1991, xviii, 234 pp., 24 cm.
Includes bibliographical references (pp. 220–227) and index.

D085. **PEASANT ECONOMY, CULTURE, AND POLITICS OF EUROPEAN RUSSIA, 1800–1921.** Edited by E. Kingston-Mann and T. Mixter, with the assistance of J.Burds. Princeton, NJ: Princeton University Press, c1991, xviii, 443 pp., ill., map, 24 cm.
Based on papers presented at an international conference held at the University of Massachusetts at Boston in Aug. 1986.
Includes bibliographical references and index.

D086. **PERESTROIKA: THE HISTORICAL PERSPECTIVE.** Edited by C. Merridale and C. Ward. London (England), New York, NY: Edward Arnold, 1991.

Result of the 3-year King's College Research Centre Project on Soviet History and Politics 1988–1991.

Includes bibliographical references and index.

D087. Petelin, B.Y. **ORGANIZED JUVENILE CRIME.** JPRS Report (Soviet Union: Sociological Studies), Jan. 10, 1991, pp. 27–32.

Translation of an article originally appearing in the Soviet magazine Sotsiologicheskiye Issledovaniya, Sept. 1990, pp. 92–98.

D088. Pipes, R. **THE RUSSIAN REVOLUTION.** New York, NY: Vintage Books, 1991.

Reprint. Originally published, New York, NY: Knopf, 1990. Includes index.

D089. Polmar, N. and Noot, J. **SUBMARINES OF THE RUSSIAN AND SOVIET NAVIES, 1718–1990.** Maps and submarine drawings prepared by W.J. Clipson. Annapolis, MD: Naval Institute Press, c1991, xv, 370 pp., ill., maps., 29 cm.

Includes bibliographical references (pp. 347–355) and indexes.

D090. Porter, T.E. **THE ZEMSTVO AND THE EMERGENCE OF CIVIL SOCIETY IN LATE IMPERIAL RUSSIA 1864–1917.** San Francisco, CA: Mellen Research University Press, 1991. Distinguished Dissertations Series, Vol. 18.

Based on the author's thesis (Ph.D.).

Includes bibliographical references and index.

D091. Rabinowitch, A. **PRELUDE TO REVOLUTION: THE PETROGRAD BOLSHEVIKS AND THE JULY 1917 UPRISING.** Bloomington, IN: Indiana University Press, 1991.

Includes bibliographical references and index.

D092. Rapoport, IA.L. **THE DOCTORS' PLOT 1953.** Cambridge, MA: Harvard University Press, 1991, viii, 280 pp., ports, 24 cm.

Translation of: Na ruezhe dvukh epokh. Includes index.

D093. Ratushinskaia, I. **IN THE BEGINNING.** Translated by A. Kojevnikov. New York, NY: Knopf, 1991, 317 pp., 25 cm.

Translated from Russian.

D094. Read, C. 1946–. **CULTURE AND POWER IN REVOLUTIONARY RUSSIA: THE INTELLIGENTSIA AND THE TRANSITION FROM TSARISM TO COMMUNISM.** Houndmills, Basingstoke, Hampshire: macmillan, 1990, xii, 266 pp., 23 cm.

Includes bibliographical references (pp 253–261) and index.

D095. Rettino, E. and Rettino, D.K., 1949– . **PSALTY IN THE SOVIET CIRCUS.** Designs and illustrations by D. Wehlacz. Dallas, TX: Word Pub., 1991.

Word kids! Separated from his family on a visit to the Soviet Union and taken to jail for minor violations, Psalty finds comfort in a remembered Bible verse.

D096. **REVOLUTION IN RUSSIA: REASSESSMENTS OF 1917.** Edited by E.R. Frankel, J. Frankel and B. Knei-Paz. Cambridge (England), New York, NY: Cambridge University Press, 1991.

Essays first presented in preliminary form at a conference held in Jerusalem in Jan. 1988 as a tribute to Israel Getzler. Includes index.

D097. Richards, S., 1950– . **EPICS OF EVERYDAY LIFE: ENCOUNTERS IN A CHANGING RUSSIA.** New York, NY: Viking, 1991, xiv, 366 pp., 24 cm.

D098. Riehn, R.K., 1928– . **1812: NAPOLEON'S RUSSIAN CAMPAIGN.** New York, NY: Wiley, 1991.

Includes bibliographical references and index.

D099. Riordan, J. **PLAYING TO NEW RULES: SOVIET SPORT AND PERESTROIKA.** *Soviet Studies*, Vol. 42, Jan. 1990, pp. 133–145.

Today the inheritors of the sports system evolved during the Stalin, Khruschev and Brezhnev years find themselves in a quandary: to what extent should they break with the past? How sharply and through what new forms should change be brought about? In the field of culture, and specifically of physical culture, how should they dismantle the various by now well entrenched fetished institutions and values?

D100. Rittersporn, G.T., 1948– . **STALINIST SIMPLIFICATIONS AND SOVIET COMPLICATIONS: SOCIAL TENSIONS AND POLITICAL CONFLICTS IN THE USSR, 1933–1953.** Chur, New York, NY: Harwood Academic Publishers, c1991.

Translation of: Simplifications Staliniennes et complications sovietiques.
Includes bibliographical references and index.

D101. Roberts, I.W., 1927– . **NICHOLAS I AND THE RUSSIAN INTERVENTION IN HUNGARY.** New York, NY: St. Martin's Press, 1991, xi, 301 pp., ill., maps, 23 cm.

Includes bibliographical references (pp. 277–285) and index.

D102. Roi, Y. **THE HISTORICAL LINK BETWEEN SOVIET DOMESTIC DEVELOPMENTS AND JEWISH EMIGRATION.** Jerusalem Quarterly, No. 53, Winter 1990, pp. 137–144.

The factors in the Soviet domestic scene that the author would like to discuss are the following: (1) regime policy and general socio-political trends: (2) the nationalities questions; (3) the Soviet Jewish situation.

D103. Ross, S. **THE U.S.S.R. UNDER STALIN.** New York, NY: Bookwright Press, 1991.

Witness history.
Includes bibliographical references and index.
Examines the social and economic changes in the Soviet Union during Stalin's regime and discusses the nation's devastation by World War II.

D104. Rummel, R.J. (Rudolph J.). 1932–. **LETHAL POLITICS: SOVIET GENOCIDE AND MASS MURDER SINCE 1917.** New Brunswick, NJ: Transaction Publishers, c1990, xvii, 268 pp., ill., 24 cm.

Includes bibliographical references (pp. 245–257) and indexes.

D105. **RUSSIA IN THE ERA OF NEP: EXPLORATIONS IN SOVIET SOCIETY AND CULTURE.** Edited by S. Fitzpatrick, A. Rabinowitch and R. Stites. Bloomington, IN: Indiana University Press, c1991.
Includes bibliographical references and index.

D106. Salzman, N.V. **REFORM AND REVOLUTION: THE LIFE AND TIMES OF RAYMOND ROBINS.** Kent, OH: Kent State University Press, c1991.
Includes bibliographical references and index.

D107. Saves, S. and Vandelin, J. **PHOTOS OF RUSSIA TODAY.** New York, NY: Pantheon Books, 1991.
Translation of: Niin Suuri on Maa.

D108. Schneier, W. **TIME BOMB.** *Nation*, Vol. 251, Dec. 3, 1990, pp. 682–684,686–688.
Review article of Khrushchev Remembers: The Glasnost Tapes focuses on the book's seeming confirmation that executed spies Julius and Ethel Rosenberg were of "significant help" (in Stalin and Molotov's alleged words) in obtaining American nuclear secrets for the Soviets. An investigation for the Nation has uncovered a deception: The highly touted Khrushchev tape on the Rosenbergs is of such dubious authenticity that any serious scholar would have to declare it worthless.

D109. Service, R. **THE RUSSIAN REVOLUTION, 1900–1927.** Atlantic Highlands, NJ: Humanities Press International, 1991. Studies in European History.
Includes bibliographical references and index.

D110. Sheehy, G. **THE MAN WHO CHANGED THE WORLD.** *Vanity Fair*, Vol. 53, Feb. 1990, pp. 108–125,180–182,184,186–189.
Tracks down Mikhail Gorbachev, from his harrowing childhood in Privolnoye to the heart of the Kremlin - and his bond with the controversial Raisa.

D111. Shulgin, V.V. (Vasilii Vital evich), 1878–. **DAYS OF RUSSIAN REVOLUTION: MEMOIRS FROM THE RIGHT, 1905–1917.** Edited, translated, and with an introduction by B.F. Adams. Gulf Breeze, FL: Academic International Press, 1990, xx, 251, pp, ill., maps, 23 cm. The Russian series, Vol. 38.
Includes bibliographical references (pp. 2112–244) and index.

D112. **SOVIET NATIONALITIES.** *Journal of Soviet Nationalities*, Vol. 1, Spring 1990, whole issue (pp. 1–162).
Contents - The ethnic scene in the Soviet Union: the view of the dictatorship, by J.A. Armstrong. The Soviet ethnic scene: a quarter century later, by J.A. Armstrong. Soviet nationalities in crisis, by S.F. Starr. John Armstrong's functionalism and beyond: approaches to the study of Soviet nationalities politics, by M.R. Bessinger. An assembly of nations or an all-union Parliament?, by V.A. Tishkov. Youth and nationality in the U.S.S.R., by M.B. Olcott. Ethnicity and support: findings from a Soviet–American public opinion poll, by E. Mickiewicz.

D113. **SOVIET SOCIAL PROBLEMS.** Edited by A. Jones, W.D. Connor and D.E. Powell. Boulder, CO: Westview Press, 1991, ix, 337 pp., ill., 23 cm.

Includes bibliographical references and index.

D114. **THE SOVIET TAKEOVER OF THE POLISH EASTERN PROVINCES, 1939–1941.** Edited by K. Sword. New York, NY: St. Martin's Press, 1991.

Result of a conference held at the School of Slavonic and East European Studies, University of London, in April 1989.

D115. Steininger, R. 1942–. **THE GERMAN QUESTION: THE STALIN NOTE OF 1952 AND THE PROBLEM OF REUNIFICATION.** Translated by J.T. Hedges. Edited by M. Cioc, New York, NY: Columbia University Press, c1990, xvii, 186 pp., 24 cm.

Translation of: Eine vertane Chance. Includes bibliographical references (pp. 159–182) and index.

D116. Susokolov, A.A. **ETHNIC GROUPS CONFRONT A CHOICE.** *Soviet Review*, Vol. 31, May–June 1990, pp. 80–96.

The purpose of the present article is to present briefly some results of sociological studies of ethnic relations and to show what may be gleaned from these results for purposes of forecasting and regulating these relations.

D117. Szayna, T.S., 1960– . **THE ETHNIC FACTOR IN THE SOVIET ARMED FORCES: THE MUSLIM DIMENSION.** Santa Monica, CA: Rand Corp., 1991.

Prepared for the United States Army, March 1991. R-4002-A.

D118. Teague, E. **AIRBRUSHING IN THESE DAYS OF GLASNOST.** *Report on the U.S.S.R.*, Vol. 2, Nov. 9, 1990, pp. 11–14.

Since the advent of glasnost, the Soviet Party press has been unearthing archive materials that demonstrate how Stalin had Trotsky and other rivals were airbrushed out of group photographs in which they appeared with Lenin. Even today, however, it seems that there is still work for the airbrushers to do.

D119. Thompson, E.P. **HISTORY TURNS ON A NEW HINGE.** *Nation*, Vol. 250, Jan. 29, 1990, pp. 117–118,120–122.

Takes exception to those who claim that changes such as those in the Soviet Union and Eastern Europe are proof that ideological history has come to an end with the triumph of Western liberal democracy. Argues that a major factor of change overlooked by the analysis of such triumphant "Western cold warriors" has been the influence of the Western peace movement.

D120. Thompson, L.M. **SOVIET STRAITJACKET PSYCHIATRY: NEW LEGISLATION TO END THE PSYCHIATRIC REIGN OF TERROR IN THE U.S.S.R.** *Syracuse Journal of International Law and Commerce*, Vol. 16, Spring 1990, pp. 271–291.

Briefly develop(s) the history of psychiatric abuse in the Soviet Union....Provide(s) a thorough analysis of the two legal procedures for psychiatric confinement, along with an analysis of legal reforms implemented under Gorbachev.

D121. **THREE REVOLUTIONS.** Washington, DC: Regnery Gateway; Lanham, MD: Distributed to the trade by National Book Network, 1991.

Reprint. Originally published, Chicago, IL: H. Regnery Co., 1959.

Contents - The French and American Revolutions compared, by F. Gentz. Reflections on the Russian Revolution, by S.T. Possony.

D122. Tolstaya, T. **NOTES FROM UNDERGROUND: SOVIET WOMEN: WALKING THE TIGHTROPE.** *New York Review of Books*, Vol. 37, May 31, 1990, pp. 3–7.

Reviews this recent work describing the life of women in the U.S.S.R.

D123. **TRANSFORMATION IN RUSSIAN AND SOVIET MILITARY HISTORY.** Washington, U.S. Air Force, Office of Air Force History, 1990, 405 pp.

Proceedings of the Twelfth Military History Symposium, United States Air Force Academy, 1–3 October 1986.

Partial contents - The Military legacy of imperial Russia: history and the environment, by N.V. Riasanovsky. Soviet military doctrine, by R.E. Berls, Jr. Emergence of a military superpower: purpose and results, by R.B. Furlong.

D124. Tumarkin, N. **RUSSIANS AGAINST JEWS.** *Atlantic Monthly*, Vol. 266, Oct. 1990, pp. 32,34–36,40,42,45.

Russian Jews are actively seeking respect just when manifestations of extreme popular anti-Semitism have sharpened.

D125. Tumarkin, N. **THE GREAT PATRIOTIC WAR AS MYTH AND MEMORY.** *Atlantic Monthly*, Vol. 267, June 1991, pp. 26,28,37,40,42,44.

In Soviet eyes the Second World War is being transformed from heroic farce to grotesque tragedy.

D126. Turan, K. **THEY TOLD ME THAT YIDDISH WAS A DEAD LANGUAGE.** *Smithsonian Magazine*, Vol. 21, Jan. 1990, pp. 60,62–64,66,68,70–71.

Profiles the efforts of Aaron Lansky to rescue and to preserve books in Yiddish. Lauds lansky's founding of the Yiddish Book Center in Amherst, MA, and his response to the requests of diverse Jewish communities throughout the Soviet Union, especially in the Baltics, with gifts of shipments of Yiddish books.

D127. **U.S. COMMISSION ON THE UKRAINE FAMINE. INVESTIGATION OF THE UKRAINIAN FAMINE 1932–1933: ORAL HISTORY PROJECT**. Edited for the Commission by J.E. Mace and L Heretz. Washington, The Commission, G.P.O., 1990, Vol 1–3 (1734 pp.).

Case histories in the Ukranian language with short summaries in English.

D128. **THE U.S. LOOKS AT THE REVOLUTIONS OF 1989.** Winchester, MA., Americans Talk Security, 1990, 48 pp. (Serial national surveys of Americans on public policy issues, survey no. 13, report no. 2(Apr. 16, 1990)).

Describes the results of a national telephone survey of 1,000 adults completed under the direction of Market Strategies, Inc. Interviews were conducted between February 19th and March 2nd, 1990. Analysis finds that the American public is full of hope and anticipation and quite positive regarding changes in the Soviet Union, Eastern Europe, and Western Europe. Americans show a great deal of optimism and support for these developments.

D129. Vaksberg, A. **STALIN'S PROSECUTOR: THE LIFE OF ANDREI VYSHINSKY.** Translated by J. Butler. New York, NY: Grove Weidenfeld, 1991.

Translated from the Russian. Includes index.

D130. Van Atta, D. **BACK TO THE FUTURE IN THE SOVIET COUNTRYSIDE?** *Problems of Communism*, Vol. 40, Jan.–Apr. 1991, pp. 155–164.

Reviews recent works which examine the role of the collective farm in Soviet politics, government, economics, and culture. Considers directions for this institution under Gorbachev.

D131. Van Dyke, C. **RUSSIAN IMPERIAL MILITARY DOCTRINE AND EDUCATION, 1832–1914.** New York, NY: Greenwood Press, 1990, xvi, 193 pp., ill., maps, 25 cm.

Includes bibliographical references (pp. 165–179) and index.

D132. **THE VIENNA CSCE FOLLOW-UP MEETING: REPORT**. Prepared by the staff of the U.S. Commission on Security and Cooperation in Europe. Washington, DC: U.S. G.P.O.

At head of title: Committee print. 101st Congress, 2nd session, House of Representatives.

D133. Volkogonov, D.A. **STALIN: TRIUMPH AND TRAGEDY.** Edited and translated by H. Shukman. New York, NY: Grove Weidenfeld, 1991.

Translation of: Triumf i Tragedia.

Includes bibliographical references and index.

D134. Volkov, Y.E. **PERESTROIKA, EDUCATION, AND THE SOVIET ECONOMY.** *Forum for Applied Research and Public Policy*, Vol. 6., Spring 1991, pp. 89–97.

Argues that in order to tailor the Soviet education system to the needs of the scientific and technological revolution, it is necessary to make radical economic changes, reorganize the education system, and improve education and training methods. Within the next few years, the Soviet Union must increase education's share of the national budget from its present two percent to 10 to 12 percent - the level in most industrialized countries. Without this investment, Soviet education will continue to decline, and the economy and living standards of the Soviet people will continue to fall as well.

D135. Walter, J., 1788–1864. **THE DIARY OF A NAPOLEONIC FOOT SOLDIER.** Edited and with an introduction by M. Raeff. New York, NY: Doubleday, c1991.

Translation of: Denkwurdige Geschichtschreibung uber die erlebte Millitaridienstzeit des Verfassers dieses Schreibens.

Includes bibliographical references.

D136. Watts, A.J. **THE IMPERIAL RUSSIAN NAVY.** London: Arms and Armour, New York, NY: Distributed in the U.S.A. by Sterling Pub. Co., 1990, 192 pp., ill., 26 cm.
Includes bibliographical references (pp. 187) and index.

D137. Witham, L., 1952– . **RODZIANKO: AN ORTHODOX JOURNEY FROM REVOLUTION TO MILLENNIUM, 1917–1988.** Lanham, MD: University Press of America, c1991, x, 251 pp., ill., 22 cm.
Includes bibliographical references (pp. 238–242) and index.

D138. Witkin, Z., 1900–1940. **AN AMERICAN ENGINEER IN STALIN'S RUSSIA: THE MEMOIRS OF ZARA WITKIN, 1932–1934.** Edited with an introduction by M. Gelb. Berkeley, CA: University of California Press, c1991.
Includes bibliographical references and index.

D139. **THE WORLD OF THE RUSSIAN PEASANT: POST-EMANCIPATION CULTURE AND SOCIETY.** Edited by B. Eklof and S. Frank. Boston: Unwin Hyman, 1990, 234 pp., ill., 24 cm.
Includes bibliographical references (pp. 219–225) and index.

D140. Yanowitch, M. **CONTROVERSIES IN SOVIET SOCIAL THOUGHT: DEMOCRATIZATION, SOCIAL JUSTICE, AND THE EROSION OF OFFICIAL IDEOLOGY.** Armonk, NY: M.E. Sharpe, 1991.
Includes bibliographical references and index.

D141. Zemtsov, I. **ENCYCLOPEDIA OF SOVIET LIFE.** New Brunswick, NJ: Transaction Publishers, c1991, 376 pp., 26 cm.
Includes bibliographical references (pp. 361–365) and indexes.

E. SCIENCE; TECHNOLOGY; ENVIRONMENT

E001. Altshuler, I.I., Mnatsakanyan, R.A. **THE CHANGING FACE OF ENVIRONMENTALISM IN THE SOVIET UNION.** *Environment*, Vol. 32, Mar. 1990, pp. 5–9,26–30.

Excerpts of an interview of two scientific researchers in the department of geography at Moscow State University and cofounders of the Association for the Support of Ecological Initiatives established by the Soviet Foundation for Social Innovations. They authored a report on glasnost and ecology in the Soviet Union and during this interview, they talk at length about environmental problems and issues in the U.S.S.R..

E002. **ANTISATELLITE WEAPONS.** Washington, Program on Science, Arms Control, and National Security, American Association for the Advancement of Science, 1990, 11 pp. (AAAS publication no. 90-11S).

This issue paper summarizes the missions of current major U.S. satellite programs as they are publicly understood, explains possible ASAT systems that could be used to attack them, and discusses various proposals to alleviate their vulnerability, including countermeasures, deterrence, tacit cooperation, and arms control.

E003. Atta, D.V. **FARMS DECLARE "GRAIN STRIKES."** *Report on the U.S.S.R.*, Vol. 2, Feb. 23, 1990, pp. 9–11.

Like the "kulaks" of fifty years ago, farm managers say that state payments offered for their grain are so low relative to industrial prices that it does not pay them to sell to the procurement agencies....Increasing amounts of grain are being retained on the farms as livestock feed or sold "on the side" to cooperatives or at kolkhoz markets, (and) whole districts are threatening to withhold their grain unless state purchase prices are increased.

E004. Baer, D. and Elkind, J. **ENVIRONMENTAL LAW: SOVIET–U.S. COOPERATION.** *Environment*, Vol. 32, Apr. 1990, pp. 5,41–43.

Discusses the development of environmental law in the Soviet Union, and its stimulation by U.S.–Soviet cooperation to protect the environment.

E005. Batenin, V. **ALTERNATIVE POWER SOURCES IN USE IN THE U.S.S.R..** *Ambio*, Vol. 19, July 1990, pp. 220–224.

Describes development of current use of solar, wind, geothermal, biomass, and tidal-power energy sources in the U.S.S.R.

E006. Bogart, P. **SOVIET MILITARY SPACE PROGRAMS.** *International Defense Review*, Jan. 1990, pp. 23–26.

Space-based warfare is no longer a utopia. In fact, the author points out that both Superpowers have been developing relevant platforms and weapon systems since the 1960s. Whereas President Reagan used his Strategic Defense Initiative (SDI) to justify funding on ongoing programs, the Soviets' long-term space programs are unhampered by day-to-day politics.

E007. Bojcun, M. **THE LEGACY OF CHERNOBYL.** *New Scientist*, Vol. 130, Apr. 20, 1991, pp. 30–35.

Five years after the worst accident in the history of civilian nuclear power, people in the Ukraine still live in restricted zones and daily run the risk of exposure to high levels of radiation.

E008. Bonner, E. **HEALTH CARE IN THE SOVIET UNION.** Freedom at issue, No. 117, Nov.–Dec. 1990, pp. 10–14.

Dr. Elena Bonner, wife of the late Andrei Sakharov, presents her observations of the health care system in the Soviet Union. She contents that the general state of poor health is tied directly to the lack of adequate housing which promotes the rapid spread of disease.

E009. Brooks, K. **SOVIET AGRICULTURE: ELUSIVE SUPPLY RESPONSE KEEPS PRESSURE ON REFORMS.** Choices, first quarter 1990, pp. 8–11.

The first set of efforts to change things - the much heralded leasing system - has had little impact....To date, the reforms are not clearly articulated. And there is no guarantee that they will succeed when and if implemented. However, spurred by increased food shortages and the general financial crises, Soviets and their politicians have little choice: the structure of agriculture must change.

E010. Brooks, K.M. **SOVIET AGRICULTURE'S HALTING REFORM.** *Problems of Communism*, Vol. 39, Mar.–Apr. 1990, pp. 29–41.

Although a prosperous agriculture is essential for perestroika, effective reforms have largely passed this sector by. It was not until late 1987 that Gorbachev's initial agricultural policy was put to serious scrutiny and found wanting. Deteriorating agricultural finances at the farm level and the burden of burgeoning agricultural subsidies on the state budget triggered a reassessment of agricultural policy that continued throughout 1988. The result was a concerted effort beginning in 1989 and continuing on into 1990 to effect a radical change in land tenure and contractual relations.

E011. Brown, L.R. **THE ARAL SEA: GOING, GOING....** *World Watch*, Vol. 4, Jan.–Feb. 1991, pp. 20,22–27.

Twenty years from now the Aral Sea may exist only on old maps. The soaring ecological and human costs of this disaster argue for immediate action, but can the Soviets move quickly?

E012. Bush, G. and Gorbachev, M.S. **TWO WORLD LEADERS ON GLOBAL ENVIRONMENTAL POLICY.** *Environment*, Vol. 32, Apr. 1990, pp. 12–15,32–35.

Contains remarks by George Bush to the Intergovernmental Panel on Climate Change (IPCC) on 5 February 1990, Washington, D.C. and remarks by Mikhail Gorbachev to the Global Forum on Environment and Development for Survival on 19 January, Moscow.

E013. Buydos, J.F. **SOVIET UNION AND EASTERN EUROPE: STATE OF THE ENVIRONMENT.** Washington, Library of Congress, Science and Technology Division, Reference Section, 1990, 10 pp. (LC Science Tracer Bullet TB 90-1).

This guide offers a review of the literature in the collections of the Library of Congress on the state of the environment in the Soviet Union and Eastern Europe. Although only English-language sources are listed, references to materials in other languages can also be traced by means of the subject headings provided on the following page. Not intended to be a comprehensive bibliography, this guide is designed - as the name of the series implies - to put the reader "on target."

E014. Cremins, T., Newton, E. **CHANGING STRUCTURE OF THE SOVIET SPACE PROGRAMME.** *Space Policy*, Vol. 7, May 1991, pp. 129–136.

Elaborates on the implications of a number of changes occurring in the space programme, including the shift to a more legislative government, decreased centralization, increased budget openness and political accountability to a restive public, more independently minded republics, and a growth in the emphasis placed on deriving economic benefits from the space programme.

E015. **ENERGY ISSUES.** *Forum for Applied Research and Public Policy*, Vol. 6, Summer 1991, pp. 78–92.

Contents - Nuclear power in the U.S.S.R., by M.K. Launer. Soviet bureaucracy and nuclear safety, by O.M. Kovalevich, V.A. Sidorenko, and N.A. Shteinberg.

E016. **THE ENVIRONMENTAL CRISIS.** *Harvard International Review*, Vol. 12, summer 1990, pp. 4–6,8–14,16–27,56,61.

Contents - Heeding nature's tug: the global environmental agenda, by Mostafa K. Tolba. Coping with the uncertainties of the Greenhouse effect, by J.T. Mathews. Democracy and the environment in Eastern Europe and the Soviet Union, by B. Jancar. The new context of multilateral environmental negotiations, by K.W. Piddington. Challenging the international order: the "Greening" of European politics, by K von Moltke. Seizing the international environmental initiative, by A. Gore, Jr.

E017. French, H.F. **GREEN REVOLUTIONS: ENVIRONMENTAL RECONSTRUCTION IN EASTERN EUROPE AND THE SOVIET UNION.** *Columbia Journal of World Business*, Vol. 26, Spring 1991, pp. 28–51.

Eastern Europe and the Soviet Union have a unique opportunity to cull from 20 years of Western experience in addressing environmental problems. They could "leapfrog" the West in both policies and technologies. By implementing the strategies that have proved most effective, Eastern Europe and the Soviet Union could realize the greatest possible return on environmental investments.

E018. Ginzburg, H.M., Reis, E. **CONSEQUENCES OF THE NUCLEAR POWER PLANT ACCIDENT AT CHERNOBYL.** *Public Health Reports*, Vol. 106, Jan.–Feb. 1991, pp. 32–40.

Discusses nuclide fallout distribution, long-term medical, psychological, social, and economic effects, and effects of low dose radiation exposure in effected villages.

E019. Huntington, T. **SOVIET BOOSTER.** *Air and Space,* Vol. 5, Mar. 1991, pp. 90–95.

Space Commerce Corporation, founded by Art Dula, tries to market Soviet space services in the U.S. including arranging for U.S. satellites to be launched aboard Soviet boosters. But U.S. export policy classifies satellites and boosters as munitions and bans their export to the Soviet Union. Dula is looking for ways to open a window to allow for joint commercialization projects.

E020. Johnson, N.L. **THE SOVIET YEAR IN SPACE 1989.** Colorado Springs, Teledyne Brown Engineering, 1990, 179 pp.

The data contained in this report are derived solely from open source literature, including Soviet media releases and scientific journals, international technical papers, unclassified satellite tracking data, and articles appearing in the Western press.

E021. Johnson, N.L. **THE SOVIET YEAR IN SPACE, 1980.** Colorado Springs, Colo., Teledyne Brown Engineering, c1991, 173 pp.

Reviews Soviet space activities for 1990. Lists all launches, describes space station activities, communications, earth resources and reconnaissance satellites, and the Soviet space program infrastructure.

E022. Junkin, E.D. **GREEN CRIES FROM RED SQUARE.** *Buzzworm,* Vol. 2, Mar.–Apr. 1990, pp. 28–33.

Reports on the growth of the environmental movement in the Soviet Union and the ecological catastrophes that challenge the movement. Includes coverage of the First All-Union Conference on Agriculture and the Environment held in Moscow, November 1989.

E023. Khabibullov, M.R., DeBardeleben, J.T. and Sacks, A.B. **NEW TRENDS IN SOVIET ENVIRONMENTAL POLICY.** Indianapolis, Universities Field Staff International, 1990, 10 pp. (UFSI Field Staff Reports, 1990–91/No. 1, Europe).

Over the course of the past five years in the Soviet Union, since Mikhail Gorbachev's policies of glasnost and perestroika took hold, there has been increasing public awareness of and frustration with the severity of the nation's environmental problems and increasing official recognition of the scope and significance of these problems....The Soviet land area experiencing serious degradation is approaching 16 per cent of the total.

E024. Manber, J.K. **PERESTROIKA IN ORBIT.** *Across the Board,* Vol. 27, July–Aug. 1990, pp. 51–55.

Describes how Payload Systems, inc., a small U.S. company solely devoted conducting research in space, developed and funded a pharmaceutical research project that flew on the Soviet space station Mir.

E025. Marples, D. **AN INSIDER'S VIEW OF CHERNOBYL.** *Report on the U.S.S.R.,* Vol. 2, Oct 19, 1990, pp. 23–29.

Presents an interview with Yuri Risovanny, head of the foreign relations bureau in the International Department of the Pripyat Industrial and Research Association, located at Chernobyl. Risovanny has been involved in the cleanup operations for four years. An attached article reports on the disputes in the Ukraine about the future of the Chernobyl nuclear power plant.

E026. Mote, V.L. **BAM, BOOM, BUST: ANALYSIS OF A RAILWAY'S PAST, PRESENT, AND FUTURE.** *Soviet Geography*, Vol. 31, May 1990, pp. 321–331.

Analyzes the boom and bust history of the Baykal-Amur Mainline (BAM) railway. BAM, a pet project of Leonid Brezhnev, was viewed by the former Soviet leader as both a lasting legacy to his memory and a means for "quick profit." Ultimately, the decision to construct the railroad and develop its hinterland reflected a gross misunderstanding of the long-range cyclical nature of resource markets. The likely future of BAM is assessed in light of the fact that BMA will not be a paying proposition until after the year 2000.

E027. Oberg, J.E. **INSIDE STAR CITY.** *Air and Space*, Vol. 5, June–July 1990, pp. 37–42,44.

Profiles the Soviet town where the cosmonauts live and train. Describes how cosmonauts are recruited.

E028. **OCEAN ENGINEERING AND TECHNOLOGY.** *Oceanus*, Vol. 34, Spring 1991, whole issue (108 pp.).

Contents - Introduction: ocean engineering, by A.J. Williams. High-resolution optical and acoustic remote sensing for underwater exploration, by W.K. Stewart. SOFAR floats give a new view of ocean eddies, by P.L. Richardson. Robotic undersea technology, by D.R. Yoerger. A telescope at the bottom of the sea, by G. Wilkens, J. Learned, and D. O'Connor. Ocean data telemetry: new methods for real-time ocean observation, by D.E. Frye, W.B. Owens, and J.R. Valdes. The role of the microcontroller in ocean research instruments, by A.M. Bradley. The history of salinometers and CTD sensor systems, by N. Brown. Underwater technology in the U.S.S.R., by D. Given. Toward a global ocean observing system, D.J. Baker. Modernizing NOAA's ocean service, by V.K. Tippie and J.D. Cawley. Artificial reefs: emerging science and technology, by I.W. Duedall and M.A. Champ. Douglas Chester Webb: a profile, by H.M. Stommel.

E029. **PANEL ON THE STATE OF THE SOVIET ENVIRONMENT AT THE START OF THE NINETIES.** *Soviet Geography*, Vol. 31, June 1990, pp. 401–468.

A panel of geographers assesses the current state of the Soviet environment based on information released for the first time in two recent Soviet publications (Doklad, 1989; Okhrana, 1989). Topics covered include air and water quality, water resource conservation, agricultural resources, mineral resource consumption and land reclamation, toxic waste disposal, forest resources, and wildlife conservation. Other issues addressed include data reliability, glasnost' and the environment, possible consequences of regional and ethnic differences for environmental policy, and the components of a realistic environmental agenda in the context of limited financial resources and the enormous and escalating costs of clean-up.

E030. Pehe, J. **THE ECOLOGICAL DAMAGE CAUSED BY SOVIET TROOPS.** *Report on Eastern Europe*, Vol. 1, Aug. 3, 1990, pp. 28–31.

Since early march 1990, when the Soviet Union began withdrawing the troops it had been stationed in Czechoslovakia since 1968, the Czechoslovak public has gradually become aware of the extensive ecological damage that the troops have caused. The Czechoslovak government has insisted that the clean-up of the polluted sites be paid for by the Soviet Union, but the Soviets have disputed these claims.

E031. Peterson, D.J. **THE STATE OF THE ENVIRONMENT: SOLID WASTES.** *Report on the U.S.S.R.*, Vol. 2, May 11, 1990, pp. 11–14.

Discusses the approach toward solid waste disposal in the Soviet Union, a problem for which little provision is made and for which few people are prepared to take responsibility.

E032. Peterson, D.J. **THE STATE OF THE ENVIRONMENT, THE AIR.** *Report on the U.S.S.R.*, Vol. 2, Mar. 2, 1990, pp. 5–9.

Describes the extent of air pollution in cities of the Soviet Union. Includes a brief comparison with air pollutant emissions in the U.S.

E033. Piotrowski, J.L. **THE CHALLENGE IN SPACE.** *U.S. Naval Institute Proceedings*, Vol. 116, Feb. 1990, pp. 32–39.

Argues that the Soviets have an impressive array of satellites, a shuttle (here, at launch), and antisatellite capabilities that clearly display their designs for space. The United States needs to develop a space strategy and attain the capability to execute that strategy successfully. Two views on these issues are presented here. Includes companion article, "The Navy's case," by W.J. Holland, Jr.

E034. Pryde, P.R. **ENVIRONMENTAL MANAGEMENT IN THE SOVIET UNION.** Cambridge, New York, NY: Cambridge University Press, 1991.

Includes bibliographical references.

E035. **RADIATION AND HEALTH: SPECIAL REPORT.** *Bulletin of the Atomic Scientists*, Vol. 46, Sept. 1990, pp. 1,11–39.

Contents - Low-level radiation: the cancer controversy, by A.M. Steward. Chernobyl: answers slipping away, by R.P. Gale. Nuclear workers at risk, by T. Connor. Culture shock at the weapons complex, by S.J. Olshansky and R.G. Williams. Zapping the food supply, by D.B. Louria. Telling the public about risks, by J.F. Ahearne.

E036. Rapoport, IA.L. **THE DOCTORS' PLOT 1953.** Cambridge, MA: Harvard University Press, 1991, viii, 280 pp., ports, 24 cm.

Translation of: Na ruezhe dvukh epokh. Includes index.

E037. Rodinov, S.N. **A CLIMATOLOGICAL ANALYSIS OF THE UNUSUAL RECENT RISE IN THE LEVEL OF THE CASPIAN SEA.** *Soviet Geography*, Vol. 31, Apr. 1990, pp. 265–275.

A climatological explanation is elaborated for the recent (post-1977) rise in the level of the Caspian Sea, preceded by falling levels over much of this century. An examination of major components of the Caspian water balance is followed by a study of more general changes, first in global climate, then in the climate of the Caspian's drainage basin. Shifting general circulation patterns over the North Atlantic (a strengthening of the North Atlantic Oscillation) are proposed as triggering increased precipitation in the volga basin, accelerating an increase in river flow feeding the Caspian.

E038. Rozengurt, M. **THE SOVIET WATER CRISIS: EXPOSING AN ENVIRONMENTAL DISASTER.** Boulder, CO: Westview Press, 1991.
Includes bibliographical references.

E039. Schultz, S.S. and Rafferty, M.P. **SOVIET HEALTH CARE AND PERESTROIKA.** *American Journal for Public Health,* Vol. 80, Feb. 1990, pp. 193–197.
This report briefly describes the current state of Soviet health and medical care, Gorbachev's plans for reform, and the prospects for success. In recent years the Soviet Union has experienced a rising infant mortality rate and declining life expectancy. The health care system has been increasingly criticized for its uncaring providers, low quality of care, and unequal access. The proposed measures will increase by 50 percent the state's contribution to health care financing, encourage private medicine on a small scale, and begin experimentation with capitation financing.

E040. **SCIENCE AND TECHNOLOGY U.S.S.R.: LIFE SCIENCES.** Washington, Foreign Broadcast Information Services, 1991, 26 pp.
JPRS-ULS-91-003, January 10, 1991.

E041. **SCIENCE AND TECHNOLOGY U.S.S.R.: LIFE SCIENCES.** Washington, Foreign Broadcast Information Service, 1991, 75 pp.
JPRS-ULS-91-002, January 9, 1991.

E042. **SCIENCE AND TECHNOLOGY U.S.S.R.: SCIENCES AND TECHNOLOGY POLICY.** Washington, Foreign Broadcast Information Services, 1991, 39 pp.

E043. Shockley, H.P. **FINAL RESOURCE USE FOR CONSUMPTION IN THE SOVIET UNION THROUGH 2000.** Santa Monica, Calif., Rand Corporation, 1991, 31 pp. (Rand Note, N-3162-USDP).
Estimates the range of potential resource claims that may be exerted in the next decade for consumption in the Soviet Union. The study separates consumption into five sectors: health, education, food supply, and nonfood consumer goods and services.

E044. Sorokovikova, N.V. **THE OVERALL EFFECT OF AUTOMOBILE TRANSPORTATION ON THE NATURAL ENVIRONMENT.** *Soviet Geography,* Vol. 31, Feb. 1990, pp. 116–125.
The aggregate effects of a variety of impacts generated by motor transport on the natural environment in the Upper Oka River basin are examined (through factor analysis) and maps of roadside pollution intensity are generated. The two factors identified, representing the effects of higher-order and local roads, respectively, provide a basis of regionalization of the Upper Oka basin according to the impacts generated by automobile traffic. The pattern of regional impacts identified, in turn, provides the basis for policy recommendations on how to reduce the level of roadside pollution and minimize other negative environmental impact of road transport.

E045. **SOVIET ENERGY DATA RESOURCE HANDBOOK: A REFERENCE AID.** Washington, U.S. Central Intelligence Agency, available from NTIS, 1990, 43 pp. SOV 90-10021, May 1990.

E046. **THE SOVIET ENVIRONMENT: PROBLEMS, POLICIES, AND POLITICS.** Edited by J.M. Stewart. Cambridge (England), New York, NY: Cambridge University Press, 1991.

Selected papers from the Fourth World Congress for Soviet and East European Studies, Harrogate, July 1990 - P. Includes index.

E047. **SOVIET REQUIREMENTS FOR WESTERN TECHNOLOGY: A FORECASTING METHODOLOGY.** (S.l.) Technology Transfer Assessment Center, Central Intelligence Agency (1991?), 2 volumes.

Presents a proof-of-concept for a methodology which demonstrates how the Soviets use Western technology in future military systems, and forecasts Soviet requirements for Western technology....The paper provides a brief overview of the Soviet process for identifying Western technologies required for development and production of future weapon systems. The methodology, which simulates this process, is presented with a detailed case study of its application in the area of microelectronics.

E048. Steward, J.M. **BAIKAL'S HIDDEN DEPTHS.** *New Scientist*, Vol. 126, June 23, 1990, pp. 42–44,46.

For the first time since the Russian Revolution, foreign scientists have a great opportunity to probe the depths of Lake Baikal - the most fascinating freshwater ecosystem on earth.

E049. Steward, J.M. **THE GREAT LAKE IS IN GREAT PERIL.** *New Scientist*, Vol. 126, June 30, 1990, pp. 58–62.

Siberia's sacred sea - gibber than Belgium and older than any other lake - Baikal is threatened by pollution from industry and agriculture.

E050. **THE STRUGGLE TO SAVE OUR PLANET.** *Discover*, Vol. 11, Apr. 1990, pp. 35–43,46–49,51–53,55–59,61–62,64,66–70,72,74,76–78.

Contents - Down in the dumps, by D. Grossman and S. Shulman. The numbers game, by D. Berreby. Ecoglasnost, by T. Waters. Playing dice with megadeath, by J. Diamond. Green giants, by D. Steward. Invisible garden, by R. Kunzig. The poison eaters, by S. Chollar.

E051. **TECHNOLOGY AND THE FUTURE STRATEGIC ENVIRONMENT.** Edited by K.B. Moss, Washington, DC: Wilson Center Press, Lanham, MD: Distributed by arrangement with University Press of America, c1990, p. cm.

Includes bibliographical references.

E052. Turnbull, M., 1947– . **SOVIET ENVIRONMENTAL POLICIES AND PRACTICES: THE MOST CRITICAL INVESTMENT.** Aldershot, Hants (England), Brookfield, VT: Dartmouth, c1991, xiv, 215 pp., 23 cm.

S. Revell, consultant, A. Main, consultant, D.J.I. Matko, R. Berry, translator, W. Joyce, translator, W.V. Wallace, project administrator.

Includes bibliographical references and index.

E053. Van Winkle, J., Zycher, B. **FUTURE SOVIET INVESTMENT IN TRANSPORTATION, ENERGY, AND ENVIRONMENTAL PROTECTION.** Santa Monica, Calif., Rand Corporation, 1991, 49 pp. (Rand Note N-3173-USDP)

Partial Contents - Introduction. Transportation in the 12th five-year plan. Condition of the Soviet railroads. The biggest constraints on economic growth. Railroad capacity and maintenance. Motor vehicle transportation. Energy. Investment in the fuels and electricity sectors. Nuclear safety retrofit. Environmental issues and resource demands in the Soviet economy. Water supply. Air pollution. Overview of Soviet environmental policy. Prospects for future investment in environmental protection.

E054. Worsnop, R.L. **UNCERTAIN FUTURE FOR MAN IN SPACE.** Washington, Congressional Quarterly, 1991, pp. 174–187. (Editorial Research Reports, 1991, No. 12)

Contents - Mission to Mars? Space shuttle's problems. Role of astronauts. Probability of disaster. U.S.-Soviet competition.

E055. Zaharchenko, T. **THE ENVIRONMENTAL MOVEMENT AND ECOLOGICAL LAW IN THE SOVIET UNION: THE PROCESS OF TRANSFORMATION.** *Ecology law Quarterly,* Vol. 17, No. 3, 1990, pp. 455–475.

This article surveys some of the changes and challenges in Soviet laws concerning the environment (referred to as ekologicheskoye pravo or ecological law), reviewing the Soviet Union' grave environmental problems and the new prominence of environmental issues on the Soviet political agenda. It provides an overview of the history and existing structure of Soviet legislation concerning environmental protection and suggests other changes to Soviet ecological laws that could provide more effective legal protection for the country's environment.

SUBJECT INDEX

AUTHOR INDEX